Critical Essays on Post-Colonial Literature

Fourth Revised and Enlarged Edition

Bijay Kumar Das

ATLANTIC
PUBLISHERS & DISTRIBUTORS (P) LTD

ATLANTIC
PUBLISHERS & DISTRIBUTORS (P) LTD

7/22, Ansari Road, Darya Ganj, New Delhi
Tel.: +91-11-4077 5252, 2327 3880
E-mail: orders@atlanticbooks.com
Web: www.atlanticbooks.com

Reprint 2026

Published by Atlantic Publishers & Distributors (P) Ltd.

Printed & bound in India by Atlantic Print Services

Acknowledgements

Acknowledgements are due to the following journals and books in which some of the essays first appeared: *The Commonwealth Review; Critical Practice; The Critical Endeavour; The Journal of Indian Writing in English; The Ravenshaw Journal of English Studies; Recent Indian Fiction; Indian Fiction of the Nineties; Changing Faces of Women in Indian Writing in English; The Continuity in the Flux—Orissa; The Literary Half-Yearly*; and *The Literary Criterion.*

BIJAY KUMAR DAS

Preface to the Fourth Edition

The Third Edition of the book, *Critical Essays on Post-Colonial Literature* came out in 2012. In the meanwhile, many books (both creative and critical) have appeared in the field of postcolonial literature. Hence, there is a need to update the book keeping in mind the requirements of the researchers all over the English speaking world. To fulfil this need, I have added four new chapters viz. 26, 27, 28 and 29 to the book and updated the bibliography. The four new chapters are: "Multi-theoretical Approaches to Five Seminal Twentieth Century Novels Across the World", "Reconfiguring Partition Narratives in Three Select Indian English Novels", "Two Centuries of Indian English Poetry: The Making of a Canon", and "*An Era of Darkness*: A Journey from Colonialism to Postcolonialism".

This book is designed as a reference book for students pursuing postgraduation, M.Phil, and the researchers in the subject. It will also serve as a handbook on postcolonial studies for the teachers.

I am thankful to Atlantic Publishers and Distributors (P) Ltd., New Delhi, particularly to its Honorary Advisor, Dr. K.R. Gupta for bringing out the revised and enlarged edition of the book in time.

BIJAY KUMAR DAS

Preface to the First Edition

The term "Commonwealth Literature" fell into rough weather in the hands of writers from the erstwhile British colonies, when it was drawn upon them that the writers of the colonizer (i.e., England) do not form a part of this body of literature. Hence, a new term, "Postcolonial Literature" was coined to suggest decentring of the colonial literature. Two books, *The Empire Writes Back* (1989) by Bill Ashcroft, Gareth Griffiths, and Helen Tiffin, and *Encyclopedia of Post-Colonial Literatures in English* edited by Eugene Benson and L.W. Conolly proved to be the last nail in the coffin of Commonwealth Literature and popularized the term Postcolonial Literature.

In this book, an attempt has been made to analyze some of the outstanding postcolonial writers like Arundhati Roy (Booker Prize winner 1997), Vikram Chandra (Commonwealth Prize winner 1996), Derek Walcott (Nobel Prize winner 1992), Margaret Atwood (Booker Prize winner 2000), Jayanta Mahapatra, Dom Moraes, Nissim Ezekiel, Keki N. Daruwalla, Kamala Das, Shiv K. Kumar, Anita Desai, Shashi Deshpande, and Ruskin Bond (all Sahitya Akademi Award winners) in the light of postcolonial theory. Apart from analyzing individual authors, an attempt has also been made to show the trends in postcolonial poetry, Orissan contribution to postcolonial Indian English literature, and above all, postcolonial English studies in India.

I have enjoyed reading the authors included in this book and shall feel rewarded if the book finds favour with the readers. A Select Bibliography has been provided in the end, both by way of acknowledgement and by way of bringing to the notice of the readers the materials available in the field.

Last but not the least, I am thankful to Atlantic Publishers and Distributors (P) Ltd., New Delhi, particularly to its Chairman, Dr. K.R. Gupta, for bringing out the book in time.

BIJAY KUMAR DAS

Contents

1

Trends in Post-Colonial Poetry

In the closing decades of the twentieth century, the term post-colonialism has gained currency and what is more, it has eclipsed terms like post-modernism, post-structuralism and so on. Before plunging into the subject of this paper indicated by the title given above, I would like to explicate the term 'post-colonialism' for the benefit of those who seek an introduction to it.

The establishment of the British Commonwealth of Nations has followed a definite course. The British had an extended empire during the nineteenth century and this empire had a fairly strong impact on all its territories. These territories were of two kinds — those like Canada, New Zealand and Australia in which the English people colonized and established their culture and those like India and Nigeria where they were rulers by force and imposed their institutions and norms. The process of self-determination and the granting of political independence to each country of the Empire continued in quick succession. By the Statute of Westminster, Australia, Canada, New Zealand and South Africa were made free and equal partners and independent nations in 1931. In 1947, India became free and at the same time Sri Lanka (Ceylon, a former colony), was granted independence. The break-up of the British Empire with resulting development of newly independent nations and the assertion of an independent cultural and political identity led to the growth of Commonwealth Literature.

Commonwealth Literature refers to the literature written in English only in the Commonwealth countries outside the Anglo-American tradition. In Australia, New Zealand and Canada, on the one hand, and in Asia, Africa and West Indies, on the other, the English language whether as an inherited or an acquired language has been employed as the medium of creative expression in diverse cultural contexts. 'English' being the distinguishing mark of

'Commonwealth Literature', this literature excludes the literatures written in their native languages in the Commonwealth Countries, even though these literatures are more authentic than the literature in English. Some of the creative writers in Commonwealth Countries asserted their right to use English not like the British but in their own way.

Commonwealth Literature gained currency in 1960s. Despite the sharp differences in context in which the Commonwealth writers function, Commonwealth Literature presents an immense landscape alive with creative energy and instinct with promise.

"But in 1962 a bold step was taken, and the writing in English language from all the countries which were at one time a part of the British Commonwealth, was christened as 'Commonwealth Literature'. The term appeared to be descriptive and appropriate. Though some critics like Canada's George Woodcock sneered at this christening as an attempt to build academic principalities, the term gained currency, and a number of scholars have been using it without embarrassment", says S.K. Sarma (1985 : 67).

But till now the term remains controversial and unsettled, for some critics the term "Commonwealth" has political connotation and overtones. Moreover, some countries keep on opting out and again coming in, into the Commonwealth Group of Nations, and thereby, make the term Commonwealth Literature open ended.

An alternative term to Commonwealth Literature is mooted, i.e. Third World literature. But all countries of the Commonwealth Group of Nations do not come under this term. And again, this term has unmistakable political overtones. In this connection Arthur Ravenscroft makes an interesting observation:

The literatures of those Commonwealth countries that can conveniently be regarded as belonging to the Third World are either very much concerned with 'the turning world', as in Africa and the Caribbean, or look back to great cultural phenomena unrelated to Europe's Renaissance, as in India — despite Raja Rao's interest in the Albigensian heresy in the *The Serpent and the Rope*. The really interesting literature in English of India begins with Mulk Raj Anand's *Untouchable* and R.K. Narayan's *Swami and Friends* in 1935, of Black Africa with Sol T Plaatje's *Muhdi* in 1930 and Amos Tutuola's *The Palm-Wine Drinkard* in 1952, of the Caribbean with Claude Mckay's *Home to Harlem* in 1928, or alternatively with C.L.R. James's *Minty Alley* in 1936. There were earlier writings in verse and prose, but these titles are markers of the rising tide which proclaim that quarter of the twentieth century, at least a decade after the end of the first of Europe's two holocausts (1989 : 23).

The second alternative to the term "Commonwealth Literature" is suggested by a phrase "New Literature in English". This to my mind, is a misnomer, for it may mean apart from creative writing in English, translations into English in the Commonwealth Countries.

The term Commonwealth Literature fell into rough weather in the hands of writers from the erstwhile British colonies, when it was drawn upon them that the writers of the colonizer (i.e., England) do not form a part of this body of Literature. Hence, a new term, post-colonial literature is coined to suggest de-centring of colonial literature. Two books, *The Empire Writes Back* (1987) by Ashcroft, Gareth Griffiths and Tiffin and *The Encyclopedia of Post-Colonial Literatures in English* by Eugene Benson and Connolly proved to be the last nail in the coffin of Commonwealth Literature and popularized the term post-colonial literature.

I would briefly quote a few theorists of post-colonial literature, before I give a resume of post-colonial poetry for that will make the protean term intelligible to the readers. Let me first refer to the widely known book, *The Empire Writes Back*.

We use the term post-colonial to cover all the culture effected by the imperial process from the moment of colonization to the present day. This is because there is a continuity of preoccupation throughout the historical process initiated by European imperial aggression, say the authors (qtd in Mukherjee, 1996 : 8).

As Stephen Slemon puts it:

the question of the 'post-colonial' is grounded in overlapping of three competing research or critical fields, each of which carries a specific cultural location and history. In the first of the these fields, the term 'post-colonial' is an outgrowth of what formerly were 'Commonwealth' literary studies — a study which came into being after 'English studies' had been liberalized to include 'American' and then an immediate national or regional literature (Australian, Canadian, West Indian), and as a way of mobilizing the concept of national or geographical difference within what remains a unitary idea of 'English'. The second of these critical fields, in contrast, employs the term 'post-colonial' in considering the valency of subjectivity specifically within Third and Fourth-World cultures, and within black, and ethnic, and First-Nation constituencies dispersed within First-World terrain. The institutionalizing of these two critical fields has made possible the emergence of a third field of study, however, where nation-based examinations of a variable literary Commonwealth or a variable literary "Third World, give way to specific analyses of the discourse of colonialism (and neo-colonialism), and where studies in cultural representativeness and literary mimeticism give way to the project of identifying the kinds of anti-colonialist resistance that can take place in literary writing... 'Post-colonial' studies in 'English' now finds itself at a shifting moment, where three very different critical projects collide with one another on the space of a single signifier — and what will probably be a single course offering within an English studies program. Not surprisingly, this situation has produced some remarkable confusions, and they underpin the present debate over the specificity of the 'post-colonial' in the areas of literary and critical practice (Griffiths, 1996 : 33).

Another theorist, T. Vijay Kumar argues that the type, in 'post-colonialism' foregrounds at least three aspects of the term:

> Firstly, by splitting the word into two the hyphen effectively prevents/defers the integration of the colonial past into the post-colonial present. The lack of integration can be seen in 'post-colonial' history, culture, and literature. When used to refer to the history or culture of a society, the term privileges one phase or strand over all others that go into the making of a post-colonial situation. When we refer to a literature as 'post-colonial' we do not only over-emphasize its continuing concern with the colonial experience, but also hinder its integration into the tapestry of literatures written in the 'local' languages. I am obviously thinking here of Indian literature in English and its relationship with the literatures in other Indian languages. Surprisingly, but perhaps expectedly, only Indian literature in English is referred to as 'post-colonial' literature, as if only those who write in English have been subject to the colonial experience. The decontextualisation of this literature is complete when it is categorised as 'post-colonial' because neither the category nor the term exists in other Indian literatures/languages.
>
> Secondly, by separating 'post' and reducing it to a dependent prefix, the hyphen succeeds in centring 'colonialism'. The effects of such centring are many. One, it facilitates both the

> erasure of the specificity, multiplicity, and unfamiliarity of post-colonial situations, and the totalization of their differences under the unitary and familiar sign of colonialism. Two, by marginalising 'post' it strips the colonial subject of agency and forecloses any promise of change in his post-colonial situation (for instance *Empire Writes Back* which claims to be "concerned with the world as it exists" finds in all post-colonial literatures "a continuity of preoccupation"). Three, the centring of colonialism empowers 'post-colonial' critics, at least those who see the colonial experience everywhere as the same, to draw up universal models for post-colonial societies. In *Empire Writes Back* Ashcraft et al., present the American example as "paradigmatic for post-colonial literatures everywhere". In Nationalism, Colonialism, and Literature Eagleton, Jameson, Said, on the other hand, try to project the Irish literary experience as the "prototype for the explosion of the new literatures in English around the world." In this way 'post-colonialism' becomes a free-floating theory with universal application. Four, the centring of colonialism as the common factor among post-colonial societies falsifies history and betrays the colonial powers' desperate attempt to remain relevant and mediate the dialogue among the post-colonial societies.
>
> Lastly, besides working against integration and centring colonialism, the hyphen also conditions the way in which 'post-colonial' discourse is constituted as a category. Since colonialism is installed at the centre, only those discourses which continue to engage with it from their marginal position are reckoned as 'post-colonial' (1996 : 196-98).

According to Harish Trivedi post-colonialism means something different in the Indian context:

> Unlike with feminism or post-structuralism or even Marxism, the discourse of post-colonialism is ostensibly not about the West where it has originated but about the colonized other. For the first time probably in the whole history of the Western academy, the non-West is placed at the centre of its dominant discourse. Even if it is in part a sort of compensation for all the colonial material exploitation, the academic attention now being paid to the post-colonial is so assiduous as to soothe and flatter. Never before, for example, was Indian writing (though crucially, writing only in English) so widely represented in a monumentally canonical

> metropolitan work as in the *Routledge Encyclopedia of Post-colonial Literatures in English* (1994). It was, moreover, self-represented, with the entries on Indian authors and themes being written not by metropolitan critics but by as many as sixty-seven Indian academics (including several contributors to this volume), often with just the kind of self-reflexive, interrogative complicity which marks much of the Indian academic engagement with post-colonialism. And an even higher proportion of contributors with Indian names is to be found in the critical anthology *Colonial Discourse and Post-colonial Theory*, edited by Patrick Williams and Laura Chrisman (1994), (1996 : 232).

There are critics like Adil Jussawalla and Arun P. Mukherjee, who raise objection to the term, 'post-colonial'. Jussawalla says: "the problem with the word 'post-colonial' is that it always invokes the former coloniser". He argues further by saying that the 'colonisation' of Australia and Canada was different from ours that they could scarcely be called British colonies in the sense we were. Arun Prabha Mukherjee also views the term post-colonial as signalling 'the present of the past' and assails its "homogenizing, assimilationist and hegemonic" tendencies. She asserts:

Now I believe that theory is not born of an immaculate conception but emerges of the conditions of living. So my hunch is that "post-colonialism" or "post-colonial theory" which claims that "all" literatures from the above mentioned geographical area "share" certain formal and discursive features, which have been identified as "resistance" and "subversion" of the imperial "centre" and can, therefore, be treated as a collectivity under the name "Post-colonial literature", called "Post-colonial literatures" by those a bit more conscious about charges of homogenisation, was born because of the peculiar working conditions of post-colonial critics. That is, when one puts together a course, one is called upon to provide a rationale for what is excluded from and included in the course. "Post-colonial theory" provides the rationale for "English 4000: Post-colonial literature". It is the instrument which sees the hidden similarities among the these discrete texts from diverse areas of the world and thereby provides a prefabricated grid which the novice can use in his/her reading of these texts (1996 : 14).

Bill Ashcroft provides an answer to the above observations of Arun P. Mukherjee, when he says,

To assume that the word 'post-colonial' encapsulates a unified and homogeneous experience is to disregard the material consequences of colonialism upon which post-colonial discourse is constructed. But to exclude some societies from the term for tawdry motives of political correctness is both to ignore the material effects of colonization (themselves very different in different situations) and the huge diversity of ordinary and sometimes hidden response to it throughout the world. It is fall into a form of categorisation still controlled by imperial discourse (Griffinths 1996 : 25).

Semantically post-colonialism means something that has a concern only with the national culture after the departure of imperial power. But in actual practice, it has to be understood only in reference to colonialism. Like colonialism, post-colonialism is 'a state of consciousness', a crucial stage in the continuum of our cultural process and self-awareness. Colonialism involves two types of imperialism — political and cultural. Therefore, myth and history, language and landscape, self and the other are all very important ingredients of post-colonialism.

Post-colonial theory claims that the major theme of literatures from post-colonial countries can be taken as resistance to the former coloniser. It further assumes that the writers who write back to the centre are representing the people of their society authentically.

Post-colonial theory in using terminologies like 'the oppressed', 'the colonized peoples', and 'the indigenous' to describe post-colonial societies, it suppresses internal hierarchies and divisions in these societies. What is disturbing is that it confers the 'Subaltern' status on the entire post-colonial world. Moreover, it states clearly that post-colonial writing must be in English, or in 'English' as emphasized by the authors of *The Empire Writes Back*. They explain:

We distinguish into this account between the 'standard' British English inherited from the empire and the English which the language has become in the post-colonial countries (1996 : 238).

Vijay Mishra and Bob Hodge in a critique of the book, *The Empire Writes Back* felt the need to 'distinguish sharply between two kinds of post-colonialism'.

The first is that what we call oppositional post-colonialism, which is found in its most overt form in post-independent (i.e., independent?) colonies at the historical phase of post-colonialism (with a hyphen). The second form is a complicit post-colonialism

... an always present underside within colonization itself (Trivedi 1996 : 236).

Following Mishra and Hodge, Francis Barker *et al.*, in their introduction to colonial discourse/post-colonial theory state that they have "distinguished between 'post-colonial' used as a temporal marker and 'post-colonial' etc. to indicate the analytical concept of greater range and ambition as in 'post-colonial theory' or the post-colonial condition" (*Ibidem* : 237).

Post-colonial poetry refers to poetry written in English in the erstwhile British colonies. It is not correct to say that the post-colonial writers (poets included) write back to the former colonizer. In fact, they write to establish their individual identity independent of their colonizer and try to show that not only they have gained independence from the latter but successfully made the colonizer's language (i.e., English) as a vehicle for creative expression. The result is that English literature has yielded place to literatures in English and the medium has been transformed from English to other Englishes (or englishes). Each former colony uses English in its own way (the Queen's English is out of fashion) and that is why we get African English, Australian English, Caribbean English, Canadian English, Indian English etc. in the post-colonial age.

Post-colonial poetry should be construed in relation to colonial poetry, and appreciated as 'resistance' and 'subversion' of former colonizer. Hence, national identity, landscape, rituals, and national culture and tradition form the core of post-colonial poetry. The current trend in post-colonial poetry is to assert one's national identity and glorify the landscape of his/her country. The leading post-colonial poets in Africa, Australia, Canada, India and West Indies write to underline their national identity and highlight their landscape. The poets of Africa in whose works the image of 'Africa' comes alive are Okot p'Bitek, Dennis Brutus, Wole Soyinka, J.P. Clark, Christopher Okigbo, David Rubadin, Noemia De Sousa and Feavien Ranaivo. "The artist" says Wole Soyinka "has always functioned in Africa Society as the recorder of mores and experiences of his society and as the voice of vision in his own time" (1986 : 15-16). Dennis Brutus's poetry bears testimony to Soyinka's observation as it is the outcome of Brutus's suffering in life because of his fights for freedom, justice and peace in South Africa. According to Jasper A. Onuekwusi, Brutus's poetry "is a direct response to the unsavoury demands which a horrible socio-political situation makes on his personality. Every page of his poetry bristles with images of searing pain, spilling blood, contorting hearts or Wrecking nerves. In his poetry words are charged with lethal colours. From Brutus we read poetry that shocks, simulates, agitates, activates and educates us about the South African society. In fact, Dennis Brutus's poetry is inseparable from South African reality. He is the altruistic voice of the people who has gone through almost all the experiences which any coloured South African may undergo" (1988 : 60). In a way, his poetry is an artistic rendition of a socio-political discourse of the South African situation. As Brutus puts it:

> Only I speak the others' woe
> Those congealed in concrete
> On rotting in rusted ghetto-shacks
> Only I speak their wordless woe
> Their uncirculated simple lust.

African poets make best use of their native tradition in their creative writings and they are very successful in acclimatizing the traditional belief to English language. They do not follow the British poets blindly and show the courage to write poetry in their own way. It is in this aspect African poetry has affinity with post-colonial poetry. C.D. Narasimhaiah has rightly observed this trait in African poetry in the following words:

> Similarly the African poet summoned courage to affirm 'Black is beautiful' and reject Bach and Mozart as rhythms fit for Yeats and Eliot, as for him he wishes to laugh, cry, grimace which elevated the drum beat into poetry. Where generally the English poet showed fear and anxiety in the face of death, here in what may be called an African Ode to Autum, the poet (Wole Soyinka) explores in the traditional Yoruba way the metaphysical dimensions of life and death through agricultural images of the harvester witting for the fruit of life, death (Das 1995 : 10).

Poets like Wole Soyinka and Christopher Okigbo have tried to infuse their sense of belonging and belief into the texture of their poetry. Thus, Soyinka writes:

> And no one speaks of secrets in his land
> Only, that the skin be bared to welcome rain
> And earth prepare, that seeds may swell
> And roots take flesh within her, and men
> Wake naked into harvest-tide.

The African poets have a sense of 'belonging' and pride in using English in their own way (In Southern and West Africa English has become in the words of Chinua Achebe, 'an African language' for literary purpose) and hence, their poetry assumes an identity which is both lovable and enduring. Here are a few examples:

I thank you God for creating me black
For making of me
porter of all sorrows,
setting on my head
The World.

(*I Thank you God*)

The negro labourer in Liverpool
That from his motherland
A heart heavy
with the load of a century's oppression
Gloriously sought for an identity
Grappled to clutch the fire of manhood
In the land of the free
But here are only the free dead
For they too groping for a light

(*A Negro Labourer in Liverpool*)

Noemia De Sousa gives poignant touch to African consciousness in a poem called, "If you want to know me":

Africa from head to foot
This is what I am.
If you want to understand me
come, bend over his soul of Africa
in the black dock worker's groans
the chopes' frenzied dances
the changanas' rebellion
in the strange sadness which flows
from an African song through the night.

These African poets are trying to reinforce their sense of liberty and freedom through their poetry. The image of "Africa" dominates their thinking process and they seek an identity which is both enduring and lovable. David Diop's "Africa" is a bright example of a poet's desire to celebrate the country.

Africa my Africa
Africa of proud warriors in ancestral savannahs
Africa of whom my grand mother sings.

On the banks of the distant river
I have never known you
But your blood flows in my veins.

(*Africa*)

The "image" of Australia in Australian poetry has undergone a sea change since William Wentworth wrote his poem "Australasia" at the Cambridge University for the Chancellor's God Medal Poetry competition in 1823. The image of the native land has become central to the modern Australian poets such as A.D. Hope, Judith Wright, Mary Gilmore, Douglas Stewart and James McAuley. The poets seem to echo McAuley when he writes:

And I am fitted to that land, as the soul is to the body
I know its contractions, waste and sprawling indolence
They are in me and its triumphs are my own
Hard won in the thing and bitter years without patience.

Judith Wright expresses an ageless antiquity of her young country in the image of "The Cycads" and the way it effects the poet.

Their smooth dark flames flicker at time's own root...
Only the antique Cycads sullenly
Keep the old bargain life has long since broken;
and cursed by age, through each chill century
they watch the shrunken moon, but never die,
for time forgets the promise he once made,
and change forgets that they are left alone....

The making of an image of the "native land" and the "native idiom" are the two characteristics which are common to all post-colonial poets. Nowhere one finds a better expression of the image of Australia than in A.D. Hope's poem, "Australia". The beginning of this poem is abrupt.

A nation of trees, drab green and desolate grey
In the field uniform of modern wars
Darkens her bills: those endless outstretched paws
of Sphinx demolished or stone lion worn away.

C.D. Narasimhaiah makes a pertinent point when he says:

Precisely here does the poet's shocked sensibility seek its stimulus from legend and history. The sources he seeks his strength from are the ones with which his own situation has striking affinities, and they are implicit in the following:

Yet there are some like me turn gladly home
From the lush jungle of modern thought, to find
The Arabian desert of the human mind,
Hoping, if still from the deserts the prophets come
Such savage and scarlet as no green hills dare
Springs in that waste, some spirit which escapes
The learned doubt, the chatter of cultured ape,
Which is called civilization over there.

Here is a poet who recognises the Judo-Christian tradition that he is heir to and the other which also took its birth in the Arabian desert — both point to a rich possibility in his own seemingly unpromising and unsuspected situation. And as we come to the end of the poem we realize that this poet, if he took savage delight in laying bare the dismal geography and history of his own land, refuses all the same to be cowed down by them, on the contrary, feels challenged to bring forth the hidden resources, his own and the land's (1995 : 204-05).

David Rowbotham reiterates in 'The Brown Island' the history and identity of his country in no uncertain terms. He says:

We were patient and we conquered. The island
rolled beneath our weight and steadied down..

....
We know the place was briefly called Australia.
We changed the name and even the seas then
resounded as you hear them, echoing the hearer,
and the brown island learned to speak our tongue.

Australian landscape comes alive in Judith Wright's poetry. For her Australia 'has been the outer equivalent of an inner reality, first and persistently, the reality of exile; second though perhaps we now tend to forget this, the reality of newness and freedom'. This double aspect of the Australian mind, Judith Wright discusses in her book, *Preoccupations in Australian Poetry* (Melbourne: O.U.P., 1965), David Malouf, a leading Australian poet in the 1970s too has given beautiful images of 'Australia' in his poetry.

In the post-colonial Canadian Poetry there is the employment of the image of the native land in all walks of life. G.D. Roberts and Archibald Lampman are pioneers of Canadian Poetry. Duncan Campbell Scott has contributed immensely to the formation of national consciousness in Canadian Poetry. Important Canadian Poets include A.J.M. Smith, P.K. Page, Margaret Avison, Margaret

Atwood, Anne Wilkinson, Charles Mair, Robert Finch, Dorothy Livesey and A.M. Klein. In a poem called "Notes towards a poem that can never be written," Margaret Atwood depicts the Canadian predicament which could be the predicament of any post-colonial poet of our time.

> In this country you can say what you like because no one will listen to you any way, it's safe enough, in this country you can try to write the poem that can never be written the poem that invents nothing and excuses nothing, because you invent and excuse yourself each day.

A.J.M. Smith expresses his determination to sing his song to continue the poetic tradition like W.B. Yeats (on whose memory he wrote a poem title "Ode on the Death of William Butler Yeats") singing to "the lords and ladies of Byzantium", Smith will "sing to the barrenrock" the difficult "lonely music" like "an old proud king in parable". Landscape has become an integral part of Canadian poetry. Thus, Margaret Atwood writes:

> that the hills Which the eyes make flat as a wall, welded together, open as I move to get me through ..... .
>
> what ever I do I must keep my head. I know It is easier for me to lose my way forever here, than in other landscapes
>
> (*Journey to the Interior*)

The theme of landscape and national identity makes a rewarding study when applied to Indian English poets. Indian landscape has inspired the Indian English poets to create newer and more fascinating images of 'India' that have not been created before. Images of 'India' are handled with a consummate skill and keenness of intellect in Shiv K. Kumar's specifically Indian poems like, 'Indian Women', 'An Indian Mango Vendor', 'Transcendental Meditation', 'A Hindu to His Cow', 'Rickshawallah', 'My Correspondent', 'Karma' and Aftermath'. Kumar's treatment of the theme of love (i.e. man-woman relationship) in terms of the elements of Indian landscape has the weight of a poetic reconciliation of the spirit and the country. He incorporates the heat and dust, the sun and flood, the crowd, the senses of poverty and deprivation into the texture of his moods. For example, 'The Sun Temple at Konark' catches the spirit of Vyatsayana's 'Kamasutra' in verse:

> Rhythm and fire
> this riotous sea of navels, breasts
> and lips — will never break

into prevarication
for the perfect logos
in the act of affirmation.

In 'Summer in Calcutta', Kamala Das describes a world which is harsh, Sun-pierced tropical world full of smells of rotten garbage and death, where men have 'limbs like carnivorous planes'. The lanes are 'fevered', the trees dusty and leafless, cheeks 'sun-stained'. Only the marigolds and bougainvillea survive and courtesans with 'tinsel and jasmine in their hair'. The poet harshly feels 'a hunger to take in with greed, like a forest fire that/consumes'.

Nissim Ezekiel's poetry emanates from life. India's poverty, the rituals observed in the country and her people in all walks of life attract the attention of the poet. Ezekiel's Bombay is located in the present and this city is as much within him as without. As Professor J. Birje-Patil has rightly observed. Ezekiel's originally lies in his projection of Bombay as a metaphor which defines the alienation of the modern Indian intellectual brought up in the Judaeo-Christian and Greco-Roman traditions and being forced to come to terms with a culture whose response to life is controlled by a totally different metaphysics (1976 : 209). This city of Bombay has become central to Ezekiel's poetic thought and an integral part of his poetics.

Jayanta Mahapatra's various themes in terms of the elements of the landscape have the weight of a poetic reconciliation of the spirit and the country, a subconscious empathy with the topographical and human aspects of the Orissan landscape. As Professor K. Ayyappa Paniker rightly suggested, 'the Sun of the Eastern coast of India' shines through his poems. The Eastern sea sends its morning wind through them. Mahapatra, a child of the Sun and the sea, delights in invoking the god of fire and the god of· water in poems like 'Sunburst', 'The Exile', 'Indian Summer Poem', 'This Stranger, My Daughter' and 'The Beggar Takes it as Solace.' 'Puri is a living character in several of these poems' (1978 : 129). The history and myths of his land coupled with the vision of Mahapatra present an integrated experience. The Orissan landscape comes fully alive in his poetry, particularly in 'Relationship'. Not only Puri and Konark but Chilika, Chandipur and a few other religious and historic places occupy the still centre of his poetry.

New Zealand gained significance in the 1930s and it sought for reality in the distinctive character of the country, 'the individually of New Zealandness'. Poets like R.A.K. Mason, A.K.D. Fairburn,

Denis Glover and Curnow rose to prominence and wrote their best poetry in the 1930s. Most of the New Zealand poets believed in tradition. Nationalism too has a great appeal for them. As Andrew Gurr has rightly suggested, "While Holcroft and poets like Charles Brasch concerned themselves with expressing the physical character of their country, the environment, Curnow's especial preoccupation in his poetry was with the heredity, New Zealand's history" (1973 : 103). Allen Curnow's *A Small Room with Large Windows* (O.U.P., 1962) is a significant volume which contains poems like 'House and Land', 'The Unhistoric Story', 'A Victim', 'Discovery', 'The Navigators', 'Sailing or Drowning' and 'Landfall in Unknown Seas' dealing with various aspects of New Zealand history. In 'Sailing or Drowning', it is the 'green myth' which connects the past and the present making 'the evening and the morning one'. Curnow writes:

> Simply by sailing in a new direction
> You could enlarge the world.

Derek Walcott, Wilson Harris and Edward Brathwaite have given the West Indies poetry a new direction and established its identity. Edward Brathwaite's 'The Arrivant's : A New World Trilogy', Wilson Harris's 'From Eternity to Season', and Derek Walcott's volumes of poems like 'Another Life', 'The Castaway and other poems', 'In a Green Night' and 'The Gulf and other poems' exhibit the image of the native land in its reality. Walcott takes the stand of an intellectual West Indian right from the beginning of his poetic career. He describes the predicament of the West Indian. The culture of the West Indies which is an amalgam of various cultures forms the subject matter of Walcott's poetry.

Against the backdrop of the colonial exploitation, the West Indies poet has to choose between the cultural past and native tradition, on the one hand, and the English language, on the other. The last stanza of the poem expresses Walcott's dilemma as a poet. Walcott not only tries to acclimatize an indigenous tradition to English language but he also struggles hard to keep up multi-cultural commitment and, therefore, it appeals to people cutting across continents. The last stanza of the poem contains a series of questions — partly rhetorical, for Walcott has chosen to retain both his native tradition and the acquired English language. Thus, he concludes:

> I who am poisoned with the blood of both,
> Where shall I turn, divided to the vein?
> I who have cursed

The drunken officer of British rule, how choose
Between this Africa and the English tongue I love?
Betray them both or give back what they give?
How can I face such slaughter and be cool?
How can I turn from Africa and live?

To conclude, I should say that post-colonial poetry can be appreciated better as a 'resistance' to the former colonizer and an assertion of national identity, which fully explains the theory of post-colonialism.

WORKS CITED

Ashcroft Bill, Gareth Griffths and Helen Tiffin, *The Empire Writes Back*. London; Methuen, 1987.

Brije-Patil, J., "Interior Cadences: The Poetry of Nissim Ezekiel," *The Literary Criterion* 12 : 2-3 (1976).

Das, Bijay Kumar, *Aspects of Commonwealth Literature*, New Delhi: Creative Books, 1995.

Griffiths, Gareth, "Representation and Production: Issues of Control in Post-colonial Cultures," *Post-Colonialism: Theory, Text and Context*, 1996.

Gurr, Andrew, "The Two Realities of New Zealand Poetry", *Readings in Commonwealth Literature*, ed. William Walsh London: Oxford University Press, 1973.

Jasper A. Onuekwusi, "Pain and Anguish of an African poet: Dennis Brutus and South African Reality", *The Literary Criterion* 23 : 1-2 (1988).

Kumar, T. Vijay, "Post-Colonial or Post-Colonial? Re-locating the hyphen", *Post-colonialism: Theory, Text and Context*, 1996.

Mukherjee, Arun P., "Interrogating Post-colonialism: Some Uneasy Conjunctures", *Post-colonialism: Theory, Text and Context*, 1996.

Mukherjee, Meenakshi, quoted in "Interrogating Post-colonialism", *Interrogating post-colonialism: Theory Text and Context*, ed. Trivedi, Harish and Meenakshi Mukherjee, Shimla: Indian Institute of Advanced Study, 1996.

Narasimhaiah, C.D., *Essays in Commonwealth Literature*. Delhi: Pencraft International, 1995.

Ravenscroft, Arthur, "Third World Literature: Purpose or Indulgence," *The Commonwealth Review* 1 : 1 (1989).

Sarma, S. Krishna, "Commonwealth or Uncommonwealth? Quarrels over Naming this, 'New Literature'," *Indian Scholar* 7: 1-2 (1985).

Soyinka, Wole, "The Writer in the Modern African State", *The Writer in Modern Africa*, 1986.

Trivedi, Harish, "India and Post-colonial Discourse", *Post-colonialism: Theory, Text and Context*, 1996.

2

Indian English Poetry: Retrospect and Prospect

In order to trace the development of Indian English poetry in its proper perspective one has to take into account the origin and continuity of this body of poetry beginning with Henry Derozio's first publication, *Poems* in 1827. Critics tend to divide the whole gamut of Indian English poetry into two periods: pre-Independence and post-Independence poetry and unfortunately either denigrate one or eulogize the other. One group outright condemns the poetry written before Indian Independence in 1947 and eulogizes post-Independence Indian poetry in English. Take for instance, R. Parthasarathy's pronouncement that Indian verse in English "did not seriously begin to exist till after the withdrawal of the British from India" (3). In an introduction to his anthology, *Two Decades of Indian Poetry 1960-1980*, Keki N. Daruwalla writes: "I must say here that it is fairly easy to denigrate whatever the earlier Indian poets wrote and then contrast their failures with modern Indian poetry in English."

He further states that "the final indictment of the earlier poets will not be on the score of their prosody or their archaic, dandified georgianisms, but that they were untouched by either the reality around them, drought, famine, plague, colonial exploitation or by the reality within, namely erosion of faith and the disintegration of the modern consciousness." (Introduction)

But there are also critics who denounce the post-1960 Indian poets and poetry in English. Reviewing two anthologies *Stranger Time: An Anthology of Indian Poetry in English* edited by Pritish Nandy and *Ten Twentieth Century Indian Poets* edited by R. Parthasarathy, R.W. Desai observes:

> Looking through the poems in these two volumes, one has the feeling that the writers would have been well advised to have started their poetic careers by writing nursery rhymes

> — I speak with all seriousness. After at least five years this regimen, followed by another five heroic couplets in iambic pentameter they would have been ready to make a careful study of the discipline that a Nissim Ezekiel — an exception in these pages under review — has attained to in two of his finest poems: "Enterprise" and "Philosophy" (*Ten Twentieth Century Indian Poets*, pp. 30 and 31).

Before making an assessment of the post-1960 Indian poetry in English, I should, for the sake of arriving at a balanced view on the subject, dwell at some length on these two extreme viewpoints held by two militant groups — traditionalists as well as modernists. V.K. Gokak in his introduction to *The Golden Treasury of Indo-Anglian Verse* and in his *Studies in Indo-Anglian Poetry* traces the growth and progress of Indian poetry in English and showers praise on almost all the poets whom he includes in his anthology. To him Sarojini Naidu is the Yeats of India and Sri Aurobindo a great innovator in the art of versification. He classifies the Indian poets in English before Independence into two groups: neo-symbolists and neo-modernists. The neo-symbolists dive deep into mysticism and the neo-modernists's vision is coloured by humanism. C.D. Narasimhaiah speaks of Toru Dutt, Sarojini Naidu and Sri Aurobindo in *The Swan and the Eagle*. He writes about Toru Dutt in the following words:

> For an Indian girl in her teens to demonstrate in English such acquaintance with Greek mythology, Christian and Hindu symbolism, a rare feeling for words coupled with a reliance on speech rhythms, an enviable control of the Sonnet form and above all to vindicate with such seeming playfulness the strength of her own tradition — it is not surprising that Edward Thompson so often critical of Tagore (on whom he writes a whole book) should bracket Toru with Sappho and Emily Bronte (29).

On Sarojini Naidu he writes: "where she succeeded in keeping her emotion somewhat tidy, her sentiment genuine and her rhythms faithful to the folk songs of South India she did compose some very good verses as in the poems, 'Corn Grinders,' 'Indian Weavers,' 'Festival of Serpents' (Song of Radha the Milkmaid) and 'Leile.' In 'To a Buddha Seated on a Lotus,' the poet rejoices inaccessible desire and heavenward hunger and in doing so she sums up the central philosophy of the Vedantas" (21). C.D. Narasimhaiah is more eloquent in his praise of Sri Aurobindo, whom be considers hot only as a distinguished poet but a critic too. He even goes to the extent of telling that English language has gained from Sri Aurobindo. He comes to this conclusion by comparing Sri Aurobindo with Joseph Conrad. Thus, he observes:

> Like Conrad who broadened the descriptive range of the English language, it may be said of Sri Aurobindo that he made the English language accommodate certain hitherto unknown (inconscient) areas of experience both through his prose work "Life Divine" and through his epic, *Savitri*, not to speak of the numerous translations from Sanskrit poetry and drama as well as his other less known but important works (30).

Speaking of Sri Aurobindo A.K. Srivastava asserts: "it is conveniently forgotten that Aurobindo is probably the only example of an Indo-Anglian poet who nearly succeeds in hammering out an idea in English which is peculiar and unique to the genius of the Indian people even if certain ingredients of his poetry such as high seriousness, epic grandeur, verbal artist, heightened metaphor, today seem dated" (34).

M.K. Naik wonders: 'it is strange that certain Indian critics who reverently genuflect before "The Wreck of the Deutschland," "Ash Wednesday" and "The Four Quartets" should turn up their (not always well shaped) noses at these mystical lyrics, perhaps because some Westerners, who probably have neither the time nor the inclination to try to understand their complex symbolism have dismissed them [Aurobindo works] as too ornate' (25). In M.K. Naik's view Sarojini Naidu "was a true nightingale who has had the misfortune to the branded a mere mynah" (26).

Reacting to the poetry written in English by Indians before Independence two anthologists P. Lal and K. Raghavendra Rao assert: "we claim that the phase of Indo-Anglian romanticism ended with Sarojini Naidu" (6-7) and go on to say that the necessity to poetry of "the private voice, especially because we live in an age that tends so easily to demonstrations of mass approval and hysteria. For this reason we celebrate the lyric form as the best suited for a capsule minded public" (6-7). Adil Jussawalla writes: "To my mind... 'Savitri' a poem on the relation of the spirit to matter, unwinding like an interminable Sari through twelve books and about 2400 lines is one vast onion of a poem. The layers gradually fall away to reveal nothing" (76). R. Parthasarathy writes, "'Savitri' fails as a poem because Ghose's talent and resourcefulness in the use of English were limited" (Iyengar 13). And Keki N. Daruwalla says, "it is rather unfair to pick on Sri Aurobindo because no other Indian poet was half as bad, none so nebulous or verbose or who so thoroughly confused, the inflated with the sublime" (14). In course of an article in *The Humanities Review* (July-Sept. 1979), Parthasarathy says, "It [pre-1947 poetry] has the vitality, or what was left of it, of an enslaved nation." Rightly K.R.S. Iyengar takes Parthasarathy and Daruwalla to task in course of an article entitled "Indian Poetry in English: Yesterday-Today-Tomorrow" (*The Literary Criterion*, Vol. XVIII, No. 3, 1983).

On the other hand, there is another group who glorifies modern Indo-English poetry on, parochial considerations. Moreover, some modern poets-turned-anthologists-turned-self-styled-critics who denounce the poetry of pre-Independence era, have an axe to grind — i.e., to win attention to post-Independence Indian English poetry. There are purists (like R.W. Desai whom I have quoted in the beginning of this article), to whom the best modern Indo-English poet would appear as pseudo-Keats, second-rate Tennyson, third-rate Hardy and fourth-rate Eliot. It seems to me that a good deal of poetry of our time can be highlighted without denying, denigrating the poetry of our predecessors or taking a parochial and what George Woodcock calls "literary incestuousness" attitude to recent Indian poetry in English.

To my mind serious contemporary poetry in English came to be written not just after Independence but in the sixties and after. In short, the modern Indian English poetry has come to mean post-1960 Indian poetry in English. This poetry has already acquired a distinct character of its own. There appeared on the scene a large number of Indian poets in English in the sixties and after, making the task of the reader difficult to judge. In an interview not long ago, on being told that "according to one anthology of Indian English poetry, there are over 300 poets writing today," A.K. Ramanujan is reported to have said, "I say good luck to them. Three hundred is not a large number for such a long country" (*The Humanities Review*, Jan.-June 1981, p. 12).

The post-1960 Indian poetry in English has proved increasingly robust, varied, responsive the time and enjoyable. It has acquired a distinct character and discovered its own voice. The voice is discovered by the poet's genius for intimately registering the idiom of his own world. Modernity in post-1960 Indian poetry in English which essentially means a break with the past has three identifiable manifestations: one, a past-oriented vision which is associated with a sense of loss and hopelessness, a sort of cultural pessimism, two, a future-oriented vision, associated with a desire to remake the world, three, a present-oriented attitude, historical, amoral, neutral, stoic, ironic, ambivalent, absurdist. This modernity has two modes of "expression" — one, it might result in one turning inward going on one's "voyage within," two, it might result in an ironic observation of reality in "voyage without."

Poets like A.K. Ramanujan, R. Parthasarathy and Kamala Das turn inward to get into their roots. There is a need to return to one's own linguistic tradition to write poetry effectively. Parthasarathy, as it were, gives a clarion call to the Indo-English poets to return to their respective linguistic traditions. He wonders:

> How long can foreign poets
> Provide the staple of your lines?
> Turn inward. Scrape the bottom of your past.
>
> (*Rough Passage*)

It seems natural to conclude that a poet with a live natural past behind him, aware of his roots and perhaps prejudiced by those roots, has a greater probability of writing significantly than one who has no knowledge of any Indian language other than English. An awareness of Indian may be helpful to get at one's roots. I have in mind A.K. Ramanujan's *Selected Poems* (1976) in which some of the titles of the poems such as "A Hindu to his Body," "The Hindoo: he doesn't hurt a Fly, or a Spider either," "Some Indian Uses of History on a Rainy Day," "Small town, South India," "Old Indian Belief" and the sequence called "Prayers to Lord Murugan" are indicative of the subject. Ramanujan tries to assimilate the Kannada and the Tamil traditions, where his deepest roots lie, into English. His determination to seek his roots is expressed in "Conventions of Despair":

> I must seek and will find
> my particular hell only in my Hindu mind.

On a close reading of Ramanujan's poetry one comes to a conclusion that "Indianness" in his verse is enough to indicate a complex interaction of psychological forces kept under linguistic and formal control. His poetic sensibility operates more in terms of the landscape of the mind, the interior landscape in which memories of India are re-lived with a gusto which belongs to the present.

Taking a clue from Ramanujan to acclimatize the English language to an "indigenous tradition like Tamil, Parthasarathy writes:

"I saw my tasks as one of acclimatizing the English language to an indigenous tradition." In fact the tenor of *Rough Passage* is explicit: it initiate a dialogue between myself and my Tamil past" (Ijes 52).

Similarly, Kamala Das works out her emotional and sexual traumas in poems of unexceptional frankness reminiscent of medieval Sahaja poets who espoused free love as a means of realizing oneself. Traditionally Nayar women were sexually uninhibited because the practice marumakkathayam ("matrilineal system of inheritance and succession") and Kamala Das's bold treatment of sexual relations is an offshoot of her Nayar background. While Ramanujan's mind seems to be perpetually busy probing the areas of strength and weakness of his Hindu heritage, Kamala Das highlights with boldness the sexual permissiveness and uninhibition rooted in her native culture and produces arresting effect on her readers. Parthasarathy is caught in the dilemma of revealing his identity exposed to two cultures — the Indian and the Western.

Poets like Nissim Ezekiel, Keki N. Daruwalla, Margaret Chatterjee, and Lila Ray who are unable to share the indigenous tradition take a different attitude, ahistorical, amoral, neutral, stoic and ironic. Their expression results in an ironic observation of reality, "voyage without." Here, Jayanta Mahapatra and O.P. Bhatnagar join them in making pointed, objective and thought-provoking observations on the reality around them. These poets too have tried, and succeeded to some extent, in evolving a new kind of idiom of post-1960 Indian English poetry. Ezekiel has taken a lead in this direction.

Ezekiel's contribution to Indian English idiom lies in his attempt to re-create Indian characters in their situations. The tone seems to be mocking but Ezekiel reproduces these characters as they appear in their real life. The language is these poems is based on colloquial speech rhythm and the tone is conversational. Poems like "Healers," "Hangover," "The Professor," "Irani Restaurant Instructions" are cases in point. Here Ezekiel uses English the way most semi-literate Indians write, speak, perhaps understand it.

Nissim Ezekiel is a trend setter. His poetry emanates from life. India's poverty, the rituals observed in the country and her people belonging to all walks of life attract the attention of the poet. A leper beggar in a railway station, a woman beggar elsewhere and the beggars, hutment dwellers and pavement sleepers in Mumbai — all appeal to him and he describes them in a cool, detached and matter-of-fact tone. He tries to catch the public ear with "a poetry of popular impersonation" (33) (G.S. Fraser's coinage) trying to imitate the talks of Indian politicians, clerks, reporters, professors, of officials and so on. Ezekiel's award-winning book, *Latter-Day Psalms* contains a number of poems in which the poet makes an attempt to re-create Indian characters in their situations. The tone may appear to be mocking but Ezekiel faithfully reproduces these characters as they appear in their real life. The idiom of these poems is made of colloquial speech and the tone is conversational. Poems like "Very Indian Poems in Indian English," "Healers," "Hangover," "Touching," "Family" and a few others belong to this category.

Ezekiel incorporates the heat and dust, the sun and floods, the sense of poverty and deprivation into the texture of his verse. The image of "India" pervades all through his poetry. The changing reality of love and the human relationship, on the one hand and the unchanging contours of Indian landscape, on the other, are as it were the "spiritus mundi" from where he draws all his images. The commitment to 'Self' and the city of his living (i.e. Mumbai) helps him to create central images like those of his hero, the city and the women. In Ezekiel's *The Unfinished Man* and *The Exact Name* (poems from which have been included in *Latter-Day Psalms*), one notices that the city has moved forward to a prominent position in the poet's consciousness.

Another achievement of post-1960 Indian poetry in English is that by harking back upon the personal failures, losses and agonies, the poets express themselves in a confessional mode or assume some kind of imaginary "self" or even put on a mask to achieve the reader's total participation. Adil Jussawalla writes, "the value of the confessional is that by exposing those dark areas which are normally concealed, it might touch some of the deepest points in the reader's own subconscious and so uncover what is worth uncovering" (84-85). The love poetry of Kamala Das, Gauri Deshpande, and Shiv K. Kumar just does that. However, Shiv Kumar refuses to be identified as a confessional poet. In an interview with Atma Ram, he comments: "I have often been labelled as a 'confessional' poet, and indeed in tone and structure my poetry may be called 'autobiographical.' But what readers fail to comprehend is the fact that a poet often invents facts and experiences camouflaging them as 'real and authentic' — to achieve the reader's total participation. It's more a strategy of the imagination that a transcript of empirical reality" (qtd in Naik 127).

But the fact remains that behind his love poems there lies frustration in love. Not only he but other post-1960 Indian poets in English write unconventional love poems with ease and the poems bear the stamp of their experience and imagination. They no longer write in the manner of Sarojini Naidu, the nightingale of India, who poured her love into a constellation of love poems called "The Temple." Kamala Das is in the main a poet of love from the woman's point of view, at least from the point of view of simple, normal and adult woman to whom the centre is the act of love. The hot-blooded sincerity of feeling, the complexity of moods, the urgency and above all a wider dramatic range, make her love poems animating and enjoyable. Nissim Ezekiel's "Passion Poems" and "Nudes," Daruwalla's "You were the first," Shiv K. Kumar's "To a Prostitute," "Kovalam Beach," "Aftermath" and "To a Young Wife," O.P. Bhatnagar's "Adam and Eve" and A.K. Ramanujan's "To Wife" are some of the outstanding poems of love in post-1960 Indian poetry in English. The point to note here is that these poets are unconventional in their attitude to love and hence their love poems arise a kind of curiosity in the heart of the readers.

To my mind some post-1960 Indian poets in English have shown mastery of verse in ironic social comment. Poets who excel in this area are Nissim Ezekiel, A.K. Ramanujan, Shiv K. Kumar, O.P. Bhatnagar and Keki N. Daruwalla. They are, to speak the least, brilliant commentators on the Indian scene. Politics, marriage, love black marketing, rioting, joint family, rituals, brain drain and a number of social events come in for criticism in their poetry. But I should hasten to add that they are not propagandists. What they intend to do is to create an awareness among the people and to make them alive to the problems of the day and that is just a strategy to get their poetry more and more acceptable and enjoyable too. Post-1960 Indian poets in English should be complimented on being aware of the change that takes place in the society daily and this sharpens their sense of adaptability.

Jayanta Mahapatra, Nissim Ezekiel, O.P. Bhatnagar, Shiv K. Kumar, R. Parthasarathy, Kamala Das and a host of others underline the typical Indian sensibility in their poetry. For instance, Mahapatra's *Relationship* (1980) and two recent volumes, *Burden of Waves and Fruit* (1988), *Temple* (1989) reveal a distinct Indian sensibility that immediately arrests one's attention. History, myths, legends, folklore all go together to establish a distinct idiom and identity in these volumes.

I would like to make a few observations on the position of post-1960 Indian poetry in English. For far too long, and at insufferable length, the validity and viability of the poetry written by Indians in English has been debated, sometimes ironically enough, by some of the poets themselves and their admirers who seem to have an endless capacity to agonize over this non-issue but more often by the detractors of this comparatively nascent art form who have used every gadget in Western critical apparatus to try to destroy it. Questions like the "locale" of Indian poetry in English and its audience have been raised endlessly and fruitlessly. Even people like Khushwant Singh have tried to further classify Indian poetry in English to Punjabi Poetry in English and O.P. Bhatnagar has very rightly contested this point in his essay "The Situation of Indian Poetry in English: An Introduction," and brushed aside this narrow classification. The fact is that Indian poetry in English (for that matter Indian Literature in English) is Indian first and anything else afterwards. Its base is pan-Indian and it has audience all over the country. So the debate over its "locale" and audience seems to be futile.

Serious Indian English poetry began only in the nineteen sixties and after. There has not been enough time for a tradition to take roots. Moreover, the Indian English poet is concerned with the "Indianness" of his experience. The validity of Indian English poetry depends on the creation of a new idiom — let us say, Indian English idiom distinct from the idioms of the writers all over the world who write in English. African writers in English and Caribbean writers in English have discovered their own English idioms and established the validity of their literatures. Thus, there is a demand, as it were, for the creation of an Indian English idiom, to give authenticity and identity to post-1960 Indian poetry in English, independent of and different from the world literatures written in English including English and American literatures. To my mind post-1960 Indian poets in English particularly Nissim Ezekiel, Kamala Das, Shiv K. Kumar, Gauri Deshpande, Keki N. Daruwalla, O.P. Bhatnagar and a few others have succeeded to some extent in creating a new Indian English idiom.

In Ezekiel's poetry one encounters a number of Indian words (Hindi words in particular) in italics. Words like "goonda", "guru", "Indirabhen," "Rama Rajya," "ashram," "burkha," "bhikshuks," "Chapati," "Pan," "mantras" and a few other Indian words are used with a purpose to create new Indian English idiom. Kamala Das and Shiv K. Kumar use a new kind of unconventional vocabulary in their love poetry. A new Indian English idiom hitherto unknown in English poetic diction is used in poetry. Words like "menstrual blood," "the musky sweat between the breasts," "the jerky way he urinates," "my pubis," "lesbian," "hetero," "frigid," "queer," "Scandal scent," "Lipstick," "eunuch," "blood-stain," "schizophrenia," "eczema," "anaemia," "ischemia," "ursine" and the likening of husband's hand to a "hooded snake" that "clasps my pubis" suggesting violence and the likening of heart to an empty cistern "Waiting through long hours fills itself with coiling snakes of silence" and the likening of love to a "swivel door," "when one went out another came in" are certainly new to Indian English poetic diction.

Indian English poetry has now taken for its theme various Indian subjects from legend, folklore to contemporary Indian situations. Our poets no longer sit in ivory towers and sing about birds and cuckoos. They are alive to their contemporary situations. They are conscious artists who "look before and after" and try to bring innovations both in form and content of their poetry. They are conscious of creating a new idiom and employing new imagery in their poetry. There is variety in the post-1960 Indian poetry in English. They do not write poetry in the conventional English poetic diction but in live Indian English language. They speak to us in our own situation and in a language that is spoken, heard and understood by the English educated Indians of our country. Indian English poetry is as much Indian as any other poetry — say Oriya, Bengali, Hindi poetry — is or ought to be. The existence and validity of Indian poetry in English are beyond question now. It has not only come to stay in India but has also found recognition abroad. For example, it has gone as far as Leeds, Chicago and Adelaide. It has been offered as a course in some British, American, Singapore, and Australian universities. Some of our poets have won recognition and prizes, abroad. Indian poetry in English is no longer "Matthew Arnold in a Saree" or "a dog walking on its hind legs" and post-1960 Indian poets in English have discovered their own voices and developed their Indian sensibilities. One happy aspect of post-1960 Indian poetry in English is that it has been able to escape the clutches of Anglo-American influence. The earlier influence of Eliot, Pound, the later Yeats, Wallace Stevens, Dylan Thomas, Ted Hughes, Robert Lowell, Sylvia Plath and Roethke has now been overcome. This poetry has now been taken seriously at home and courses are offered on it at various Indian universities. This has also been accepted as a topic for M.Phil. and Ph.D. dissertations both at home and abroad. The National Academy of Letters, New Delhi, has honoured six of our poets — Jayanta Mahapatra for his book *Relationship* in 1981, Nissim Ezekiel for his book of verse *Latter-Day Psalms* in 1983, Keki N. Daruwalla for *Keeper of the Dead* in 1984, Kamala Das for *Collected Poems* Vol. 1 in 1985, Shiv K. Kumar for *Trapfalls in the Sky* in 1987 and Dom Moraes for *Serendip* in 1994. Some of our Indian English poets have also won the Commonwealth Poetry Prize. Indian poetry in English has come to stay along with poetry written in other Indian languages. This poetry can now stand comparison with the poetry written in English in the Commonwealth as well as in the Third World Countries. The future of Indian poetry in English in immense.

WORKS CITED

Amur, G.S. "Poetry as Subterfuge: An Introduction to Shiv K. Kumar's Poetry," *Aspects of Indian Writing in English*, Ed. M.K. Naik. Madras: Macmillan, 1979.

Daruwalla, Keki N. *Two Decades of Indian Poetry 1960-80*. New Delhi,Vikas Pub. House 1980.

Desai, R.W. "But Where's the Sculpture of Rhyme?," *The Indian Literary Review*, 2 : 1, 1979.

Fraser, G.S. *The Modern Writer and His World*. Penguin, 1970.

Iyengar, K.R.S. "Indian Poetry in English, Yesterday-Today-Tomorrow," *The Literary Criterion*, 18 : 3, 1983.

Jussawalla, Adil. "The New Poetry," *Readings in Commonwealth Literature*, Ed. William Walsh, Oxford, 1973.

Lal, P. and K. Raghavendra Rao. *Modern Indo-Anglian Poetry,* New Delhi. A. Chaya Devi, 1959.

Naik, M.K. "The Achievement of Indian English Poetry," *The Humanities Review*, 4 : 1-2.

Narasimhaiah, C.D. *The Swan and the Eagle*. Indian Institute of Advanced Study, 1969.

Parthasarathy, R., ed. *Ten Twentieth Century Indian Poets*. Delhi: O.U.P., 1976.

——. "Tradition and Freedom". *The Indian Journal of English Studies,* 21 (1981-1982).

Srivastava, A.K. "The Siren Muse: Reflections on the Parent Phase of Indian English Poetry," *Meru*, 1 : 1, 1980.

3

Akademi Award Winning Indian English Poetry as Post-Colonial Text

Though the Central Sahitya Akademi was established in 1954, it has not honoured any Indian English poet with its Annual Award till 1980. It is in 1981 that Jayanta Mahapatra received the first ever Akademi Award for his book of verse, *Relationship*. Since then five more Indian English poets have been honoured by the Akademi with its Annual Award. They are Nissim Ezekiel for his book, *Latter-Day Psalms* in 1983, Keki N. Daruwalla for his book, *Keeper of the Dead* in 1984, Kamala Das for her book, *Collected Poems* Vol. 1 in 1985, Shiv K. Kumar for his book, *Trapfalls in the Sky* in 1987 and Dom Moraes for his book, *Serendip* in 1994. The purpose of this paper is to examine validity of these six books of verse as post-colonial texts, and show how far these six poets have been able to give a direction to post-colonial Indian English poetry.

In 1947, we have not only won our political freedom from colonial rule but also our cultural freedom to write creative literature (including poetry) in English in our own way. Post-colonial Indian English poets at once registered a protest against writing in the manner of their predecessors (i.e., colonial Indian English poets) who wrote by imitating the nineteenth century British poets and also successfully overcame the influence of the contemporary (i.e., the twentieth century) Anglo-American poets. Hence, post-colonial Indian English poets take two definite courses: one, they tend to identify with contemporary India by evoking the landscape of the country and two, they evoke the tradition and culture of the country in order to assume an identity of their own and bring a kind authenticity to their poetry which distinguishes it from other post-colonial poetry written in the former British colonies. The six books of poetry which won Central Sahitya Akademi Award show convincingly the authenticity of post-colonial Indian English poetry by evoking the landscape, history, tradition and culture of our country in English language.

If colonialism involves two types of imperialism — political and cultural, post-colonialism overcomes them by resisting and subverting former colonizer. Hence, myth and history, landscape and language, self and the other, become the ingredients of post-colonialism. The emphasis on national identity, landscape, rituals, tradition and national culture forms the core of post-colonial Indian English poetry. The theme of landscape and national identity makes a rewarding study when applied to the Akademi Award winning poets — Jayanta Mahapatra, Nissim Ezekiel, Keki N. Daruwalla, Kamala Das, Shiv K. Kumar and Dom Moraes. In them one detects a certainty of touch that seems to reflect a confidence in the direction and purpose of their writing as well as an integrity of images of India, style and subject matter. Jayanta Mahapatra's *Relationship*, first published by the Green field Review Press, New York in 1980 has also undergone an Indian re-print in 1982 (Chandrabhaga Society, Cuttack) after being chosen for the Central Sahitya Akademi Award in 1981. This book is no collection of mere observation: a place here, a character there, a non-strenuous meditation or two, inevitable landscapes, but a determined integrated set of sections built into the theme. The poem is set in Orissa — a land of 'forbidding myth'. The first section of the poem, though over worked with images, manages to convey the impossibility of unravelling the mystery of life. The heroic past of the land of Orissa has been recalled with regret.

> Time
> and the boat,
> and the initiation into the mystery of peace,
> the sailing ships of those maritime ancestors,
> who have vanished in the black Bay without a
> trace,
> that only live in the sound of the waves
> flinging themselves into the dark fringes
> of this land from Chilika to Chandipur.

The first Section of the poem serves as an exposition when references are made to the Mahanadi, the prime river of the state, the temple of Konark, the ancient harbours like Chilika and Chandipur. There is a search for roots and the heroic Oriya past is vividly remembered and recalled with a sense of nostalgia. The glory and pride of our ancestors exhibited in the climatic Kalinga war in 261

B.C. which turned Ashok the Great into a deeply religious man is now a long-lost trait in our racial character and behaviour. The river Daya is a witness to our ancestor's heroic effort which has become a sort of myth for us. Once heroic and militant race is no more than mere memory now for its successors proved to be unworthy of keeping the glory of their ancestors afloat and drifted away from their ideals. Thus, the poet notices a sharp contrast in the descending order between the past and the present marking an overwhelming decline in values of life in our time. Thus, the poet laments.

> It is hard to tell now
> what opened the anxious skies
> how the age old proud stones
> lost their strength and fell,
> and how the waters of the Daya
> stank with the bodies of my ancestors;
> my eyes, close now
> because of the fear that moves my skies;

What to speak of the revival of the lost glory by gaining military strength, even to write about it has not been taken kindly by the preceding generation which leads the poet to say that, 'Now you do not even want me to write my poem./ Of those words which spit blood and vomit and speak of malice'. The burden of the last generation 'Burden of your peace, Father', the responsibility of the present generation ('Theme song of my life that burns my tongue') and the concern for the future generation ('Voices of children always wronged') seem to visit the poet now and thus he wants to 'draw my body out of a thousand years.'

The landscape of Orissa thrills the poet and he becomes an integral part of it. Observing the annual migrating birds from far North Siberia to the water of lake of Chilika on Orissa's Southern shores and the rich harvest of rice in December, the poet composes his lines linking the landscape to the agony of the present generation. The agony springs from the fact that while the birds and animals react naturally to the seasons of the year, the poet is cut off, as it were, from the heroic traditions of his ancestors. He knows, 'I can never come alive/ If I refuse to consecrate at the alter of my origins' and thus, 'a prayer to draw my body out of a thousand years'. This realisation helps the poet to explore the myth of the land particularly the 'golden deer' which deluded Rama and Sita the epic hero and heroine of the *Ramayana* who have passed into the Hindu consciousness as god and goddess to seek the meaning in life. Mahapatra speaks of the myth of Sun God and Konark temple. He has a purpose behind the recountings of 'the myth of sleep and action' and is fully aware of the anguish 'passing from man to man'.

There is, as it were, an attempt to dovetail the myth with contemporary reality in order to portray the anguish and predicament of modern man in our time. In section ten, Mahapatra refers to Lord Buddha and how Buddhism came to Orissa — the past is brought alive for a moment, 'of broken empires and of vanquished dynasties/ and of ahimsa's whimpers.' The poet now standing among these ruins drifts through his weariness, listening to the voices of his friends and 'writing poems' with the 'Smells of the rancid fat of the past'. The present would be better understood, appreciated and endured in the light of the past and one would learn how to live from other people's lives. Mahapatra rightly says,

> What one endures
> and one will continue to endure, a kind of
> world
> that comes up of all the love he has known.

An allusion is made to the Oriya folk-tale in which a princess was turned into a flowering tree by an evil charm in the line, the banished princess and the magnolia tree as well, to show an awareness of pervading myth and the conclusion is drawn on the observation that, 'in your dance is my elusive birth' which is a spiritless soul of memory'. Relationship is built on history, myth and vision. The myths of the 'native land' and living past of Orissa coupled with the artistic vision of Mahapatra present an integrated experience. The image of the 'native land' comes fully alive in this poem when the poet tries to re-create the myth in Modern terms and succeeds too to a great extent. The landscape of Orissa artistically portrayed becomes evocative and it gives 'a local habitation and a name', to the poem and appeals to us in our situation.

If Mahapatra writes poetry by evoking history, myth and the tradition of his land of birth, Ezekiel has clearly shown that a poet can write good poetry on contemporary society without harking back to the tradition. He has discovered his voice by identifying himself with modern India, and the city of Bombay (Mumbai) becomes the nerve-centre of his poetry. As a true modern Indian English poet, he creates his poetry out of both "slums and skyscrapers" and accepts life as it comes. Ezekiel's 'growth of mind' is helped by unhabitable condition of the city. If Wordsworth could measure his life with 'mountains and valleys', and Eliot with 'coffee spoon', then Ezekiel does so with 'slums and skyscrapers'. Therein comes his resolution:

> I cannot leave this island
> I was born here and belong

What makes a poet belong to a particular country necessarily involves nationality, and his identity is to be found in being rooted in the soil. A poet's response to the landscape of his country, his sense of tradition and culture of the land of his birth and many factors go together to make him assume an identity of his own. Nissim Ezekiel is right when he says that "there is no single Indian flavour which alone can claim the designation ('Indianness') and that its value too depends on the host of generative factors which should never be simplified for purposes of praise or blame".

Ezekiel is deeply rooted in the Indian soil. In him one discerns a certainty of touch that seems to reflect a confidence in the direction and purpose of his writing as well as an integrity of images of India, style and subject-matter.

Ezekiel incorporates the heat and dust, the sun and floods, the sense of poverty and deprivation into the texture of his verse. The images of 'India' pervade all through his poetry. The changing reality of love and the human relationship on the one hand and the unchanging contours of Indian landscape on the other, are, as it were, the spiritus mundi from where he draws all his images. The commitment to 'self' and the city of his living (i.e., Bombay) help him to create central images like those of his hero, the city and the woman. In *The Unfinished Man* and *The Exact Name* (poems from which have been included in *Latter-Day Psalms*), one notices that the city has moved forward to a prominent position in the poet's consciousness.

The author as a person may be absent from his work, but he is present in it 'as a certain functional' principle 'which limits, excludes, and chooses' in order to bring an organic relationship between the various texts of the author. Ezekiel resolves to 'be my own guest in my own one-man lunatic asylum' and determines 'to sing/the song of my experience'. As a man strives to exist in a modern urban society, to search for truth and to realize identity with the self and the community, his struggles, failures and frustrations reveal not only his own inward nature but also the insufficiency and frailty of the fallen city, — an image which has already been discussed in the beginning of this chapter. "Urban" is a very compact poem so far as the imagery is concerned. The city that 'like a passion burns' is an image of the bride, and in an ideal sense, a complete sexual union would mark the realization of fullness and identity. Since the persona merely 'dreams' and shies away from her, the use of the keyword 'kindred' in the last line turns out to be ironical. Thus, what the persona achieves is a kind of illusory union with the 'city' and this forms a kind of habitual response to it.

Without commitment to life and living, all rituals turn out to be mechanical. 'Lovers, when they marry, face Eternity with touching grace' become meaningless when marriage does not ensure love, and hence, the poet employs the image of 'Primal Fall' by way of a contrast. In "Marriage" and "Case Study", Ezekiel talks of mechanical responses to different social acts and commitments. The actions of the persona, 'a foolish love affair', 'useless knowledge', involvement in politics, marriage and vocation, are part of programmed social ritual that one is expected to perform. The commitment to 'self' and the city of his living helps him to create central images like those of his hero, the city and the woman which in turn counter his sense of alienation.

Ezekiel writes a new kind of poem in which he examines a typical Indian situation and tries to re-create the characters in their true colours. He makes an effort to bring alive those characters before the readers so that they (the readers) will take them as authentic and real. Poems like "Healers", "Hangover", "Jewish Wedding in Bombay" and "Very Indian Poems in Indian English", "Undertrial Prisoners", "Song to Be Shouted out", "Touching" and "Family" in *Latter-Day Psalms* belong to this category. In India many people are after faith-cure. Many people are credulous and superstitious by nature, so they are by the 'healers' of faith. Ezekiel takes a look at such a subject in a poem called "Healers":

> The unplanned city has a death-wish
> everybody the business, buying cures,
> so the healers come in droves.

These 'healers' pose to know the secret of all 'cures', and it does not matter if their patient is a man or a woman, vegetarian or non-vegetarian, married or unmarried. They prescribe the same kind of cure for all. As the poet puts it:

Know your mantra, meditate,
release your kundalini
get your shakti awakening and float with the spirit
to your destination.

In "Hangover", the poet exposes the people who are double dealers. They preach one thing and practise the other. Between the word and the deed falls the shadow. He describes a scene in a five-star hotel where people talk of Marx but order expensive dishes and express lip sympathy for the suffering people and eat costly and nutritious expensive food. Contradiction in action and hypocritical nature of these people are summed up in the following two lines:

The expensive menu and the shadow of Marx
The Biryani Hyderabadi and the sighs for Bangla Desh.

Shifting the responsibility and turning a deaf ear to the spirit of law, the authorities try to explain away such things casually. It is due to the callousness of the appropriate officials and the bottleneck created by the so-called democratic system in the administration of the country that people suffer disproportionately to their crime. Thus, it is not law that has failed us but we have failed it. In "Undertrial Prisoners", Ezekiel brings to our notice the delayed process of the trial of prisoners which sometimes results in harassing innocent people for no fault of theirs. Undertrials are kept behind the bars for years together before the actual trial takes place. We are yet to modernize our method of trial. Thus the poet writes:

We have our rules
made long ago
he's got to wait
the law says so,
it's not our fault
he lives in jail
he did something wrong
and he can't pay bail ....

Ezekiel reflects on another situation in which an overbearing wife shouts at her sober husband. In our country the attitude of woman towards man has changed in recent years. Gone are the days when a wife used to be devoted to her husband and worshipped him. In "Song to be shouted out", the poet presents the picture of a docile husband whose wife demands from him a lot of answers on his return from office:

I come home in the evening
and my wife shouts at me,
Did you post that letter?
Did you make that telephone call?
Did you pay that bill?
What do you do all day?...

Did you bank that cheque?
Did you buy those tickets?
Did you ask if cheese is in stock or not?
What do you do all day?

The decent husband has only to say,

Shout at me, woman,
What else are wives for?

Like some of the post-colonial Indian English poets, Ezekiel is sensitive to the stresses and challenges of the modern world — a world of screaming headlines and double dealings. He is determined to come to grips with the real problems of the day — political, social and economic. He tries to catch the public ear with "a poetry of popular impersonation" (G.S. Fraser's coinage), trying to imitate the talks of Indian politicians, clerks, reporters, professors, officials and so on.

Ezekiel not only recreates Indian characters in their situation but he recreates the language as well. The tone may appear to be mocking as the poet becomes an ironist or even a parodist but he faithfully recreates these characters as they appear in their real life. Ezekiel's friendliness and sympathy with the poor and common people redeem his poetry from being caricatures of people. Gieve Patel draws our attention to this aspect of Ezekiel's poetry in the following lines: "It [friendliness] redeems also the "Very Indian Poems in Indian English", prevents them from becoming unkind caricatures of people who do not know the language they use, in fact gives their language warmth and a kooky status. Friendship permeates Ezekiel's world, touches poem after poem goes about its business trying to repair creation's lapses. It alleviates the grotesqueries of poverty, squalor and brutishness" (1989 : XXVI).

Ezekiel's language is typical Indian English and the voice that speaks through the poems is honest and emphatic. He recreates the characters in their own situation, and thereby lends authenticity to them. The readers once used to it will not let this variety of English die. This new idiom gives a distinct identity to Ezekiel's poetry. What distinguishes Ezekiel from other poets writing in English either in India or elsewhere, is his fashioning of a new language of poetry to express modern man's experience in a faithful and accurate way. Like Eliot, Ezekiel brought everyday conversational language closer to poetry and made it the medium of his poetry. In "The Professor" Ezekiel describes an encounter between a retired Professor and his former student in everyday conversational language that gives a sense of immediacy to the subject. The introduction serves as a kind of renewal of the past in realistic terms:

> Remember me? I am Professor Sheth.
> Once I taught you geography. Now
> I am retired, though my health is good.

Then the protagonist (i.e., Professor Sheth) gives an account of his family before switching over to subjects of common interest like family planning and contemporary living. He says,

> These are the days of family planning.
> I am not against. We have to change with times.
> Whole world is changing. In India also
> We are keeping up. Our progress is progressing.
> Old values are going, new values are coming.

The implicit irony in 'our progress is progressing' brings home the protagonist's dissatisfaction with the rate of progress in our country. Finally, he turns to his old student by humourously contrasting his past with the present, before he closes the dramatic monologue by inviting him (i.e., the student) to call on him during his next visit. He says,

> You were so thin, like stick,
>
> Now you are man of weight and consequence.
> That is good joke.
> If you are coming again this side by chance,
> visit please my humble residence also.
> I am living just on opposite house's backside.

The poem is in the form of a dramatic monologue and the language is typical Indian English. The word 'backside', which has different connotations, is used instead of 'behind'. This poem evokes a real scene in the Indian context.

Poems like "Songs for Nandu Bhinde", "Song to be Shouted Out", "Touching", "Family", "Soap", "The Way it Went",

"Healers", "Hangover", "Ganga", "Goodbye Party for Miss Pushpa T.S.", and "Guru" are written in this mode. Ezekiel in these poems has used an idiom 'really used by men'. Ezekiel does not invoke the moon, stars, and the 'ocean of bliss' and creates his metaphors and similes from everyday life. He handles his language with meticulous care, skill and sophistication.

Ezekiel's irony is woven into the very texture of his poetry. His irony is direct. As Shiv K. Kumar rightly says, "his [Ezekiel's] irony comes through more incisively in his poems written in Indian-English, which is a mix of Indian vernacular and half-baked English" (1992 : 4).

Poems like "Morning Prayer", "Case Study", and "Night of the Scorpion" make use of irony. In fact, irony is the hall-mark of good poetry and even great poetry. Thus, "Night of the Scorpion" ends with an undertone of irony:

> My mother only said
> Thank God the Scorpion picked on me
> and spared my children.

One encounters the frequent use of irony, paradox and metaphor in a number of Ezekiel's poems. Ezekiel has the gift of story-telling. Moreover, he can create poems out of ordinary incidents and situations that one encounters in everyday life. He takes a situation, examines it, and describes it in such a way that it immediately assumes a kind of social significance. Thus, he turns his personal emotion into "structural" emotion which finally becomes artistic emotion.

Ezekiel is a conscious artist. The centre of poetic interest in him lies in the process of adjustment between the knowledge derived from experience or personal feelings and the knowledge which imposes a pattern. To read his poetry is to watch an actor enacting his coming play in all its facets — love, sex, commitment to life on the stage, it is to know him inside out. He deals with love and sex directly and boldly. Ezekiel stands with W.B. Yeats for 'profane perfection of mankind' in which sense and spirit are fully and harmoniously exploited. He writes:

> This longing is for nakedness:
> Soul naked, body naked ......
> And let him understand, that in the working
> of his mind the body takes a hand.
>
> (*Nakedness*)

Ezekiel considers love and the consummation of it as the Spring of life. And, therefore, he emphasizes fulfilment in love leading to marriage. He says,

> Life can be kept alive
> By contact with the unknown and the strange,
> A feeling for the mystery,
> Of man and woman joined, exhaustion
> At the act, desire for it again.
>
> (*To a Certain Lady*)

Ezekiel seems to say, 'hail wedded love', for it brings fulfilment to life. Like D.H. Lawrence, he sees marriage and procreation as a mystery:

> Between the acts of wedded love
> A quieter passion flows,
> which keeps the nuptial pattern firm
> as passion comes and goes,
> And in the soil of wedded love
> Rears a white rose.
>
> (*Marriage Poem*)

So strongly does he hold this view that he projects the union of man and woman as a key to our survival in this world. Like T.S. Eliot, he also sees marriage as a process essentially of this world and part of the cycle of time:

> Destroying or creating, moving on or standing still,
> Always we must be lovers,
> Man and wife at work upon the hard
> Mass of material which is the world.
>
> (*To a Certain Lady*)

Ezekiel's poetry is a veritable apotheosis and dramatization of personality through passion and affirmation. His characters — Miss Pushpa T.S., the Railway Clerk, the Professor, the English teacher, Ganga, the maid-servant, Guru, and host of others symbolize the achievement of personality. They are individuals as well as types. His world is warm, palpable and dynamic, his personages are vividly present and recognizable in terms of 'chief intensity' as the poet himself.

In his memorial lecture on Yeats, Eliot said, the great poet is the man who 'out of intense and personal experience is able to express a general truth: retaining all the particularity of his experience to make it a general symbol'. This is what Ezekiel's poetry does by revealing Indian reality in our situation. His 'scorpion' in "Night of the Scorpion" has become a household name and a living myth. Ezekiel's greatest contribution lies in making the English language able to carry the weight of his Indian experience and at the same time keeping it fit to communicate with the English-speaking people all over the world.

Keki N. Daruwalla is the third Indian English poet to win the Central Sahitya Akademi Award for his book of verse, *The Keeper of the Dead* in 1984. He has successfully evoked the Indian landscape in his poetry and availed himself of contemporary reality to such an extent that he ranks among the front ranking post-colonial Indian English poets like Nissim Ezekiel, A.K. Ramanujan, R. Parthasarathy, Jayanta Mahapatra and a few others. In his introduction to *Two Decades of Indian Poetry* 1960-80, Daruwalla writes:

My poems are rooted in landscape which anchors the poem. The landscape is not merely there to set the scene but to lead to an illumination. It should be the eye of the spiral. I try that poetry, relate to the landscape, both on the physical and on the plane of the spirit. For me riot-stricken town is landscape (1980 : 21).

The landscape has a deep impact on life and it is integrated with seasons. No wonder, that it has great influence over the lovers. In a poem titled "From the snows in Ranikhet" (To a friend newly married), Daruwalla writes:

It's pleasant thought that seasons
will in each other blend
while you move along a landscape
of yearning that will end
in the precincts of your bodies
which you'll seed and tear and rent.

Large scale deaths in India because of disease and lack of medical facilities upset the poet and he writes a lot of poems on this theme in *The Keeper of the Dead*. Death is the central metaphor in this volume. Daruwalla as it were, 'was much possessed by death/And saw skull beneath the skin'. In 'Pestilence in Nineteenth Century Calcutta', Daruwalla depicts the large scale deaths in Calcutta in the Nineteenth century, when people died of common diseases.

In a poem titled "The Parsi Hell" Daruwalla unambiguously states his death consciousness which is largely shared by Indians althrough the ages in the following words:

> Throughout life a man carried his death
> even as a woman carries her child.

If creation of a new idiom in English is one of the characteristics of post-colonialism, then Daruwalla's claim to be a post-colonial poet cannot be overlooked. He wants to use new idiom and create new themes by writing about contemporary Indian reality, subverting the tradition so that Indian English poetry will assume an identity of its own. In a poem called "The King Speaks to the Scribe", Daruwalla suggests:

> Write whatever
> you chance on. Don't look for a white-quartz boulder
> Anything will do, a mass of trap rock
> or just a stone sheet. And the language simple
> something the forest folk can understand.

Kamala Das is the fourth Indian English poet to have been awarded by the Central Sahitya Akademi for her book of verse, *Collected Poems* (Volume I) in 1985. Born in Kerala, and brought up in Calcutta, she has also lived in Delhi and Mumbai, in a sense she has felt the pulse of the whole of India. Her imaginative world derives its power to involve the reader from its rich mimetic content while its enduring quality comes from verbal imagery drawn from many sources. Thus, she grapples with ideas and abstractions, images of men and women on several planes, the complex of emotions centring round human activities such as love, sex, companionship and problems relating to her own art. Her feminine sensibility finds its true and fullest expression in her love poems. Indian sensibility is transparent in her poetry and the use of Radha Krishna myth makes a more appealing to the Indian readers. Krishna, the eternal lover is a living consciousness among Indians and epitome of love. The utterance of His name brings joy to millions of people in India. In a poem called 'Ghanashyam' Kamala Das invokes Lord Krishna with a heart filled with devotion and joy.

A poet may assume an identity by referring to national myths, so that when the myths are employed, the link is immediately established in the minds of the people. The use of national myths helps to create an identity for the poet. Post-colonial poets in their effort to create an identity of their own by way of resisting and subverting the colonizer, make use of national myths. Kamala Das has exactly done that by evoking Mira Bai myth in her poetry. The sudden disappearance of Mira, a devotee of Lord Krishna has become a living myth and legend in our country. Like Mira all devoted and religious minded women desire to merge with the ultimate consciousness — i.e. Lord Krishna. In a poem titled, 'Radha' a virgin girl after the first embrace says crying: 'Everything in me/ Is melting, even the hardness at the core/O Krishna, I am melting, melting, melting'. In another poem, 'Krishna' the protagonist surrenders with the following words:

> Your body is my prison, Krishna,
> I cannot see beyond it,
> Your darkness blinds me.
> Your love words shut out the wide word's din.

In her poetry, apart from love, Kamala Das describes a world which is harsh, sun-pierced tropical world full of smells of rotten garbage and death, where men have 'limbs like carnivorous plants'. The lanes are 'fevered', the trees dusty and leafless, cheeks 'sun-stained' only the marigolds and bougainvillea survive, and courtesans with 'tinsel and jasmine in the hair'. The poet herself feels "a hunger to take in with greed, like a forest fire/that consumes." As Eunice de Souza rightly suggests that "against a background of this brought landscape on to which the poet projects so much of her inner sense of dirt and sexual disgust, Kamala Das plays out her rules of unhappy women, unhappy wife, mistress to young men. Mother, reluctant nymphomaniac pining for the lost joys of innocence and childhood" (1977 : 22).

Kamala Das subverts the conventional myth of marriage by refusing to submit to the husband blindly. She is in the main a poet of love, of love from the woman's point of view. To her the centre is not blind worship of the husband but the consummation of love. She goes to the extent of advocating love outside marriage because love for her has become 'swivel door/when one went out another came in'.

Like Ezekiel, Das uses conversational and colloquial language to re-create the characters in their situation. Her poetry is lucid, scrupulously honest in its effort to be accurate, and sincere. There is no traditional love-ritual, no hyperbole, and no hypocrisy in it. The tone is conversational, the attitude is defiant against deifying either the lover or the beloved and the voice that speaks through the poems is thoroughly honest. Courage, conviction and honesty are the hallmark of her poetry. She expresses a feminine sensibility that demands equality with man and examines love relationship from a woman's point of view. She does not imitate Anglo-Americans but uses words as naturally as they come to her. She does not experiment with English language but uses it in a typical Indian way with native accent and collocation. She is not obsessed with the use of English language either in the manner of the British or the Americans. She uses English as an Indian speaks, writes and perhaps understands it. It is in this sense that she is a modern Indian English Poet.

Shiv K. Kumar is the fifth Indian English poet to have been honoured by the Central Sahitya Akademi for his book of verse, *Trapfalls in the Sky* in 1987. The theme of landscape and national identity makes a rewarding study in Kumar's poetry. He grapples with ideas and abstractions, images of men and women on several plains, the complex of emotions centring round human activities such as love, sex, companionship and problems relating to his own art. The poet's primary commitment is to the image and symbol through which he apprehends reality. Telescoping of images and multiplied association is characteristic of Kumar's poetry. Indian landscape has inspired the Indian English poets like Kumar and a few others to create newer and more fascinating images that have not been created ever before.

Trapfalls in the Sky is in three sections:

'On Native Grounds', 'Under Alien Skies' and 'Genesis'. Kumar gives a distinct touch to his Indian sensibilities in these sections. In a poem titled, 'An Indian Mother's advice to her Daughter before Marriage' is a typical example of how Indian mothers tender advice to their daughters to get in on in married life.

> A man's memory is myopic
> like a sparrow's; once filled up
> he hardens into a bedrock.
> And often at night you may find
> yourself alone, pulling feathers
> Out of your pillow. But be patient.
> If he's gone out fishing down the dark
> river, he'll be back
> for in spite of his appetite, a man
> cannot swallow both ends of the rainbow.

Like Ezekiel, Kumar is against mechanical performance of rituals. He is in favour of the subversion of tradition and rituals and, therefore, irony becomes a favourite mode in his poetry. Instead of river Ganga cleansing us, we need to cleanse it to get rid of water pollution. Thus, he writes:

> It's only when they are carried down the river of time
> that iron sinks into their souls.
> The waters then get sullied by ritual and dogma-
> ashes and bones,
> wilted floral offerings to the dead,
> and the noontime sweat oozing from the saffron-
> striped foreheads of the crocodiles
> whose yawning jaws chant mantras in some obsolete
> tongue.
>
> May be if someone could dismantle all scaffoldings
> along the mother river's waistline
> and ask the dead to seek immersion
> in other confluences,
> the little fish will then bleach these waters
> for the sun's lasers to probe her limpid groin.

As a post-colonial poet, Kumar makes an attempt to come to terms with contemporary reality. The picture of the capital city of India (i.e. Delhi) is brought alive in a poem called "O'Delhi". To read the poem is to know 'the horror and boredom' of life in this city and it is to see it inside out. Kumar recalls his harrowing days when he landed in Delhi as a refugee. In a 'frigid morning' when Kumar landed in Delhi, which received him with open arms.

> ... I felt redeemed
> as you threw open your gates — Kashmir and Ajmeri
> to welcome indoors a fugitive from another land.
> I savoured your hospitality.

But this Delhi is no more. The poet, who like Adam inherited 'a new garden' asks Delhi: 'what have you done to yourself?' And then makes a prophesy:

> I prophesy that you too will fall
> like Nireveh and Babylon
> and no new Indraprastha will rise
> from your barren ashes.

Kumar's treatment of the theme of love in terms of the elements of Indian landscape has the poetic reconciliation of the spirit and the country. He incorporates the heat and dust, the sun and flood, the crowd, the sense of poverty and deprivation into the texture of his moods. Images of 'India' are handled with a consummate skill and keenness of intellect in Kumar's poetry. Unlike other post-colonial Indian English poets Kumar writes a number of poems on the West and sees it from the Indian view point. His poetry fits into the definition of post-colonial literature which states that the post-colonial writer writes back (*The Empire Writes Back)*. Two sections of *Trapfalls in the Sky* ('Under Alien Skies' and 'Genesis') are about the West, Kumar's poetry exhibits both 'subversion' and 'resistance' — the two important traits of post-colonial literature.

Dom Moraes is the sixth Indian English poet to win the Central Sahitya Akademi Award for his book of verse, *Serendip in 1994*. The title, Serendip is taken from the old name of Sri Lanka, called 'Serendip'. Dom Moraes makes it clear in the introduction to the Book.

Ceylon was at one time known to travellers by this name. The associations it has acquired are such that 'Serendip' now seem a mythical place. As a child I lived for two years in Ceylon, and in its forests encountered the Veddahs, shy tribesmen who are said to have been the first inhabitants of the island. My recollections of these people, and of pilgrims with lamps climbing Adam's peak, are very clear, and on these sonnets I have tried to turn them into myth and symbol (1990 : 10).

Like Kamala Das, Moraes writes about Ceylon (Sri Lanka), a former British colony and brings the landscape of that country alive in his poetry. The interaction between the colonial past and post-colonial present gives rise to a new kind of poetry in *Serendip*. Moraes' interest in anthropology has contributed a lot to the second sequence of poems 'Steles' in this volume. He has got 'the feel' for places of archaeological sites and museums. The dead seems to be absorbed into the place and landscape of the country, and 'memories feel your nostrils'. Landscape, and nostalgic harking back to the past, love and death all attract his attention. His poetry is sometimes about himself, it includes his fears, obsessions and desires. But he achieves a kind of perfection in his poetry by transcending the personal feeling and making it universal. He may have "some regrets and memories" but 'not unhappy to have lived'. His poetry is an affirmation of life.

The six Akademi Award Winning books of poems are post-colonial texts both in thematic content and in articulation of words, phrases, images and above all, in the 'subversion' and 'resistance' of not only the former colonizer but also the colonial Indian English poets. These post-colonial poets have convincingly established anti-colonial nationalism which succeeded in overcoming the cultural imperialism of the West. To conclude, I should say that post-colonial Indian English poetry not only reminds us of Eliot's counsel 'home is where one starts from' but also Ezekiel's assertion 'home is where we have to gather grace'.

WORKS CITED

Daruwala, Keki N., ed. *Two Decades of Indian Poetry,* Ghaziabad: Vikas Publishing House, 1980.

——. *The Keeper of the Dead,* Delhi: Oxford University Press, 1982.

Das, Kamala, *Collected Poems,* Vol. I, Trivandrum: The Poet, 1984.

Eunice, de Souza, Kamala Das, *Osmania Journal of English Studies,* 13 : 1, 1977.

Ezekiel, Nissim, *Latter-Day Psalms,* Delhi: Oxford University Press, 1982.

Kumar, Shiv K., *Trapfalls in the Sky,* Madras: Macmillan, 1986.

——. *Contemporary Indian Literature in English,* New Delhi: Manohar Publication, 1992.

Mahapatra, Jayanta, rep. *Relationship,* Cuttack: Chandrabhaga Society, 1982.

Moraes, Dom, *Serendip,* New Delhi: Penguin Books, 1990.

Patel, Gieve, *Nissim Ezekiel: Collected Poems, 1952-88,* Delhi: Oxford University Press, 1989.

4

The Crisis of Identity in the Poetry of Derek Walcott

It has been rightly said that one can take a person out of his country but not the country out of his mind. In the post-colonial age, the concept of 'Home' has become extremely complicated. In the closing decades of the twentieth century the expatriate experience has given rise to expatriate literature — thanks to the massive migratory movements of various people across national and continental boundaries. Though the destinations differ, the reasons for migration seems to be the same for all the Commonwealth expatriate writers — that is, to reach a larger audience the world over through the English language. Therefore, the Commonwealth writers from Africa, West Indies, India, Australia, Pakistan migrate either to England or to America with a hope to win the attention of a large number of readers cutting across countries and continents. But this expatriate experience invariably results in a sense of loss, for it involves an unbearable rift from one's origin and tradition. The expatriate writers face the dilemma of choosing between the language of their creative expression (i.e., English) and the country of their birth-resulting in the crisis of identity. As Chinua Achebe rightly says:

(Colonialism) did bring together many peoples that had hither to gone their several ways. And it gave them a language with which to talk to one another. If it failed to give them a song, it at least gave them a tongue for singing (1975 : 57).

It is heartening to note that post-colonial writers accept both (i.e., the native land and the English language, their migration notwithstanding) and reject neither. What Miss Robin Hyde, a New Zealand writer says in this context is equally applicable to all post-colonial expatriate writers including Derek Walcott:

"It's just dawned on me that I'm a New Zealander and surely, the legends of the mountains, rivers and people that we see around us should mean more to us than the legends of any country on earth" (1990 : 229).

A good writer is one who assimilates both the cultures — of his native land and the land of his present living — and makes a multi-cultural commitment to transcend the individual consciousness and thereby achieves universality. Derek Walcott, the Caribbean Nobel Laureate in Literature for 1992, is one such expatriate poet who has achieved universality for his multi-cultural commitment.

The Swedish Academy, explaining its decision, said, "three loyalties are central for him — the Caribbean where he lives, the English language and his African origin." Born in the island of St. Lucia in the West Indies, Walcott was educated at St. Mary's College, Castries, St. Lucia and at the university campus of the West Indies, Mona, Jamaica. His father, Warwick Walcott, was English and had great interest in the theatre and opera. His mother was a prominent social worker and a producer of amateur dramatics. Though he has a chair in English at Boston University, U.S.A., where he works, he still retains his West Indies nationality. This is by way of introduction to his life. His volumes of poetry include *In a Green Night* (1962), *The Castaway* (1965), *The Arkansas Testament,* his autobiographical poem, *Another Life, The Gulf and Other Poems* (1969), and his latest poetic work *Omeros* (1990) a majestic Caribbean epoch in sixty-four chapters.

In Walcott one is aware of a treble impulse — that of his African origin, the West Indian birth and upbringing and the recent American stay which keep him at a distance from his environment. He is caught in a dilemma to choose between the country of his origin, on the one hand, and the English language, on the other. Cameron King and Louis James, bring out this aspect of Walcott's poetry: "Reacting against demotic imprecision of language, he declares that as a literary artist he seeks" (1973 : 289).

> As climate seeks its style, to vote
> Verse crisp and clear as sunlight
> Cold as the curl'd wave...
>
> (*Islands*)

In another poem, Codicil Walcott states that, "To change your language you must change your life." The dilemma of choosing between one's tradition and medium of expression is beautifully expressed in "A Far Cry from Africa." It is a very significant poem for it gives expression to multi-cultural commitment for which he was awarded Nobel Prize for literature. "If there is any dominant principle for literary prize giving that influences the Swedish Academy," writes Stephen Breshow, "it is: a strong regional voice that transcends its topical locality, through the depth and breadth of its poetic resonance and through its global human implications. The publication of Walcott's *Omeros* in 1990 absolutely certified this same long-standing quality of his work. *Omeros,* a rare modern verse epic, places Walcott's birthplace of St. Lucia at the centre of his epic cosmos, builds its local islanders into epic heroes, magnifies their conflicts into epic battles, visits the exotic shores of Africa, North America, and Europe on Odyssean journeys and gives voice (in a lyric mode that departs from traditional epic form) to the epic writer himself, Walcott as the lonely, exiled 'Homer'. In the manner of Joyce and Yeats, Walcott has merged a profound, rhapsodic reverie upon his remote birthplace — its people, its landscape and its history — with the central, classical tradition of Western civilization" (1993 : 267).

What's unique to Walcott is his multi-cultural consciousness that successfully binds his native tradition and present profession of teaching and writing in English together. Those critics who charge him with neglecting the indigenous West Indies tradition and embracing 'the dominant culture of European imperialists', are silenced by his 'historical themes of the African diaspora, his colourful St. Lucian characters, and the epic largesse of *Omeros*' (*Ibidem* : 268). Walcott is inspired by Antillean natural settings and Port of Spain, Trinidad and Castries, St. Lucia form as it were, his central 'cityscapes'. Walcott's closely drawn characters appear in his two epic — length poems, *Another Life* and *Omeros.* This epic mode suits his poetic talent to develop more generalized human typologies which blend into larger and universal themes.

Like T.S. Eliot, who integrated the history of England into the texture of his poem *Four Quartets,* Walcott too revokes the Caribbean history in his attempt to place it along with the European history in course of his poetry. Breslow makes it clear in the following words:

"From the outset of his poetic career through his recent completion of *Omeros,* Walcott has sketched and resketched discrete fragments, long passages, and cosmic eons of history unfolded in the Caribbean. Beginning at the zero point, the "blank pages turning in the wind," and the infinite void of blue azure and Caribbean sea imaged in many of his poems, Walcott has set out to reconfigure and to reprioritize Caribbean history. From his post-colonial vantage point, the poet has been freed to "reverse the sights" on European history, on the prior heralded exploits of imperialist expansion, the "conquest" of indigenous people, slave-trading, and colonial cultivation. In most of the "official" European and American histories of colonial grandeur, the slaves have been mere footnotes to essentially white texts. The true history of Caribbean blacks, as of the Caribbean Indians before them, remains largely unwritten. This vast and sad ignorance permeates even the present generation, as Walcott's persona, Shabine, reflects in "The Schooner Flight" (from The Star-Apple Kingdom, 1979) : "Who knows/who his grandfather is, much less his name?" His history is only one that his "masters please". "Official" histories are most frequently promulgated on some notion of "progress," and "progress" is quite hard to discern within the backwash of present-day colonial vacuums, as Shabine goes on to lament in "The Schooner Flight": "Progress leaving all we small islands behind.... Progress is history's dirty joke" (*Ibidem* : 270).

Walcott does not forget the landscape of his country and keeps: his umbilical cord intact. Once Walcott wrote: "I needed to become omnivorous about the art and literature of Europe to understand my own world. I write my own world because I had no doubt that it was mine, that it was given to me, by God, not by history, with my gift" (1974 : 27). In a poem called 'A sea-chantey', he recalls his past and sings the song of his ancestors. He writes:

> A young sailor is playing
> His grandfather's chantey
> On a trembling mouth-organ
> The music curls, dwindling
> Like smoke from blue galleys
> To dissolve near the mountains.

Walcott does not disown the past and the torture of the colonizers is still fresh in mind. "A Far Cry from Africa" states the dilemma the minds of the poet — how to reconcile the past with the present in the post-colonial era, becomes the burden of his poetry. The agony of colonial torture is still fresh in his mind. As Walcott puts it:

> A wind is ruffling the tawny pelt
> Of Africa. Kikuyu, quick as flies

Batten upon the bloodstreams of the veldt.
Corpses are scattered through a paradise.

The gruesome picture of torture inflicted by the colonizers is suggested by the image of "worm" which vitiated the atmosphere. This is a recurrent image in Walcott's poetry. He is bitter against the colonial policy. He revolts against the injustice meted out to the natives of Africa. The discrimination against race and colour is brought out in the following lines:

Statistics justify and scholars seize
The salients of colonial policy
What is that to the white child hacked in bed?
To savages, expendable as Jew?

The voice of humanity is drowned in the hatred of man for his fellow human beings as the colonizers choose to discriminate against people on grounds of colour and race. With a touch of pathos tinged with irony, Walcott records:

The violence of beast on beast is read
As natural law, but upright man
Seeks his divinity with inflicting pain.

The result of inhuman torture is the "native dread/of the white peace contracted by the dead." Man's cruelty to man has resulted in "a waste of our compassion."

Against the backdrop of the colonial exploitation, the West Indies poet has to choose between the cultural past and native tradition, on the one hand, and the English language, on the other. The last stanza of the poem expresses Walcott's dilemma as a poet. Walcott not only tries to acclimatize an indigenous tradition to English language but he also struggles hard to keep up multi-cultural commitment and, therefore, he appeals to people cutting across continents. The last stanza of the poem contains a series of questions — partly rhetorical, for Walcott has chosen to retain both his native tradition and the acquired English language. Thus, he concludes:

I who am poisoned with the blood of both,
Where shall I turn, divided to the vein?
I who have cursed
The drunken officer of British rule, how choose
Between this Africa and the English tongue I love?
Betray them both or give back what they give?

How can I face such slaughter and be cool?
How can I turn from Africa and live?

Walcott is caught between a commitment to the English cultural traditions — 'the English tongue I love' — and the national identity of the Caribbean. This idea of multi-cultural commitment is further reinforced in *Omeros* where he celebrates the "many strands" in his life:

I'm just a red nigger who love the sea,
I had a sound colonial education
I have Dutch, nigger and English in me
And either I'm nobody or I'm nation.

Love for the English language, concern for the native country and nostalgia for the African origin combine in his poetry and enable him to fulfil the multi-cultural commitment which make him a universal poet.

Derek Walcott has an open mind. And he puts down no shutters and puts on no blinkers. By transcending the limitation of his native tradition and through his multicultural commitment, he has assumed an identity of his own, that is both enduring and lovable.

WORKS CITED

Achebe, Chinua, "The African Writer and the English Language", *Morning Yet On Creation Day,* 1975.

Breslow, Stephen, "Derek Walcott: 1992, Nobel Laureate in Literature", *World Literature Today,* 67 : 2 April 1993.

King, Cameron and Louis James, "In Solitude for Company: The Poetry of Derek Walcott", *Readings in Common-wealth Literature,* ed. William Walsh, London: Oxford University Press, 1973.

Narasimhaiah, C.D. ed., quoted. *An Anthology of Commonwealth Poetry,* Madras: Macmillan, 1990.

Walcott, Derek, "The Muse of History: An Essay." *Is Massa Day Dead. Black Moods in the Caribbean,* ed. Orde Combs, New York: Anchar, 1974.

5

The Poetry of Nissim Ezekiel and the Question of the Reader Response

The question that puzzles an Indian reader is how to approach Nissim Ezekiel's poetry, particularly when he has shown a double impulse of being a native and an alien at the same time? It takes us to the next question: how does his poetry affect the reader? The communication from an author to a reader through the text has ever been a delicate problem which baffles the critics all through the ages. The problem becomes all the more difficult in our time because we no longer accept the proposition that it is the author's 'text' nor the opposite — that is, the reader's 'text'. May be it is both and neither. If 'text' is not what the author makes it to be but it is as the reader takes it to be, then we can say that the 'text' and reader not only act upon one another but there are many reversible reactions between them. The purpose of this paper is to make a study of Ezekiel's poetry in the light of the recent Reader Response criticism.

Ezekiel is an Indian Jew of Ben-Israel origin. That is why, in spite of his being a natural citizen of India, the sense of 'alienness' abides. This dilemma in life does not escape the notice of the critics. As William Walsh rightly observes:

> One is aware of a double impulse in the poet, which, on the one hand, keeps him at a distance from his environment as he clutches to his private history and aspirations, and which on the other, by means of a free and painful act of will, reconciles him to his environment (Walsh, 1979 : 106).

Ezekiel is not unaware of this dilemma in his life. In course of an interview given to *World Literature Written in English* he states:

"My background did make an outsider but it's too easy to talk being an outsider. I don't want to remain negative: I feel I have to connect and turn the situation to the positive" (Beston, 1977 : 2). R. Parthasarathy emphasizes this aspect in his introduction to *Ten Twentieth Century Indian Poets*, and quotes Ezekiel: "I am not a Hindu and my 'background makes me a natural outsider: Circumstances and decisions relate me to India'" (Parthasarathy, 1976 : 28).

Apart from saying in interviews, Ezekiel also states the question of belongingness in three of his important poems.

This is the place
where I was born. I
know it
well.

(*After Reading a Prediction*)

I have made my commitments now,
This is one: to stay where I am.

(*Background Casually*)

I cannot leave the island,
I was born here and belong.

(*Island*)

Ezekiel being culturally distanced from India's heritage, tries to identify himself with modern India. He takes a detached view of contemporary Indian situation both — ahistorical and amoral. After knowing Ezekiel's stand as a writer, let us analyse his poetry on the basis of Reader-Response criticism.

The most important thing in Reader-Response criticism is that the reader must be made to feel for himself the new meaning of the text. To do this he must actively participate in bringing out the meaning and this participation is an essential precondition for communication between the reader and the writer. The author creates as it were an image of himself and another image of his order and the successful reading is that in which the created characters, writer and reader can find complete agreement. On being asked a question. "Do you have in mind the audience, your readers when you write?", Ezekiel wrote:

"No but I am not indifferent either to a hypothetical reader. I do not put into a poem what would baffle me as a reader. I imagine readers who are at least as intelligent and human as I am or more but not less" (In reply to a questionnaire sent by this writer).

In an interview given to *Gentleman* Ezekiel said:

> To start with, my own inspiration is and always was 'my inner life'. And writing is, for me, a way of coping with the tension between my inner life and the outer life. Looking back, this, from the earliest days, seems to be the main source of my writing. Every other source is somehow related to it — even the experiences of other people. My poems are often introspective and, therefore, express self-criticism, and self doubt. I also write about my relationship with other people, love, sex, the individual in society, etc. (Ezekiel 1984 : 97).

In order to understand and appreciate a poet's work from the stand point of the Reader-Response criticism, we will do well to remember that the empirical self of the poet goes extinct as he starts creation. And his poetry is marked by the implied personality which is the point of view embodied in it. On the other hand, we should take note of the fact that a poet often invents facts and experiences camouflaging them as real in order to elicit the reader's total participation.

Nissim Ezekiel's poetry resembles 'Confessional Poetry' and in tone and structure it may be called autobiographical. But all that he describes in first person has not necessarily happened to him. It has happened to people around him and he merely describes. But many readers take the first person in the poem as the empirical self of the poet. A literary work is now known as a 'text' and the way an individual reads it as a text on the basis of a theory of meaning is known as reading. Depending upon the kind of reading one makes, we have the 'implied reader', the 'ideal reader', or the 'super reader' and the 'real reader'. Ezekiel refuses to take his entire poetry as a search for identity or as autobiographical. In course of an interview given to Dr. Frank Birbal Singh, Ezekiel states:

> I don't think every thing I write or say or do should absolutely and unconditionally have what I have discovered to be my identity. That would suggest psychological insecurity. I would prefer to claim that nine times out of ten my being human is more important than anything else in the whole world (Ezekiel, 1992 : 173).

Ezekiel's poetry thematically could be grouped under the following heads: "Very Indian Poems in Indian English", poems of human love including 'Passion Poems', and 'Nudes 1978', poems on contemporary situation including 'Poverty poems', 'Ten Poems on Greek Anthology Mode', 'Edinburgh Interlude', 'Hymns' and 'Latter-Day Psalm'. Of these, 'Very Indian Poems in Indian English', 'Passion Poems' and 'Nudes 1978' are variously read by different readers. Meanings in these poems are not quite clear. They offer a kind of suspended meaning to the reader to explore depending upon his perception.

Let us take a close look at his 'Very Indian Poems in Indian English', and erotic poems like 'Passion Poems' and 'Nudes 1978'. Most of the poems under the category of "Very Indian Poems in Indian English" are situational poems. Ezekiel writes a good deal of situational poems. Some readers call them parody and Ezekiel a parodist. Others say that they are comic poems written to be laughed at and, therefore, they resent such kind of poetry. Ezekiel himself asserts that here there is a 'faithfulness of temperament' (Ezekiel, 1992 : 161).

Ezekiel wrote a lot of situational poems. Almost all his "Very Indian Poems in Indian English" are situational poems in which he re-creates the Characters in their own situation. The poem could be read and appreciated in relation to the situations that underlie them, and according to the conventions of poetry — 'poetry of popular impersonation' (G.S. Fraser's coinage, Fraser, 1970: 30) or situational poetry demands upon the reader to be aware of the background or acquainted with the socio-cultural ethos against which this poetry is written in order to be understood and appreciated properly. A well-known Reader-Response critic Jonathan Culler rightly maintains that while there will be variations in the assimilation of the system by actual readers, their emphasis falls upon the common system. The system itself will set the limits to the individual response. However, within the limits a wide variation is possible. In his well-known essay, 'The Pursuit of Signs', Culler says,

> Variation in Interpretation are not an obstacle, they are rather the fact with which one starts. What one is attempting to explain is the fact that for any work there is a range of interpretations which can be defended within the conventions of reading (Culler, 1981; 124-25).

The conventions of Poetry are impersonal, while the individual response is the dialectic of the personal and the impersonal. Let us take some of his poems for a close study. "Goodbye Party for Miss Pushpa T.S.", "The Railway Clerk", "The Patriot", "The Professor",

"Soap", "Song to be Shouted Out" and "Dead end Story" are often variously interpreted by different readers. To some these poems appear as parody and even worse, caricature. Some readers take them as a piece of satire and for others the note of irony is unmistakable. But if one starts reading these poems against the background of Indian English idiom actually used by half-educated Indians, and the actual use of English in Indian situation one cannot help taking them seriously. Moreover, a poet cannot put words into the mouth of the character which he does not know at all. In other words, in order to re-create characters in their situation faithfully, one has to use the language they actually speak and that is what Ezekiel has done. It is in this sense to Ezekiel is faithful to his characters. He does not laugh at these characters, he merely reflects. Miss Pushpa, T.S. is taking leave of her colleagues on the eve of her foreign trip to improve her prospects, and a farewell party is organized to bid her a warm send off. And this is how the poem goes:

> Friends,
> Our dear sister
> Is departing for foreign
> In two three days
> And
> We are meeting today
> To wish her bon voyage.
> She is most popular lady
> With men also and ladies also
> Whenever I asked her to do anything
> She was saying, 'Just now only
> I will do it'. That is showing
> Good spirit. I am always
> Appreciating the good spirit.
>
> (*Goodbye Party for Miss Pushpa T.S.*)

The Railway Clerk who does his work sincerely gets no promotion because he is not a graduate and he has no extra income, for nobody gives him bribe. Hence, the complaint and resultant frustration.

> Every day there is so much work
> and I don't get over time.
>
> ...
>
> My job is such, no one is giving bribe,
> While other clerks are in fortunate position,
> and no promotion even because I am not graduate.

I am never neglecting my responsibility
I am discharging it properly.
I am doing my duty,
but who is appreciating?

(*The Railway Clerk*)

The Professor, who met an old student of his, tells him about his family, and country in a matter of fact tone. The situation is brought alive with the use of present progressive tense:

These are the days of family planning
I am not against. We have to change with times.
Whole world is changing. In India also
We are keeping up. Our progress is progressing.
Old values are going, new values are coming
Everything is happening with Leaps and bounds.

(*The Professor*)

In India we normally use present progressive tense in place of simple present tense. The characters in the aforesaid poems do exactly the same. But what is important here, is that the voices that speak in these poems are thoroughly honest. In a sense Ezekiel's characters are individuals as well as types.

Like "Very Indian Poems in Indian English", the 'Passion Poems' and 'Nudes 1978' are variously interpreted by different readers. Some dismiss them just as erotic poems having no literary value and to others these poems merely mean a vulgar display of sex and sensuality. In these poems Ezekiel has actually raised a question by seeking to differentiate between nakedness and nudity. In India, in the temple walls we see many erotic arts where men and women are shown in different poses of sexual union. If in art nobody questions nudity, then why should we object to the description of sex act in poetry, Ezekiel seems to ask. A foreign critic, Bruce King, to my mind reads these poems in their proper perspectives when he observes:

> 'Nudes 1978' is a remarkable sequence of fourteen unrhymed sonnets, each different in structure. They are among Ezekiel's better poems of the later period. While W.H. Auden popularized in recent times the idea of a loose narrative made up of a string of poems, each a variation on the sonnet form. Ezekiel, in treating of sexuality and love-making in his poems, takes the sonnet back to its more normal subject matter of love and desire. But here, as implied by the title, desire is examined with critical self-consciousness. The title suggests a series of

> nude portraits like a painter's work on a theme during a period of time. This is furthered by the distinction between naked and nude, the former usually referring to bareness, being unclothed, whereas nude is more cultured, more a term from the arts. A model, a dancer, an actor may be nude without shocking the cultured whereas a naked person violates most social norms. The naked is scientific, the nude is cultured. We see the world with a naked eye. People are nudists not nakedists. Ezekiel uses this distinction both to examine the social arts that accompany seduction and to draw a parallel between his poems and a painter's series of nude portraits in which formal qualities and matter are of equal interest. Thus, the poems shift rapidly between discussion of the women as forms, as an, as objects of desire, as individuals and there is a constant secondary significance, as discussion of form and experience can also refer to the art of poetry (King, 1991 : 48).

In the opening lines of *Nudes 1978* Section I, Ezekiel makes his point clear. He writes:

> This body has a name,
> or the name has a body.
> It is not the subject of my love
> but a form, an art
> in which I am absorbed.

Each of the fourteen poems in the sequence *Nudes 1978* is different. There is the shy woman, the rich woman and others who fill these poems with thoughts and incidents but the poet, in 'Artist of the nude' unable to being satisfied with either art or pornography 'resorts to something more direct', which would be a Zen-like direct knowledge of truth.

In 'Passion Poems' Ezekiel holds the ancient Sanskrit poet as his ideal and describes love and sex freely. Sex and sensuality are a part of life. Ezekiel believes that in order to accept a work of art one has to affirm sensuality. As he puts it:

> I have lost my reason —
> let it go.
> Did I create this woman
> untameable and yet
> willing to be tamed?

Only Shiva, meditating
could be immovable
in her moving presence

(*Passion Poems VIII*)

English language has a sadly limited erotic vocabulary. Any reader who is conversant with Sanskrit literature knows how our ancient poets have romanticised love and described sex act including female anatomy. Compared to that, Ezekiel's erotic poetry is nothing, it pales into insignificance.

Ezekiel excels in creating situational poems. Take, for instance. 'Night of the Scorpion' ostensibly written for a foreign audience, takes a very insignificant incident for a theme. But Ezekiel creates a memorable poem out of an ordinary situation with which Indian readers are familiar. To foreign readers it conveys an Indian ethos but to us it shows how poetry could be created out of a trivial incident or everyday reality. The speaker in the poem recalls an incident when his mother was stung by a scorpion and then goes on to describe how it happened and what followed. The poem demonstrates an unusual depth of feeling, a remarkable economy of language and a rare imaginative insight.

As I have stated in the course of this paper that the empirical 'self' of the poet goes extinct as he proceeds to create and the implied self which is a point of view embedded in the work emerges. "Hymns in Darkness" illustrates this point well. Ezekiel here makes an attempt to make us aware of the sense of reality. He tries to universalize the predicament of man through bardic imperative. Thus, he says:

I met a man once
who had wasted half life
partly in exile from himself
partly in a prison of their own making.
...
A tireless social human being
destined always to know defeat
like a twin brother.

(*Hymns in Darkness*)

A reader has to understand the background of the poems in order to understand them. The Impersonality of the reader is necessary to appreciate a work of art. As Poulet puts it:

Reading then is the act in which the subjective principle which I call 'I' is modified in such a way that I no longer have the right strictly speaking to consider it as my 'I'. I am on loan to another, and this other thinks, feels, suffers and acts within me (Poulet, 1969 : 58).

Let us take some other poems which are written in the first person narrative such as 'Jewish Wedding in Bombay' and 'The Visitor'. In the first poems 'the reluctant bridegroom of the day' is not necessarily the 'empirical self' of the poet. It is the 'implied personality' that matters here. This implied personality is the point of view embodied in the poem. What the poet emphasizes here is how we mechanically perform rituals without any belief in them. This poem is an implied criticism of modern mechanical approach to a religious question. Ezekiel writes:

> I remember the breaking of that glass and the congregation
> Clapping which signified that we were well and truly married
> according to the Mosaic Law.
> Well, that's about all. I don't think there was much that struck me as
> solemn or beautiful. Mostly, we were assumed, and so were the others
> Who knows how much relief we had?
>
> (*Jewish Wedding in Bombay*)

'The visitor' describes a superstitious person in the first-person narrative who thinks that if a crow caws three times, then a guest would come to the house. This is a common enough superstition among Indian people. The poet says:

> Three times the crow has cawed
> At the window,...
> Three times I got the message.
>
> (*The Visitor*)

Ezekiel describes the scenes he encounters in everyday life, and gives a subtle touch to them so that his characters speak to us in our situation. A beggar woman at railway station, a leper beggar elsewhere, a maid servant, a professor, a mother stung by a scorpion, a guru, a middle-aged city dweller, an undertrial prisoner all attract his attention and he faithfully portrays them in his poetry. Through them, Ezekiel seeks to reach an intense universality of meaning. To read his poetry is to watch an actor enacting his tragic-comic play in all its facets — love, politics, sex, religion, contemporary reality on the stage, it is to know him inside out. His world is warm, palpable and dynamic, and his people are vividly present and recognizable in terms of 'chief intensity' as the poet himself.

Ezekiel like W.B. Yeats knows how to make poems about the self while keeping away from it. He takes the stance of a detached observer and discusses personal emotions and conduct intellectually in abstractions. He has come to terms with reality and becomes somewhat sceptical. He uses antithesis and paradox as a device to portray contemporary reality and create a live Indian English idiom. Let us take a look at the following lines:

> A man withdrawn into himself
> may be a man moving forward.
> ...
> I am near everybody
> being near myself alone.
>
> (*Happening*)
>
> The further I move
> away from madness
> towards stability
> and a measure of sense
> the closer I seem
> to the verge of madness
>
> (*Dilemma*)
>
> The closer you come, the further you move.
>
> (*Distance*)

To know oneself is not egoism but the gateway to all virtues. Ezekiel while trying to come to terms with reality remembers Eliot's method of bringing everyday conversational language to the realms of poetry. The use of irony, antithesis and paradox helps the poet to grasp reality, 'here and now'.

How does Ezekiel's poetry affect the reader? It is very important to remember that while some of the foreign critics including William Walsh, praise Ezekiel for his desire to identify himself with modern India, others fail to read him properly. As a result, Ezekiel gets uncritical adulation or unqualified blame for not trying to acclimatize an indigenous tradition to English language, the way Ramanujan, Parthasarathy and even Jayanta Mahapatra have done in their poetry. One should not take either the praise or the blame seriously.

Ezekiel's poetic pilgrimage begins with a longing 'to own a singing voice and a talking voice/A bit of land, a woman and a child or two' and reaches an Olympian height when empirical self gets transcended obliterating the individual desire. Hence, Ezekiel moves forward expressing his desire to do some public good before he hears his 'last song'. He writes:

> I want my hands
> to Learn how to heal
> myself and others
> before I hear
> my last song.
>
> (*At* 62)

Ezekiel has 'abundance, variety and complete competence' for which Eliot praised Tennyson so much. Reader Response Criticism could be made use of in the explication of his poetry, provided the reader takes the conventions of his poetry along with its variety into consideration. Ezekiel's poetry is at once representational and non-representational. Reader-Response criticism will be helpful in evaluating Ezekiel as a poet as it takes the whole gamut of his poetry as a dialectic of the personal and the impersonal.

WORKS CITED

Beston, John B. *World Literature Written in English*, Arlington: University of Texas (April), 1977.

Culler, Jonathan. *The Pursuit of Signs*, Ithaca, New York: Cornell University Press, 1981.

Ezekiel, Nissim. *Gentleman* (July), 1984.

Ezekiel, Nissim. *Selected Prose*, Delhi: Oxford University Press, 1992.

Fraser, G.S. *Modern Writer and his World*. Penguin Books, 1970.

King, Bruce. *Three Indian Poets*, Madras: Oxford University Press, 1991.

Parthasarathy, R. *Ten Twentieth Century Indian Poets*, Delhi: Oxford University Press, 1976.

Poulet. "Phenomenology of Reading", *New Literary History* (October), 1969.

Walsh, William. "Small Observations on a Large Subject", *Aspects of Indian Writing in English*, Madras: Macmillan Company of India, 1979.

6

Margaret Atwood's *Surfacing* as an Eco-Feminist Novel

Margaret Atwood's novels, *The Edible Woman* (1969), *Surfacing* (1972) and *The Handmaid's Tale* (1985) are regarded as feminist novels, and Atwood is taken as a feminist writer. Her other texts like *Survival* (1972) and *Bodily Harm* (1981) too reveal her feminist attitude in unmistakable terms. *Surfacing* has been interpreted variously: as a novel of self-discovery, as a blue-print for revolution, as an anti-colonial novel, and finally as a feminist novel. Each of these interpretations though right in its own way, is inadequate to make a full explication of the novel. I think the novel can be adequately explained in terms of ecofeminism and hence, this paper seeks to interpret it as an ecofeminist novel. At the outset, I would briefly discuss feminism and ecofeminism in literature of our time and then proceed to analyse *Surfacing* in terms of ecofeminism. First, I begin with feminism.

Feminism is an ideology which seeks not only to understand the world but to change it to the advantage of women. Simone de Beauvoir's phrase 'the second sex' with reference to woman cut ice. He opines that woman's idea of herself as inferior to man and dependant on him springs from her realisation that 'the world is masculine on the whole, those who fashioned it, ruled it and still dominate it today are men' (de Beauvoir, 1949 : 298). Though the biological distinction between male and female is an accepted fact, the notion that woman is inferior to man is no longer acceptable to women in general and feminists in particular. Simone de Beauvoir asserts that 'one is not born but becomes a woman' (*Ibidem* : 273). The old prejudice against woman as being weaker than man in all respects is also reflected in the language system — particularly in English one notices the pronoun is largely male-oriented. Now there is not a single position in the society, including administration and government which is not being occupied by woman. Today we have women Presidents, Prime Ministers, Scientists, Commanders, administrators and what not. Thus, the feminist movement aims at overthrowing social practices that lead to the oppression and victimization of women lock, stock and barrel. In the words of Shirin Kudchedkar, "it disputes the conflation of sex and gender categories and releases women from confinement to gender roles. It aims at making woman the subject of her own story and not the object of male desire and male satisfaction or a whipping block for male frustration. Women come to realize the inauthenticity of the lives lead and struggle to discover for themselves their own impulses, reactions, desires and needs. Their quest is for self-knowledge and self-realization which can in turn lead to relationships based on mutual understanding and respect. Individual change and social change, both are desired goals, together with an eventual change in male perceptions and attitudes" (1996 : 34).

No wonder that Hélène Cixous has reiterated the demand for self-assertion by women writers and leaders of the feminist movement in unequivocal terms: 'Woman must put herself into the text — as into the world and into history by her own movement' (Prabhakar, 1994-95 : 126). Margaret Atwood reacted against the so-called optimism of post-feminist era in the 1980s and after (it is presumed that feminist era ended in the 1970s and post-feminist era began in the 1980s) in the following words:

"It would be a mistake to assume that everything has changed ... the goals of the feminist movement have not been achieved, and those who claim we're living in a post-feminist era are either sadly mistaken or tired of thinking about the same subject" (1982 : 370).

Feminist writers refuse to accept the 'images of women' as portrayed by male writers. They are of the view that women characters portrayed by men in literature are lacking in authenticity. In other words, men have portrayed women as they find them not as 'women' would have perceived themselves (i.e., from men's point of view, not from the view point of women themselves). This kind of attitude prompted Carlo Christ to say that 'Women have not experienced their own experience' (Christ : 5).

Colonialism and patriarchy are seen as power structures that exploit and, therefore, the former is seen as a paradigm of the latter in feminist literary criticism. In Canada colonial exploitation is seen as a kind of exploitation of both nature and women. To Northrop

Frye, Canada is 'the only country left in the world which is a pure colony, colonial in psychology, as well as mercantile economics' (1971 : III). Margaret Atwood goes a step ahead when she says that, "Canada as a whole is a victim, or an 'oppressed minority' or 'exploited', a colony for someone else's profit" (1972 : 35). Colonial power-structures have gone deep into the collective unconsciousness of Canada and have become a metaphor for feminine and nature exploitation for women writers in that country. The kind of attitude that links colonial exploitation of female and nature together gives rise to Ecofeminism.

In the words of Joyce Nelson: "Ecofeminism bridges the gap between ecology and feminism: strands of analysis which have existed side by side over past decades without necessarily intertwining. By making explicit the connections between a misogynist society and a society which has exploited 'mother earth' to the point of environmental crisis, Ecofeminism has helped to highlight the deep splits in patriarchal paradigm" (1990 : 15). Greta Gaard maintains that, "Drawing on the insights of ecology, feminism, and socialism, ecofeminism's basic premise is that the ideology which authorises oppressions, such as those based on race, class, gender, sexuality and physical abilities, is the time ideology that sanctions the oppression of nature" (1992 : 20). In a broad sense Ecofeminism seeks to do away with all kinds of oppressions and holds the belief that no attempt to liberate women will be successful without a similar attempt to liberate nature from the onslaught of modern technology and the colonialists.

I would like to further elaborate the concept Ecofeminism by quoting a paragraph from Malashri Lal. She writes:

Breaking down the definition to its detailed components, I may clarify further the terms in which ecofeminists perceive Western cultural history. Body and nature have been patriarchy's "shadow" easily projected on to woman, who through her biological rhythms and her domestic milieu is easily seen to be "close to nature". With further connotations of wilderness, non-civilised state, primitivism, unformed condition, woman in man-made society was seen to require the mediation of man to 'civilise' her away from nature and take her closer to the realm of God or morality and social ethics as designed by patriarchy. Hence, emerged what ecofeminists call a "hierarchical dualism". Man and woman are not just "opposites" but the female is subordinate and inferior to the male. Man's enterprise in subduing female nature to his will is analogous to his mechanistic and technological domination over the Earth's original environment. That which resists subjugation causes unease, fear, and a sense of evil. The exploitative relation between man and woman, and man and nature, is equated (1995 : 309-10).

In a number of novels, Margaret Atwood deals with women's experience in a male-dominated world. She presents the women characters as the victims of male-dominion and oppression, trying to create a female space for themselves. These characters refuse to play second fiddle to man and challenge the so-called theory of male-superiority. Atwood seems to hold cudgel for women. Linda Hutcheon is right in saying that, "In all her writing, Atwood shows herself to be the tireless explorer and exposer of cultural clichés and stereotypes, in particular of those that affect women" (1969 : 313).

Surfacing is divided into three parts and this division corresponds to shift in tense from present (Part I) to past (Part II) and again to present (Part III). At the surface level the story told in the novel by the unnamed protagonist is plain and simple: it describes a trip made by the female protagonist, her boyfriend Joe and two other friends, Anna and David, a married couple, to a small island in distant part of North Quebec. While the protagonist's friends treat the trip as a break from city life and a short holiday she seeks to find out what has happened to her father, who after the death of the protagonist's mother, used to live alone on the island, and has lately been reported missing. As a child, the protagonist worshipped her father, a logical and scientific man, as a God; identifying with him rather than with her mother. The journey revives her memory of the unhappy past from which she feels estranged and brings to her mind the recent traumatic events — a painful relationship with her art teacher, a married man and the forced abortion. The art teacher who was determined to crush her artistic talent and sensibility by denying her the opportunity to grow as an artist, finally played a trick on her concealing his marital status he presented her a wedding ring and convinced her of his intention to marry her. The protagonist was taken by his words and got pregnant in the process. Then she understood the exploitative behaviour of her lover who forced an unwanted pregnancy upon her and took it as a part of sexual colonialism. Although she had an abortion willy-nilly, she felt during her pregnancy that the foetus in her womb belonged not to her but to her art-teacher (fake lover), that 'he imposed it on me, all the time it was growing in me I felt like an incubator ... after it was born I was no more use'.

That is the reason why she wanted to fill her womb again with the help of Joe, her boy friend. "I'll get pregnant", I said, 'it's the right time' (1980 : 157). But she did not intend to marry. David and Anna's relationship frightened her. Anna is stripped naked for the purpose of film 'Random Samples' by her husband David and his friend Joe, the cameraman. Man and woman are shown not as complementary to each other but as victimizer and victimized respectively. The protagonist having perceived this decides to stay back on the island alone. That helps her to overcome passivity and casts her in a new role of self-assertion with individual identity. She states, "I have to recant, give up the old belief that I am powerless and because of it nothing I can do will ever hurt anyone. A lie which was always more disastrous than the truth would have been. The word games, the winning and losing games are finished: at the moment these are no others but they will have to be invented, withdrawing is no longer possible and the alternative is death" (*Ibidem* : 206).

At the deep level the novel can be interpreted better in terms of eco-feminism. Take for instance the opening sentence of the novel: "I can't believe I'm on this road again, twisting along past the lake where the white birches are dying, the disease spreading up from the South, and I notice they now have sea-planes for hire" (*Ibidem* : 7). The dying of birches is seen as a disease resulting from technological expansionism which Atwood equates with 'Americanism'. The narrator's sympathy for dying birches (which symbolizes nature) is taken as a Canadian trait and this is contrasted with the two Americans who cruelly killed the heron. But these two Americans turned out to be Canadians. This prompted Atwood to say that, 'if you look like them and talk like them and think like them then you are them' (*Ibidem* : 129).

Atwood has made an attempt to create an emphatic relationship between the wounded self of the unnamed protagonist and the damaged landscape of the island near the border country in Quebec. Her journey to Quebec with her three friends (David, Anna and Joe) made her see into the life of things and in the process she gets away from all — her friends as well as the American-Canadians who indulge in senseless cruelty to birds, trees and fish. Atwood writes:

At the midway pond the heron was still there, hanging in the hot sunlight like something in a butcher's window, desecrated, unredeemed. It smelled worse ... the death of the heron was causeless, undiluted (*Ibidem* : 129).

She realizes though belatedly that no human being can help her in discovering her identity (i.e., her real self) and, therefore, she turns to nature. Ironically enough it is only when she identifies herself with the damaged landscape that she discovers herself. She becomes 'part of the landscape' but prior to this, she discards her marriage ring, her name and her seeming identity. In this connection Jaidev makes a significant comment:

"*Surfacing*, however, addresses itself to such fundamental human issues as cruelty and violence, both of which are associated with power. In a very disquieting piece of reflection, the heroine identifies herself with the landscape so that her tragedy and that of the landscape mirror each other, reflect each other. What men do to women, they do to Nature as well. Americans desecrated this border country and killed off most of the beavers. Then, they used the term beaver as a slang for the vagina. This is wittily feminist, but it is not merely that: it is also a comment on what those who hold power tend to do to those who lack power, who are indeed innocent: they killed off beavers for the same reason that they abuse women or kill the harmless, innocent heron: "To prove they could do it, they had the power to kill". All power is used for destroying the innocents. "The innocents get slaughtered because they exist, I thought, there is nothing inside the happy killers to restrain them, no conscience or piety...." The beavers, the heron, the stunted and disfigured landscape are all thus used as variations on the theme of power and the destruction it causes, and it is almost needless to add that woman's abuse too is a variation on the same theme. Indeed, the heroine is careful to point out that just as woman and the landscape are in a symbiotic relationship, persons represented through the term American are not confined to any particular country at all" (1985 : 113).

Atwood does not spare Americans who have done damage to Canadian landscape. For her the term 'Americans' has become a metaphor for power hungry people from Hitler to this day:

"It doesn't matter what country they're from, my head said, they're still Americans, they're what's in store for us, what we are turning into. They spread themselves like a virus, they get into the brain and take over the cells and the cells change from inside and the ones that have the disease can't tell the difference. Like the late show sci-fi movies, creatures from outer space, body snatchers injecting themselves into you dispossessing your brain, their eyes blank eggshells behind the dark glasses. If you look like them and talk like them and think like them, then you are them, I was saying, you speak their language, a language is everything you do.

But how did they evolve, where did the first one come from, they weren't an invasion from another planet, they were terrestrial. How did we get bad? For us when we were small the origin was Hitler, he was the great evil, many-tentacled, ancient and indestructible as the Devil. It didn't matter that he had shrunk to a few cinders and teeth by the time I heard about him; I was certain he was alive, he was in the comic books my brother brought home in the winters and he was in my brother's scrap-book too, he was the swastikas on the tanks, if only he could be destroyed everyone would be saved, safe. When our father made bonfires to burn the weeds we would throw sticks into the flames and chant "Hitler's house is burning down, My Fair Lady-O" we knew it helped. All possible horrors were measured against him. But Hitler was gone and the thing remained; whatever it was, even then, moving away from them as they smirked and waved goodbye, I was asking. Are the Americans worse than Hitler? It was like cutting up a tapeworm, the pieces grew" (1980 : 139).

The nameless protagonist finds a reflection of her own tragedy in the Quebec landscape. In course of her homeward journey the protagonist discovers that 'nothing is the same. I don't know the way any more.' She has been alienated from the landscape of her country, for the 'Old road' has been closed for years and what she needs is 'the new one' but she does not 'know the way anymore'. This actual journey is the surface meaning while the deep meaning lies in the journey of self-discovery and assertion of her individual identity. These two kinds of meanings (surface meaning and the deep meaning) links ecology with feminism and makes the novel an eco-feminist novel.

The protagonist finally refuses to be victim. She decides to stay back in Quebec and give birth to the 'gold fish' nurturing in her womb. She does not know whether the child in her womb is a male or a female child but has made up her mind to assert herself by allowing the foetus to grow. She says:

"I cannot know yet; it's too early. But I assume it: if I die it dies, if I starve it starves with me. It might be first one, the first true human, it must be born, allowed" (*Ibidem* : 206).

With the protagonist's determination to give birth the child, the novelist has hinted that germination will take place and the implication is crystal clear — that's both women and nature will be protected provided they defend themselves against the onslaught of men over them.

WORKS CITED

Atwood, Margaret. "Introduction to The Edible Woman", *The Second Words: Selected Critical Prose*, Toronto: Anansi, 1982.

——. *Survival: A Thematic Guide to Canadian Literature*, Toronto: Anansi Press, 1972.

——. *Surfacing*, Ontario: Paper Jacks Ltd, 1980.

Christ, Carol. *Diving Deep and Surfacing: Women Writers on Spiritual Quest*, Boston: Beacon Press, 1980.

de Beauvoir, Simone. *The Second Sex,* trans. H.M. Parshley, London: Four Square Books, 1949.

Frye, Northrop. *The Bush Garden: Essays on the Canadian Imagination*, Toronto: Anansi Press, 1971.

Gaard, Greta. *Women and Environment*, Spring, 1992.

Hutcheon, Linda, Quoted. "Afterword" in *The Edible Woman*, Toronto: The New Canadian Library, 1969.

Jaidev. "Women as Metaphor: A Note on Atwood's Feminism", *The Indian Journal of English Studies,* 1985.

Kudchedkar, Shirin. "Feminist Literary Criticism", *Journal of Literary Criticism* 8 : 1, 1996.

Malashri, Lal. "Inheriting Nature: Ecofeminism in Canadian Literature", *Post-Modernism and Feminism Canadian Contexts* (ed.), Shirin Kudchedkar Delhi: Pancraft International, 1995.

Nelson, Joyce. "Speaking the Unspeakable", *Canadian Forum*, March, 1990.

Pravakar, H. "Pen as a 'weapon' in Margaret Atwood's 'Bodily Harm'", *The Commonwealth Review*, 6 : 2, 1994-95.

7

The Language of *The God of Small Things*: A Post-Colonial Study

Post-colonial theory is open to question. It unlocks many a flood gates and broadens the scope of post-colonial literature by making it open ended. For some post-colonial theorist, post-colonial literature is 'subversion' and 'resistance' of the imperial 'Centre' and for others, it is an assertion of identity both in themes and language. It is an essential precondition that post-colonial literature must be written in English. But it is no longer the Queen's English but other English (or english) and it is this 'english' that has given an identity to post-colonial literature which is both lovable and enduring. In the post-colonial era we find post-colonial literatures in the erstwhile British colonies written in varieties of 'englishes', which may be regarded as dialects of the Queen's English. Hence, we find African English, Australian English, Canadian English, Caribbean English, Indian English, and so on. Each variety of these 'englishes' has produced substantial body of literature in the erstwhile British colonies. In the light of this post-colonial theory I would like to show how Arundhati Roy's Booker Prize Award Winning novel for 1997, has been successful in creating a new Indian English idiom that at once distinguishes it from the Queen's English and other englishes (i.e. Australian English, African English, Canadian English, Caribbean English and so on).

The plot of the novel is complex and it moves both ways — backward and forward — and thereby makes the narration difficult and complicated. Thematically it centres round Ammu, her two children Raphel and Esthappen, her parents, brother, Chacko and his wife Margaret and daughter, Sophie Mol and above all, Amu's low caste lover, Velutha, the paravan. The novel opens with Raphel's coming back to Ayemenem after a failed marriage, to see Estha, her twin brother ('they were two-egg twins,' 'dizygotic') who was sent to his father after Sophie Mol's funeral and now returned to their native place after twenty-three years. The whole family has been personalized in retrospection. The twins (Estha and Raphel) lived with their divorced mother, Ammu and their blind maternal grandmother, Mammachy and their maternal uncle Chacko, once a Rhodes scholar at Oxford and lecturer in Madras Christian College, who helped his mother to run their paradise pickle business, and their maternal grandfather's youngest sister, Baby Kochamma. Chacko was married to an English Woman, Margaret (who divorced him and married Joe) and had a daughter, Sophie Mol who died later by drowning.

Ammu's love for Velutha forms the core of the novel and makes the novelist's preference crystal clear. The traditional society was not only conservative but authoritarian for it laid down who should love whom. It happened long ago and it is against this concept that the novelist protests vehemently. The right to love a man of her choice, is a woman's birth right and it should not be scuttled in the name of religion, caste, colour and class. It is in this sense that the novel could be read as a feminist novel or a post-colonial novel for both feminism and post-colonialism aim at destroying the old power structure. Roy wants to break this age old tradition to uphold the right of a woman to marry a man of her choice. Thus, she says:

"... it could be argued that it actually began thousands of years ago. Long before the Marxists came. Before the British took Malabar, before the Dutch Ascendency, before Vasco da Gama arrived, before the Zamorin's conquest of Calicut. Before three purple-robed Syrian Bishops murdered by the Portuguese were found floating in the sea, with coiled sea serpents riding on their chests and oysters knotted in tangled beards. It could be argued that it began long before arrived in a boat and seeped into Kerala like tea from a bag.

That it really began in the days when the Love Laws were made. The laws that lay down who should be loved, and how.

And how much" (1997 : 33).

'Things can change in a day' is used as a kind of refrain in the novel. It suggests that Roy is determined to break the tradition.

Who's The God of Small Things? Is it Velutha, the paravan, the maker of fine things with his superb sense of detail? Who could he been? We are told:

"The God of Loss? The God of Small Things? The God of Goose Bumps and Sudden Smiles? Of Sour metal Smells like steel bus-rails and the smell of the bus conductor's hands from holding them?" (*Ibidem* : 217).

As if in a dream sequence, Ammu went with a cheerful man who had only one arm and could do only one thing at a time. "If he held her, he could not kiss her. If he kissed her, he could not see her. If he saw her, he could not feel her."

The liberation from old bondage and tradition needs not only courage but a new language. Arundhati Roy describes Ammu's (a high caste Syrian Christian Woman) love for Valutha, (a Paravan, a low caste man) in poetic prose.

She went to him and laid the length of her body against his. He just stood there. He didn't touch her. He was shivering. Partly with cold. Partly terror. Partly aching desire. Despite his fear his body was prepared to take the bait. It wanted her. Urgently. His wetness wet her. She put her arms around him.

> He tried to be rational: What's the worst thing that can happen?
> I could lose everything. My job. My family. My livelihood. Everything.
> She could hear the wild hammering of his heart.
> She held him till it calmed down. Somewhat.
> She unbuttoned her shirt. They stood there skin to skin.

Her brownness against his blackness. Her softness against his hardness. Her nut-brown breast (that wouldn't support a toothbrush) against his smooth ebony chest. She smelled the river on him. His Particular Paravan smell that so disgusted Baby Kochamma: Ammu put out her tongue and tasted it, in the hollow of his throat. On the lobe of his ear. She pulled his head down towards her and kissed his mouth. A cloudy kiss. A kiss that demanded a kiss-back. He kissed her back. First cautiously. Then urgently Slowly his arms came up behind her. He stroked her back. Very gently. She could feel the skin on his palms. Rough. Calloused. Sandpaper. He was careful not to hurt her. She could feel how soft she felt to him. She could feel herself through him. Her skin. The way her body existed only where he touched her. The rest of her was smoke. She felt him shudder against her. His hands were on her haunches (that could support a whole array of toothbrushes), pulling her hips against his, to let her know how much he wanted her (*Ibidem* : 334-35).

Arundhati Roy fashioned a new language for fiction. Her use of language reminds us of Eliot's use of language in *Rock Choruses* and *Four Quartets*. Take for instance, Ammu's parting from Velutha after the consummation of love. Roy writes:

"She moved closer, wanting to be within him, to touch more of him. He gathered her into the cave of his body. A breeze lifted off the river and cooled their warm bodies.

It was a little cold. A little wet. A little quiet.
The Air.
But what was there to say?

An hour later Ammu disengaged herself gently.

'I have to go.'

He said nothing, didn't move. He watched her dress.

Only one thing mattered now. They knew that it was all they could ask of each other. The only thing. Ever. They both knew that. Even later, on the thirteen nights that followed this one, instinctively they stuck to the Small Things. The Big Things ever lurked inside. They knew that there was nowhere for them to go. They had nothing. No future. So they stuck to the small things" (*Ibidem* : 338).

The above quoted passage also explains the title of the novel.

While trying to give a historical perspective to Estha and Raphel, Chacko says:

"We're Prisoners of War. Our dreams have been doctored. We belong nowhere. We sail unanchored on troubled seas. We may never be allowed ashore. Our sorrows will never be sad enough. Our joys never happy enough. Our dreams never big enough. Our lives never important enough to matter" (*Ibidem* : 53).

This kind of prose at once gives a made in India stamp to Indian English novel.

But the novel is not without blemish. In her attempt to describe love and sex freely she writes a few passages which border on pornography. The behaviour of the Police Officer towards Ammu at the Police Station is a case in point.

"'If I were you,' he said, 'I'd go home quietly.' Then he tapped her breasts with his baton. Gently. Tap, tap. As though he was choosing mangoes from a basket. Pointing out the ones that he wanted packed and delivered. Inspector Thomas Mathew seemed to know whom he could pick on and whom he couldn't. Policemen have that instinct" (*Ibidem* : 8).

In an ironic undertone Roy says:

Behind him a red and blue board said:

> Politeness
> Obedience
> Loyalty
> Intelligence
> Courtesy
> Efficiency.
>
> (*Ibidem*)

The chapter 'Abhilash Talkies' reads like a Shobhaa De novel. One wishes Roy should have revised this chapter (she says that she had not revised a single word while writing this novel). In the closing chapter some of the passages border on pornography. Here is one such passage.

"Ammu, naked now, crouched over Velutha, her mouth on his. He drew her hair around them like a tent. Like her children did when they wanted to exclude the outside world. She slid further down, introducing herself to the rest of him. His neck. His nipples. His chocolate stomach. She sipped the last of the river from the hollow of his navel. She pressed the heat of his erection against her eyelids. She tasted him, salty, in her mouth. He sat up and drew her back to him. She felt his belly tighten under her, hard as a board. She felt her wetness slipping on his skin. He took her nipple in his mouth and cradled her other breast in his calloused palm. Velvet gloved in sandpaper" (*Ibidem* : 336).

Arundhati Roy can be credited with creating a new idiom and phrases like 'biological father', 'die-able age'. 'Sea-Secrets', 're-Returned', 'non-elect', 'death coiled like an angry spring', 'touchables', 'Rice-Christians', 'Clean children, like a packet of peppermints' 'as lonely as a wolf', etc.

Besides, taking up Cudgel for women's right to property and to choose their lovers, the novels also makes references to communist movement in Kerala and allusions to *the Mahabharata*. This can be taken as a representative post-colonial novel for it seeks to restructure the power centre by giving right to women to live their lives in their own way, and fashions a new language for fiction by creating a new Indian English idiom.

WORK CITED

Roy, Arundhati, *The God of Small Things*, New Delhi: India Ink, 1997.

8

Women in Introspection: A Study of Anita Desai's *Fire on the Mountain*

Speaking of the way she writes novels, Anita Desai explains "By writing novels that have been catalogued by critics as psychological, and that are purely subjective, I have been left free to employ, simply, the language of the interior. Even when two characters meet, they use this particular type of language — the language of their thoughts, their interior selves — which bas nothing to do with geography and can be written in any language" (Desai, 1992 : 225).

It is clear from the above statement that Anita Desai is more interested in the 'interior selves' than in social and political realities. Her protagonists are individuals for 'whom aloneness alone' is 'the sole natural condition, aloneness alone the treasure worth treasuring'. In the words of M.K. Naik, "they are mostly women, who, though they have reached different stages in life (from school girl to grandmother), are all fragile introverts 'trapped in their own skins'" (1982 : 241).

Anita Desai's fifth novel, *Fire on the Mountain* which won her the coveted central Sahitya Akademi Award in 1978 was published in 1977. Nanda Kaul, the protagonist of the novel asks the question: "Can I not be left with nothing"? — which I think is central to the meaning of the novel. The novel opens at a point of Nanda Kaul's life, when she has already lived the best part of it. She now lives the life of a recluse at Carignano and also likes it because of, "its barrenness". Her problem now is to delink the past from the present. She wants to cut herself off the relations but fails miserably.

The novel is in three parts. Part I, is exclusively devoted to Nanda Kaul, the former Vice-Chancellor's wife who had seen the busy life in the university. As a member of the upper-class society, Nanda Kaul had experienced and tasted the bitter-sweetness of the so-called sophisticated manners. She had seen the life steadily but not the whole. Her decision to stay at Carignano, is prompted by her desire to keep herself away from the din and bustle of city life.

"It was the place and the time of life that she had wanted and prepared for all her life — as she realized on her first day at Carignano, with a great, cool flowering of relief — and at last she had it. She wanted no one and nothing else. Whatever else came, or happened here, would be an unwelcome intrusion and distraction" (Desai, 1977 : 3).

Carignano has beautiful landscape but no activity. Nanda Kaul lives here all along like a recluse. In the words of the novelist, 'To be a free, no more and no less was all/she was prepared to undertake' (*Ibidem* : 4). As R.S. Sarma rightly observes: "Her withdrawal stands for an emotional staticity, a kind of psychic frigidity that refuses to take note of any movement around. She seeks stillness that will include any movement animate or inanimate" (1981 : 188).

She is upset by the letter of her daughter, Asha informing her about the family and more so by the news of Raka, her great-grand daughter, who comes to stay with her. She takes a book, *The Pillow Book* of Sei Shonagon and opens a chapter "A Woman lives alone," only to reaffirm her desire to live alone.

She Muses over the passage about the Woman, "Who lived alone and smiled again, in spite of herself, Wondering if Carignano would live up to that epicurean lady's ideas of how things should be". The old house, the full house, of that period of her life when she was the Vice-Chancellor's wife and at the hub of a small but intense and busy world, had not satisfied her. It was the "Vice-Chancellor's house, not her's". Now that Raka comes to give her company (as Asha writes), it becomes a headache to her.

Nanda Kaul never welcomes Raka into Carignano but restrains herself from pronouncing anything. Notwithstanding the cold reception, Raka enters into great-grand mother's house. To Nanda Kaul, "She was still an intruder, an outsider, a mosquito, flown up from the plains to tease and worry" (Desai, 1977 : 40).

Raka, looks around the house. She asks Ramlal about the place and its peculiarity. Ramlal enlightens Raka about the place.

Raka has an aptitude for quietness. Nanda Kaul discovers that Raka, "had a gift for disappearing-suddenly, silently". But the old lady's policy is not to question her but 'it annoyed her intensely that she should once again be drawn into a position where it was necessary for her to take an interest in another's activities and be responsible for their effect and outcome'. But soon it is made clear to Nanda Kaul that "Raka was a perceptive child and she was not part of Nanda Kaul's life, that she had her own place and might stay in it." So they (Nanda Kaul and Raka) workout the means by which they would live together and "each felt she was doing her best at avoiding the other but found it was not so simple to exist and yet appear not to exist."

Raka ignores Nanda Kaul so calmly, so totally that it makes the great-grandmother breathless. Anita Desai is right when she says that "if Nanda Kaul was a recluse out of vengeance for a long life of duty and obligation, her great-grand daughter was a recluse by nature, by instinct" (p. 48). Gradually, Nanda Kaul approaches Raka and talks to her. Even she offers to watch her going down the hill. She begins to communicate to her great-grand daughter her experiences, feelings, so that the child would feel comfortable. With this her desire to remain alone and determination to say 'no' to any request by the members of the family is gone. Now although she does not really wish to impose herself or her ways on Raka but she could not leave her alone. For the first time, Nanda Kaul begins to feel that Raka is more or less like herself. So She says, "Raka, you really are a great grandchild of mine, aren't you? You are more like me than any of my children or grandchildren, you are exactly like me, Raka".

Raka silently tries to fit into the mainstream of Kasauli life. She enters into the Club House, only to be disillusioned. She also notices the forest fire and enquires about its extinction. She is the only child, Nanda Kaul had ever known who prefers to stand apart and go off and disappear to being loved, and cared for. As Anita Desai rightly pointed out that, she had come to Carignano to be alone.

Raka understands Carignano and knows what it stands for and in a way values that. Nanda Kaul observes that but now her sleep is being disturbed. The thought of Raka who sleeps in the next room to her's, disturbs her mind and sleep as well.

In the meanwhile, a letter comes informing her the sudden breakdown of Tara, Raka's mother. But Nanda Kaul withholds the information and does not like to disturb Raka. She is now more drawn towards her great grand child, Raka. She tells her stories, as she did in case of her other children and grand children to give her a comfortable sleep. In the process, she tells fabricated stories about her own father and family to impress upon the child, how great and aristocratic they were.

One day she could not help, telling Raka the news of Tara's illness. Raka's face suddenly turns pale but she remains composed. Nanda Kaul curses herself for not being able to surpress the truth. In order to give the great grand child comfort, Nanda Kaul talks, all fairy tales, Raka fails to understand the talkativeness of her great grand mother, who till lately preferred not to talk to her at all.

Ila Das, one-time school as well as College mate of Nanda Kaul, comes to Carignano. She recalls her association with Nanda Kaul and her Vice-Chancellor husband. Ila Das's life has been a life of ups and downs. Nanda Kaul had helped her in the past. Even a post was created for her by her Vice-Chancellor husband, in the University. With the death of the Vice-Chancellor, Ila Das was forced to relinquish the Job. Now she lives as a social worker. She is a low-paid worker, who works against child-marriage. In the process, she has earned a good number of enemies, including the priest of that area. Staying for sometime with Nanda Kaul, Ila Das leaves Carignano. Next morning a telephone call came to Nanda Kaul, informing her about Ila Das's murder.

Like Anita Desai's fourth novel *Where Shall We go this Summer?* The novel under consideration, *Fire on the Mountain*, is in three parts. Part I, deals with Nanda Kaul's stay at Carignano. A passing reference has also been made to long time occupants of the house that Nanda Kaul took possession of. This is to show the aristocratic temperament of the educated top-ranking Indians. After the British left India, these people took pains to preserve the so-called top class consciousness. Nanda Kaul, the former Vice-Chancellor's wife wanted to spend last part of her life in such a mansion, in a hill-station. Part II, is devoted to Raka's coming into Nanda Kaul's house and her stay there. Part III, is devoted to Ila Das's recall of her past and her present occupation.

Excepting the cook, Ramlal, all three characters in the novel are women. Both of them represent and reflect distinct aspects of our present day social life. Nanda Kaul, who had seen life as the wife of a Vice-Chancellor and decided to spend the rest of her life in a hill-station, represents the neglected and uncared for children whose parents don't pull on well. Ila Das, represented the poor educated women of our country who are forced to take up any job for bread and butter (including Govt. sponsored social work). Ila Das's tragic death shocks us all. But then, that is the fate of well meaning Social Workers, in a society where blind belief has taken deep roots.

Nanda Kaul's decision to leave the family and to lead the life of a recluse in a hill station, proves to be futile. The agony of her life, being the wife of a Vice-Chancellor, like the forest fire is always burning. She feels as if her life was the life of a dream, dreamt through by the minds of others. And that is why the house where she lived with her husband, was "Not her's but his house". She also feels that her own children and grand-children have let her down. She is of no use to them after the death of her Vice-Chancellor husband. In order to live peacefully and away from the demands of family life, she goes to Carignano. But with the arrival of Raka, her great-grand child, her desire to live alone is crushed. Once again she falls into the trap of family obligation.

The attitude of three women characters of this novel namely Nanda Kaul, Ila Das and Raka reminds as of Eliot's statement in *Four Quartets*:

> "There are three conditions which often look alike/Yet differ completely, flourish in the same hedgerow/Attachment to self and to things and to persons, detachment/From self and from things and from persons, and growing between them indifference/Which resembles the others as death resembles life..." (Eliot, 1977 : 55).

Nanda Kaul, Ila Das and Raka represent Eliot's three conditions which often look alike. If Ila Das stands for attachment to self, Nanda Kaul stands for detachment and Raka stands for indifference.

As Jasbir Jain observes:

"Nanda Kaul resents the claims it had made on her, the curbs it had placed on her freedom and the deceptions it had held. While Ila romanticises it with her memories of the badminton game, the music and the Jam; it is a piece of heaven, the memory of which renders her present tolerable" (1982 : 43).

From the beginning to the abrupt and violent ending, the novel makes an observing ready. Raka's setting the Mountain on fire suggests her rejection of the society and symbolizes the purging of human weakness through fire. Desai introduces 'Novel within novel' technique to impress upon us the pangs of old age on lonely women. That is why Nanda Kaul, reads the novel *The Pillow Book* by

Sei Shonagon repeatedly. *Fire on the Mountain* depicts the predicament of women in a society that fails to satisfy their desire and fulfill their hope. The novel depicts a world which is not made safe for women. Therefore, there is need for women to understand each other. Desai brings a kind of union between Nanda Kaul and her great granddaughter, towards the end of the novel.

> There was a scratching at the window that turned to a tapping, then a drumming. 'Nani,' whispered Raka, shivering and crouching in the lily bed, peeping over the sill. Look, Nani, I have set the forest on fire. Look, Nani-look-the forest is on fire. Tapping, then drumming, she raised her voice, then raised her head to look in and saw Nanda Kaul on the stool with her head hanging, the black telephone hanging, the long wire dangling (p. 145).

This novel clearly shows the dilemma of women in a society that has become a fit place not for living but dying.

WORKS CITED

Desai, Anita. *Fire on the Mountain*, Delhi: Allied Publishers, 1977. All Page References are to this Edition.

Desai, Anita. "The Indian Writer's Problems". *Explorations in Modern Indo-English Fiction.* (ed.) R.K. Dhawan, New Delhi: Bahri Publications, 1992.

Eliot, T.S. *Four Quarters*, Delhi: OUP, 1977.

Jain, Jasbir. "Anita Desai", *Indian English Novelists* ed. Madhusudan Prasad, New Delhi: Sterling, 1982.

Naik, M.K. *A History of Indian English Literature*, New Delhi: Sahitya Akademi, 1982.

Sarma, R.S. *Anita Desai*, New Delhi: Arnold Heineman, 1981.

9

Shashi Deshpande's *That Long Silence* and the Question of the Reader Response

The question that puzzles an Indian reader is how to approach an Indian English novel? It takes us to the next question: How does an Indian English novel affect the reader? The reader looks forward to seeing how far the Indian English novelist has been successful in acclimatizing an indigenous tradition and sensibility to the English language. Some of our well-known and established novelists like R.K. Narayan, Raja Rao, Mulk Raj Anand, Anita Desai, Kamala Markandaya, Nayantara Sahgal, Manohar Malgonkar and Arun Joshi have assimilated the Indian sensibility in their novels that stand comparison with novels written in English in the Commonwealth and Third World countries of our time. New novelists like Upamanyu Chatterjee, Vikram Seth, Amitav Ghosh and Shashi Deshpande in the eighties have published interesting novels on contemporary themes that make absorbing reading. Shashi Deshpande's *That Long Silence,* which won her the Sahitya Akademi Award for 1990, tells the story of an Indian housewife who maintained her silence throughout her life in the face of hardships that threatened to break it. The purpose of the present paper is to make a study of the novel in the light of the recent Reader-Response criticism.

The most important thing in Reader-Response criticism is that the reader must be made to feel for himself the new meaning of the novel. To do this he must actively participate in bringing out the meaning, and this participation is an essential precondition for communication between the reader and the writer. The reader should have the knowledge of the tradition and cultural background against which the novel has been set. Otherwise he would not be able to decipher the images and symbols through which the novelist seeks to convey his meaning. Wayne C. Booth has described the art of reading fiction in the following words:

> The author creates, in short, an image of himself and another image of his reader, he makes his reader as he makes his second self and the most successful reading is one in which the created selves, author and reader, can find complete agreement (138).

In the opening page of the novel, *That Long Silence* the protagonist makes it clear that it is difficult to get the real picture of the novel unless the reader operates at the same wavelength as the author. Writing is, like child birth, both painful and risky. Jaya says:

> Nor am I writing a story of a callous, insensitive husband and a sensitive, suffering wife. I'm writing of us. Of Mohan and me. And I know this — you can never be the heroine of your own story. Self-revelation is a cruel process. The real picture, the real 'you' never emerges. Looking for it is as bewildering as trying to know how you really look. Ten different mirrors show you ten different faces (1).

Readers, like mirrors, reflect different types of images of the author and her created characters according to their perception and understanding. In other words, a reader performs the role of a mirror in reflecting the image of the characters of the novel.

The theme of *That Long Silence* is simple. Jaya, the heroine of the novel, recalls her married life with nostalgia. She was married to Mohan and lived with him at different places till he went away from her to clear himself of the charge of business malpractice. She bore him two children and the third child was aborted. She recalled her relationship with innumerable relatives and friends with compassion and understanding. She tried to come to terms with herself by trying to write about herself and her family and was determined to break a 'Long Silence.' The novel ends with the return of her son, Rahul, the promise of Mohan 'to return' on Friday morning and Jaya changing the idea of their marriage and learning the truth that 'Life has always to be made possible.' Behind this simple story of the novel lies the ground swell of frustration in married life of the protagonist, who failed to be closer to her husband mentally. She suffered from isolation. Despite her marriage to Mohan and subsequently becoming a mother of two children, she was lonely. Her husband could not understand her feelings as a result of which she was torn from within. Shashi Deshpande uses a beautiful image to describe Jaya's married life:

> A pair of bullocks yoked together . . . a clever phrase, but can it substitute for the reality? A man and a woman married

> for seventeen years. A couple with two children. A family somewhat like the one caught and preserved for posterity by the advertising visuals I so loved. But the reality was only this. We were two persons. A man. A woman (8).

To an Indian reader the image of a pair of bullocks yoked together suggests a world of meanings. It means that the bullocks so yoked shared the burden between themselves but no one knows whether they love each other or not. The image of the beasts performing the duty mechanically undermines the husband-wife relationship, who are united in marriage for love and not for leading a mechanical life terminating in mutual hatred and distrust. Jaya resents the role assigned to a wife in our country, who is called upon to stay at home, look after the babies and keep out of the rest of the world. She could not continue her writing as Mohan discouraged her. "I gave up my writing because of you," she said to Mohan. She was deeply distressed to know that the writer in her could not come to light because of her husband. She says:

> I had known then that it hadn't mattered to Mohan that I had written a good story, a story about a couple, a man who could not reach out to his wife except through her body. For Mohan it had mattered that people might think the couple was us, that the man him. To Mohan, I had been no writer, only an exhibitionist (144).

She did not take a risk to annoy Mohan lest that should break her marriage. She says ironically:

> Perhaps, if Mohan had been angry, if he had shouted and raged at me, if he had forbidden me to write, perhaps I would have fought him and gone on. But he had only shown me his hurt. And I had not been able to counter that. I had relinquished them instead, all those stories that had been taking shape in me because I had been scared — scared of hurting Mohan, scared to jeopardising the only career I had (144).

She was fed up with the routine work like changing the sheets, scrubbing bathrooms and cleaning the fridge, and so on.

Shashi Deshpande uses an apt image of a worm crawling into a hole to describe the state of Jaya, a budding writer doomed to dwindle into a stereotyped Indian housewife:

> Middle class. Bourgeoisie. Upper-caste. Distanced from real life. Scared of writing. Scared of tailing. Oh God, I had

> thought, I can't take any more. Even a worm has a hole it can crawl into. I had mine — as Mohan's wife, as Rahul's and Rati's mother (148).

A loveless married life which caused the wife and the husband to drift away from each other resulted in total failure. Jaya complains bitterly:

> I'll tell you what's wrong. I've failed him. He expected something from me, from his wife, and I've failed him. All these years I thought I was Mohan's wife; now he tells me I was never that, not really. What am I going to do? What shall I do if he doesn't come back? (185)

and concludes: "Nothing. Nothing between us. But after his death, nothing between me and Mohan either. We lived together but there had been only emptiness between us" (185).

Mohan has crushed both the woman and the writer in Jaya as he neither loved her nor encouraged her. Jaya has every reason to be bitter with him, for he has been responsible for her misery. With straightforward language, gentle irony and matter-of-fact tone Jaya recalls their relationship as wife and husband:

> Sensual memories are the coldest. They stir up nothing in you. As I thought of those days, of my feelings, and then looked at the man lying beside me, nothing stirred in me. Those emotions and responses seemed to belong to two other people, not to the two of us lying here together.
>
> In any case, whatever my feeling had been then, I had never spoken of them to him. In fact, we had never spoken of sex at all. It had been as if the experience was erased each time after it happened; it never existed in words. The only my answer, 'No.' Each time, after it was over, the same question; and my reply too, invariably the same — 'No.'
>
> First there's love, then there's sex — that was how I had always imagined it to be. But after living with Mohan I had realised that it could so easily be the other way round.
>
> Love...? Yes, what else could I call it but love when I thought of how I had longed for his physical presence, when I remembered how readily, almost greedily, I had responded to his touch? What else could I name it when I thought of the agony it had been to be without him, when his desires, his approval, his love, had seemed to be the most important

> thing in my life? It seems to me now that we had, both of us, rehearsed the roles of husband and wife so well that when the time came we could play them flawlessly, word-perfect (95).

Jaya tells us that they were merely rehearsing the roles for the future when they could actually live like husband and wife. They are yet to live as wife and husband even after seventeen years of their married life. Nothing can be more frustrating and depressing than this. The irony is not missed upon the readers. In India the relationship between the wife and the husband is not only cordial but intimate and enduring. To any perceptive reader the relation between Jaya and Mohan is an epitome of failure and an emblem of disgust, disappointment and depression. This is so because there was no love between them.

The images employed by Shashi Deshpande are adequate and appropriate to the theme of the novel. Two recurrent images in the novel perform a crucial role. The married couple are likened to 'a pair of bullocks yoked together' and the husband is said to be like 'a sheltering tree.' Those two images explain the meaning of the novel in a subtle way. The protagonist of the novel rejects the image of traditional women like Sita, Savitri and Draupadi and instead prefers the image of 'a pair of bullocks,' to describe a married couple. Jaya says:

> No, what have I to do with these mythical women? I can't fool myself. The truth is simpler. Two bullocks yoked together ... it is more comfortable for them to move in the same direction. To go in different directions would be painful; and what animal would voluntarily choose pain? (11, 12).

This disgust of living with a man who does not love the woman the way she expected him to do, is a burning problem that educated women have to face in contemporary society. The thought of desertion by the husband, however, unnerves Jaya, for she has not yet cast off the role of a traditional Indian woman. Through Jaya's character Shashi Deshpande has thus expressed the ambivalent attitude of contemporary educated independent-minded Indian women who can neither reconcile themselves to a new situation when their husbands ignore them and crush their ambition in life nor cast off their husbands simply because the husband is like a sheltering tree they cannot afford to live without.

Irony is the chief figure of speech used in the novel to explain the behaviour of the characters. For instance, when Mohan got the job of his choice, Jaya never questioned the means by which he got it:

> Mohan had managed to get the job. I never asked him how he did it. If Gandhari, who bandaged her eyes to become blind like her husband, could be called an ideal wife, I was an ideal wife too. I bandaged my eyes tightly. I did not want to know anything. It was enough for me that we moved to Bombay, that we could send Rahul and Rati to good schools, that I could have the things we needed ... decent clothes, a fridge, a gas connection [and] travelling first class. And, there was enough for Mohan to send home to his father — for Sudha's fees, Vasant's clothes and Sudha's marriage (61, 62).

That Long Silence depicts the plight of an educated Indian woman of our time. The significance of the novel depends on how far the reader is able to realize the situation and go along with the author in finding out the meaning. In a way, the protagonist, Jaya, is any modern woman who resents her husband's callousness and becomes the victim of circumstances. By implication the character of Jaya represents modern woman's ambivalent attitude to married life. Shashi Deshpande hints at the modern woman's refusal to comply with the wishes of the husband. The reader is free to interpret the heroine as a woman who failed her husband or otherwise. Alternatively, he may also take her as a representative woman of the contemporary society who is all set to revolt against the husband. Jaya is both an individual and a type, and the reader is free to take her in any manner he likes.

Typical Indian expressions are used in the novel to convey the feeling of Jaya and other characters in an intimate manner. Shashi Deshpande tries to re-create the characters in their own situation by using Indian proverbs and expressions. For example, when Jaya moves to a new house with her husband, and they clean it, Jaya describes their experience in the following words: "The fan moved at its fastest; nevertheless, we were bathed in sweat by the time we had done" (13).

Frequent references to Indian epics and allusions to archetypal characters like Dasarath, Ram, Sita, Draupadi and Gandhari make the role of the reader difficult, for they demand the reader's total participation in order to understand the protagonist and her problems with insight and sympathy. Folk tales and fables are also used to influence the minds of the characters and infuse a sense of morality in them. Let us take an example of how people are warned against lying, stealing and cheating:

> Tell lies now and you'll be a lizard in your next life, steal things and you'll be a dog, cheat people and you'll be a snake.

Only a reader with an insight into Indian ethos and classics can appreciate the act of sin and retribution:

> An act and retribution — they followed each other naturally and inevitably. Dasarath killed an innocent young boy whose parents died crying out for their son. And, years later, Dasarath died too, calling out for his son, 'Rama, Rama.' Yes, escape was never possible (128).

That Long Silence is a typical Indian English novel that speaks to us of our own situation. The image of the woman underwent a metamorphosis when the contemporary woman decided to cast off her traditional role of living under the shade of her husband. Jaya, the heroine of the novel, gives us the new image of the Indian woman who now tries to stand on her own legs and seeks to break the age-old silence by refusing to dance to the tune of her husband. With Jaya's assertion of life that 'Long Silence' is threatened to be broken.

WORKS CITED

Booth, Wayne C. *The Rhetoric of Fiction.* Chicago, 1963.

Deshpande, Shashi. *That Long Silence.* New Delhi: Penguin India, 1989.

10

Shobha Dé's *Sisters*: An Appraisal

A Novelist is first and foremost an individual with a personal vision. At the same time he/she is a personality living in a particular period of time, in a particular place, in a particular social environment. He/she is an individual and a member of the Society, and, therefore, society inevitably plays its part in his/her novel. The writer may be in sympathy with his/her social environment or in rebellion against it, he/she may try to reject it, but its influence will be there. The novel may not be an event in social history, but it is an assertion of the novelist's singular identity. Things and events depicted in the novel might not have happened to him/her, but he/she invents them camouflaging them as real to elicit reader's total participation. Shobha Dé precisely does that in her novels. Social concern is the main thrust of all her novels. The purpose of the paper is to show how far Shobha Dé has been successful in depicting the story of two upper class young business women in Modern India within the ambit of the art of fiction.

The theme of the novel makes an interesting reading. Mikki (Mallika), the protagonist returned home following the deaths of her parents in an air-crash. Seth Hiralal and his wife (Mikki's parents) were survived by their only daughter and heir to their vast property. Mikki returned home and oversaw their funeral and took charge of Hiralal Industries. Seth Hiralal had sired another daughter, named Alisha by his concubine, Leelaben. This secret was known to Ramanbhai, a trusted employee of the Seth. Alisha was splitting venom on Mikki for not being able to get the social sanction as Seth's daughter. She was outraged by the obituary column that the Seth was "Survived by his only child, a daughter, Mallika, studying in the US" and decided to take on her step-sister one day. Ramanbhai was running with the deer and haunting with the hound by trying to be closer both to Mikki and Alisha. He had an axe to grind. Being an educated and liberated young women without any legitimate guardian to look after her, Mikki attended many parties and came in contact with many young as well as not so young persons. Many young men were interested in her. Navin, her friend, Shanay, her distant relative (Anjanaben's son) and industrialist, Binny Malhotra were interested in her. After rejecting Shanay, Mikki got engaged to Navin. Binny made all tricks possible to win over her. As ill luck would have it the precarious financial position drove Mikki to ask for a loan from Navin before marriage. Navin's mother turned it down and Mikki reacted quickly by breaking the engagement. Binny took advantage of the situation and lured away Mikki by giving costly presents and promising financial help. Binny being an elderly person and a past master in the art of love making lured Mikki to his bed and forced her to marry him. Mikki married him much against the wishes of her well-wishers and came to grief soon. Binny showed his true colour after marriage and Mikki willy-nilly became a domestic woman. Binny continued to sleep with women of his choice and Mikki got the shock of her life to know that he had a concubine named Urmi and two children by her — a son and a daughter. Mikki was beaten and forced to leave the house by Binny. She came back to her parents' place and decided to take Alisha's help. Alisha was in no mood to oblige her. Alisha like Mikki was a free bird. She had affairs with Navin and Dr. Kurien. She was almost dead when she attempted suicide but was luckily survived by the nourishment of Dr. Kurien and Mikki, who gave blood for her. This incident brought them closer and they stayed together. Binny died in a road accident and Mikki felt very sad. She again became the owner of her property as well as the property of her late husband. Ramanbhai planned her murder but she was saved by Shanay. Alisha took her to Geneva and got her cured. Two sisters understood each other and love triumphed over hate as they decided to marry and set their house in order.

Behind this interesting and apparently simple story lies the ground swell of frustration in the lives of two women between whose desire and fulfilment falls the shadow. Their characters could be profitably analysed, if read in the light of Reader-Response criticism. The most important thing in Reader-Response criticism is that the reader must be made to feel for himself the new meaning of the novel. To do this he must actively participate in bringing out the meaning, and this participation is an essential precondition for communication between the reader and the writer. The reader should have the knowledge of the tradition and cultural background against which the novel has been set. Otherwise he would not be able to decipher the images and symbols through which the novelist seeks to convey his meaning. Wayne C. Booth has described the art of reading fiction in the following words:

> The author creates, in short, an image of himself and another image of his reader, he makes his reader as he makes his second self and the most successful reading is one in which the created selves, author and reader, can find complete agreement (138).

Women in the upper class society in India in recent years have out grown Victorian taboos. They are no more prudes in public. The concept of morality arising out of love for one and the same person is dated. They behave more or less like Restoration Comedy women who were given to the enjoyment of life through physical consummation of love before and after marriage and even outside marriage. The idea of marriage and constancy in love has undergone a sea change. Indian readers must not seek the prototypes of Sita and Draupadi in contemporary Society. The reader should do well to keep in mind this fact before trying to analyse the characters in Shobha Dé's novels. Shobha Dé dives deep into the hearts of liberated upper-class women in the contemporary society and depicts the characters as they are, not as they should have been. Sex and sensuality are a part of life and in order to accept life one has to affirm sensuality Shobha Dé seems to say, she is not concerned with the traditional concept of morality and purity in love. She depicts the lives of young men and women, particularly rich upper-class (business community) people who no longer consider faithfulness and constancy in love a virtue. That is why she depicts the people in their true colours, i.e. what they are rather than what they should have been. But the description of union between the lovers or wife and husband becomes too open and vulgar to be enjoyable. It offends our sensibility and distracts our attention. It is often said that Shobha Dé's novels border on pornography and there is a grain of truth in it. The following passages from *Sisters* bear testimony to it:

"The moon was low in the sky and had a rainbow halo around it, Binny gestured towards it, 'A good omen. An auspicious one', he said, as he took Mikki into his arms and kissed her gently at first, and then with increasing passion. She left her heart thudding against his chest. Slowly, he unbuttoned her shirt and cupped her breasts. Mikki caught her breath as Binny hauled her on to the bed and nearly tore off her clothes. He kept repeating, 'Beautiful, beautiful, beautiful', while she lay back and closed her eyes. At that moment the only thing that mattered was the feel of him over her slim body, the touch of his fingers inside her, and the slow, deliberate movement of his tongue as it explored her mouth and kept up a steady rhythm, while his legs parted hers and he began his final assault on the woman he had already claimed as his own" (Dé, Shobha).

Alisha's illicit love with Dr. Kurien has been described in great detail:

> The doctor ignored her and continued peeling his clothes off. Alisha leapt off the bed and reached him in two strides. She went for him like a wild cat, tearing into his skin with her long nails, spitting and hissing curses while her legs flew at his shins. He caught her wrists and stopped her from scratching his face. She struggled to free herself while continuing to scream obscenities. He pinioned her arms with his hands and pushed her backwards towards the roomy bed. With one leg he tripped her as she approached the edge. Alisha fell back over the heaped up pillows and he fell on top of her. He grabbed her hair and Jerked her face back, 'What more do you want from me?' he asked roughly ...'Aren't you getting enough?' His mouth attached hers and his hands pummelled her body with such force she screamed. 'Go on...yell as much as you want', he said, biting into her neck savagely. There is no one who can hear you. His thighs pinned down her legs as he entered her in a manner that was so brutal, she felt herself tear. 'Take it, take it, take', he grunted, pushing into her. 'All you rich women are the same — you want more all the time. Nothing satisfies you. Here take it all...it's free'.
>
> (*Ibidem* : 186)

Many more passages could be cited from the book to show how the description of consummation of love and sex almost borders on obscenity and pornography.

But Shobha Dé's language is not without its merit. Occasional flashes of poetic language to a great extent redeems the damage done to the texture of the novel through the long and protracted description of love and sex. Here are a few examples:

> Mikki's eyes shone as she rushed to read the tiny card that had come with the car. It said, 'To my bride-to-be. A wedding present. In memory of that night and all the nights

> to come'. Binny! She had little time to even think of their unbridled ardour that magical evening, but the gift brought back memories of those moments when the waves crashing outside hadn't been able to compete with their passion, as they'd devoured each other's bodies uninhibitedly, oblivious to everything as they'd savoured each other's smells, textures, tastes, and had surrendered themselves simultaneously and totally (*Ibidem* : 90-91).

The best passage in the book which almost brings to our mind the famous description of the touching scene of the Queen's death by Lytton Strachey in his book *Queen Victoria,* is Mikki's reaction to Binny's death and funeral. It is one of the best passages ever written by any Indian English novelist of our time. Mikki slowly begins to realise life as if she sees it in a mirror and with controlled passion and subdued grief she feels the power of love that wins always. Shobha Dé writes:

> "Mikki couldn't wait to get out of that place. She was booked on the evening flight. As she looked at the largest coffin, she imagined Binny lying inside with a sneer on his face, laughing at the grotesquerie of life, laughing at her. She suppressed the desire to join in his laughter. She thought of happier times and her expression automatically softened. Suddenly it dawned on her that she didn't resent anything about him at all. Not even his brutality towards her. Perhaps that's what they call 'true love', she thought wryly, a soft smile on her face. She looked at the other coffins and found herself feeling strangely happy for Urmi and her children. They were all together at last. Something they couldn't be when they were alive. Mikki shut her eyes and fell into a light reverie induced by the heady smell of spider lilies, roses and incense combined with the insistent beat of tiny cymbals as the priest droned on...Mikki had a beautiful vision of Binny, dressed in his sharpest suit, ascending heavenwards, floating up like he was in a gently rising hot-air balloon. He was acknowledging the crowd gathered for his funeral with a jaunty wave of his hand, his lips twisted.... she thought she saw his family — his real family — Urmi and her kids, floating happily around him, also waving and showering flower petals on everybody. Mikki felt a few descend on her shoulder...and then she jerked out of her trance as she realized the coffins were being lifted up and the people had begun throwing rose petals at the departing

> procession. Mikki watched as the men moved gracefully away, their white *kurtas* and *dhotis* standing out starkly against the bright green of the grass. It was just too beautiful. And she was glad for Binny. He would have approved ..." (*Ibidem* : 174-75).

Within the framework of a novel, Shobha Dé depicts the breaking up the institution of marriage. The new concept of marriage envisages complete sexual freedom with no notion of fidelity. In such a situation man and woman do not become one in marriage, they merely become partners in love. Economic freedom, promiscuity and uncontrolled passion resulting from 'the lust of the blood' make most men and women vulnerable and the resultant frustration in life engulfs them. That is what happens to Mikki and Alisha. However, Shobha Dé tries to redeem her protagonist, Mikki by making her deeply human. Her concern for her half-sister, determination to make amends for her father's vices and misdeeds by rehabilitating Alisha in her own house, speaks volumes of her kind nature. Even her love for Binny who ditched her shows the magnanimity of her character. Shobha Dé does not make her only a sex symbol. Her hopeless passion for love making and desire for getting on in the world finally yield place to her concern for the well-being of her half-sister, Alisha, and she seems to be "more sinned against than sinning". In this tragic world of cut-throat competition, where good intentions fatally miscarry, Mikki suffers and it is through her suffering she learns the art of living. Her final triumph comes when she wins the love and affection of her half-sister, Alisha who pined for legitimacy in life, but failed, because her father had no guts to own her in public. Shobha Dé brings these two women together, who blundered their way for a while and turned their mutual distrust to love and affection passing the bounds of social restriction. The novel is appropriately titled *Sisters*.

Shobha Dé's use of language and creation of new idioms by acclimatizing idioms from Indian languages to English language, adds to the charm of the novel. The narrative holds our breath for sensuous opulence and subtlety of variation and the result is that the novel becomes a 'best seller'. It makes a popular reading.

WORKS CITED

Booth, Wayne C. *The Rhetoric of Fiction*. Chicago, 1963.

Dé, Shobha. *Sisters*. New Delhi: Penguin Books, 1992. All subsequent references are to this edition.

11

The Author and the Text: A Study of Shobha Dé's *Snapshots*

While announcing the death of the author, Ronald Barthes conceded the entry of the author into the text through back door. Some of the Structuralists and Post-Structuralists believe that an author can enter the text as a character. The authorial voice gives sometimes a glimpse of what is happening all around us. The purpose of the paper is to examine how far Shobha Dé has entered into her novel *Snapshots* (1995) as a person and which of the characters can be said to represent the authorial voice.

The blurb of the book sets the ball rolling by saying:

> As the wine and conversation begin to flow at a reunion between six women, who were friends at school, memories start to surface — some happy, others bitter sweet and a few that are downright poisonous... Forced to confront dark secrets that they thought lay buried deep in the past, the women begin to turn against one another and the mood of the party turns nightmarish...

The world of *Snapshots* is a world of women where women begin to look at things from their point of view. They literally and metaphorically play with men and sometimes are played with by men. The novel depicts the love-play between men and women in great details. 'Morality' is a dirty word for the characters in the novel, for they believe in enjoyment of life, throwing the norms of the society out of window.

Six school mates — Aparna, Swati, Reema, Surekha, Rashmi and Noor — assemble at Reema's house on the occasion of Swati's return from the States. They go down the memory lane and ruminate over the past escapades. The theme of the novel makes an interesting reading. Swati wants her old friends to assemble in Reema's house years after they left their school and college. She tells Aparna plainly: "Why can't you just accept that I wanted to meet everybody? No tricks, no motives. It's been years. Besides, if I'd phoned just you, you wouldn't have come. Admit it. The truth is I organized this tamasha only to be able to meet you again" (181).

The novel begins with Aparna's going to Goa with Prem for a holiday. After they make love. Aparna remembers her ex-husband. Rohit and feels the difference. She gets a letter from Reema asking her to come to her (the latter's) house. Surekha, Rashmi, and Noor are also invited to meet Swati. Since they are going to meet after years, Swati suggests that they should "bring Snapshots. Albums. Old Photographs. New Photographs. Mementos of their innocent past" (13). They all talk freely about their past as well as present love-affairs — pre- and post-marital relationships with men of their choice.

Behind this apparently simple story lies the ground swell of frustration in love and mutual jealousy among these women. These women feel free to discuss their affairs with men, knowing fully well that at times some of them are being enjoyed by the same man. This is because these women are in a sense 'liberated' and belong to a particular class of Indian society. Having out grown in recent years old norms of behaviour they are no more prudes in public. The concept of morality arising out of love for one and the same person is dated. They are given to the enjoyment of life through physical consummation of love before and after marriage and even outside marriage. The idea of marriage and constancy in love has undergone a sea change in modern Indian society. Indian readers must not seek the prototypes of Sita and Draupadi in the contemporary society. They will do well to keep in mind this fact before trying to analyse the characters in Shobha Dé's novels.

Shobha Dé dives deep into the hearts of liberated upper-class women in the contemporary society and depicts her characters as they are and not as they should have been. Shobha Dé seems to say that sex is a part of life and in order to accept life one has to affirm sensuality. She is not concerned with the traditional concept of morality and purity in love. She depicts the lives of young men and women, particularly rich upper-class people who no longer consider faithfulness and constancy in love a virtue. The people are presented in their true colours — what they are rather than what they should have been. At times, however, the description of union between the lovers or wife and husband becomes too open and vulgar to be enjoyable. It offends our sensibility and distracts our attention. It is often said that Shobha Dé's novels border on pornography and there is a grain of truth in it.

The opening sentence of the novel *Snapshots* — "Prem liked to make love in public places", sets the tone of the novel. The novel is not about love but about sex, seen from a woman's point of view Shobha Dé has created characters who speak about different aspects of love, sex, and life during their conversation with friends. The problem is to reconstruct the text to find out which of the characters seems to represent the authorial voice. There are situations, in the novel, where women admire men. For example, Aparna "liked men with high ideal and lofty ambitions. Men like Rohit or like her father" (7). But she soon regrets her relationship with Rohit who let her down and left her high and dry. That pushed her to the arms of Prem, who made love to her openly and shamelessly.

Reema's pre- and post-marital affairs are outrageous. Her relationship with her brother-in-law (husband's younger brother) reminds us of the world of the Restoration Comedy where sensuality overpowers individual men and women who take love as the "lust of the blood and permission of the will".

Shobha Dé focuses on the difference between older women's and young women's attitude to marriage, love and life by juxtaposing the views of Aparna and those of her mother. If 'husband' is an awful word for Aparna, for her mother a woman is incomplete without a husband. Aparna's mother says:

> "Remember, a woman in our society is nothing without a husband. Study as much as you wish. Win prizes, get a good job. But don't let all these things affect you, give you a big head. You may be the Prime Minister of India tomorrow, but when you come home, you automatically become your husband's wife. If you forget that, you are finished. Your marriage is finished" (24-25).

The women portrayed in *Snapshots* want to enjoy life and are given to sex-antagonism. There are passages in the text to show how these women are obsessed with sex and sensual enjoyment in life. A few illustrations from the text will suffice. When the friends assembled in Reema's house, Swati got excited. Shobha Dé describes the scene as follows:

> Swati's face was swathed in smiles as she pretended she was a catwalk mannequin parading up and down, humming an MTV hit. 'I'm too sexy'. Everybody laughed. Within seconds the atmosphere altered. Swati announced. "I'm breaking all the rules today. Summon a slave. It's champagne time. Come on gals drink up. This is an occasion. The best. I haven't felt this exhilarated since I lost my virginity — and all of you know how, when, where and with whom that happened. Let's drink to innocence. Let's drink to fun. Fuck it! Let's just drink. I mean Drink" (84).

The anger against men and relief for being alone in the absence of men make these women free to enjoy life without strings. Shobha Dé reflects on such a scene with imaginative skill. Swati assures them that "... nobody's watching. Nobody will know. There aren't husbands around to spoil our fun. Or fathers, lovers, boyfriends. No men for a change. *What a bloody relief*" (91).

Sex antagonism surfaces with great vigour and intensity as these women give vent to their grievances against men in general and husbands in particular. As Reema recollects her affairs with her lover Raju and later her relationship with her husband, she becomes bitter and ironical. Memory haunts her endlessly:

> It wasn't the physical act that had stayed with her for so many years, but the expression in Raju's eyes as he raised himself over her body like a conqueror. Every man behaved similarly. Reema had concluded. Her husband was no better. And these days their love-making had to be squeezed in between her watching *The Bold and the Beautiful* and his business calls. During the cricket season, she recalled at least three sexual encounters accomplished to the drone of Test Match commentary with her husband pausing mid-trust to applaud a stylish sixer (93).

The conversation between Aparna and her mother reiterates this point. Her mother dislikes the typical behaviour of husbands, who "come home, put their feet up and order their women around". When Aparna tells her that the 'modern' ones are different, she says that "all men are just the same. And Indian husbands, the worst" (202).

Since enjoyment of life is the main goal of these upper-class women, they are against the norms of the traditional society and the joint family system. They want to do two things at the same time — that is, to ask the mother-in-law to stay away from them, and second, to tame the husband. Reema gives this advice to Surekha when the latter complains against the dominance of the mother-in-law and the obedience of her husband to his mother:

> "Your just have to assert yourself once. Once your husband becomes hundred per cent dependent on you he won't look elsewhere. Men like their comforts. And men are spoilt lazy babies. Feed them well. Fuck them regularly and sit tight. That's the way to keep them. Control them. The rest is easy. Believe me — I was in your shoes not so long ago" (151).

As we turn towards the close of the twentieth century, our attitude to love and sex has changed radically. Upper-class women are no longer shy of speaking about both love and sex even publicly. Most of the women are married early, and get bored with their husbands. They seek new relationships outside marriage, without breaking the family. Reema's advice to "Say no to divorce. Never break up the home. Have your fun quietly somewhere. But don't leave the family. That is the sensible way of handling the situation" (214) — seems to be fairly representative of the class. Swati's statements about love and sex seem to project the authorial voice. "Sex is hobby," she says. "For some it can be an all-consuming one. For others, a passing fancy" (116). "Sex is not filthy," she comments further, "Our minds make it so. Look at Khajuraho, Konarak... have any of you studied the 'Kama Sutra'? Fascinating. It's a pity we got brain washed by some frustrated, repressed idiots. I think sex is a celebration — the highest form of religion" (164). The basic difference between the modern women like Swati and others is that they 'rejoice' in their sexuality, which they do not suppress. Swati adds: "We don't dismiss it [sexuality]. We don't find it dirty. Sex doesn't threaten us. I'm not afraid to fuck. I feel sorry for all you women hanging on also desperately to out-dated ideas of purity, morality, chastity. It's pathetic" (165). Their views can be taken as the author's own views on love and sex. To my mind, the author enters into the text through Swati, if we go by Ronald Barthes' theory.

Shobha Dé's novels, including *Snapshots,* are not immoral. They are not gross or trivial. They can be termed amoral. She depicts a way of life prevalent in the upper-class society in the metropolis of our country. Since 'sex' is no longer considered a sin, the idea of constancy in love has been given a go by. Sleeping with men other than the husband is not considered immoral these days by modern people. Swati says:

> "There's nothing unnatural about it. Come on, you can tell us. I believe it's the done thing in Delhi society to sleep with your husband's brother. Wow, Reema, may be you'll start similar trend in Bombay" (104).

An overdose of sex in Dé's novels may distract the readers for a while and prompt them to question the literary merit of her fiction, but occasional flashes of poetic language save to a great extent, the novels from being a pornography. Not only Dé talks about sex, she also brings out the jealousy and quarrel between her women. Within the framework of her novels, Shobha Dé depicts the breaking up of the institution of marriage. The new concept of marriage envisages complete sexual freedom with no notion of fidelity. In such a situation men and women merely become partners in love. Economic freedom, promiscuity and uncontrolled passion resulting from 'the lust of the blood' make most men and women vulnerable and the resultant frustration in life engulfs them. Shobha Dé presents love, sex and quarrels within the ambit of fictional framework. Life is presented as it is, not as it should be. Dé's use of language and her creation of a new idiom by acclimatizing the contemporary society to the English language, adds to the charm of the novel. What is important in Dé's novels is not their unconventional theme but an unusual treatment of sensual opulence in an intimate conversational language and the result is that her novels become best sellers.

WORK CITED

Dé, Shobha. *Snapshots,* New Delhi: Penguin India, 1995.

12

The Art of Storytelling: A Study of *Love and Longing in Bombay*

The art of storytelling is an integral part of Indian Literary tradition. Its origin dates back to the Sixth Century A.D. ancient fables. Old classics like *Katha-Sarit-Sagara, Brihat-Katha* and *the Panchatantra* are famous for the art of storytelling in our country. Stories in the past were written or told (according to the oral tradition) with a bias for morality. They were didactic in nature. Vikram Chandra's *Love and Longing in Bombay* marks a departure from the conventional mode of ancient Indian story telling. The five stories in this collection woven round the classic framing device of an old man (Subramaniam) telling stories in a bar, portray contemporary life in India's most sophisticated city of Bombay (recently renamed as Mumbai). The five stories form as it were, an integrated whole and read like a full length novel.

The first story, 'Dharma' is about Major General Jago Antia (real name Jehangir Antia) who returns home in Bombay after being crippled in the war. The narrator of the story, Subramaniam begins the story with a whispering note: 'I knew a man once who met a ghost' and added, "some people meet their ghosts, and some don't. But we are haunted by them" (Chandra, 1997: 5). Jago Antia, as the story unfolds is haunted by the spirit of a small boy. The story begins with an ominous note:

"On the day that Major General Jago Antia turned fifty, his missing leg began to ache" (*Ibidem* : 5).

Having resigned his job on medical grounds he came to Bombay, his ancestral place, 'to sell the house'. Amir Khan, the caretaker of the house supported Jago Antia on this point and urged him: 'Sell it, I'm tired of it'. Todywalla, to whom Jago Antia wanted to sell it, cried foul: 'there is something in that house'. Jago Antia dismissed it as nonsense and told Thappa "I will sleep to night quietly and so will you. No more of this foolishness." As he moved inside the house with Thappa, he heard a voice asking with a sob "where shall I go?".

An exorcist, named Thakker came to find out the spirit and he opined that it was a child. He explained:

"It is most powerful because it is a child and because it is helpless and because it is alone. Only one who knows it and who is from its family can help it. Such a person must go up there naked and alone. Remember, alone and naked, and ask it what it seeks" (*Ibidem* : 23).

Jago Antia went there alone and 'kicked off his shoes and unbuckled his belt and whispered' : 'what can you want from me? I was a child too'. He went down the memory lane in a flashback and shut his eyes. Chandra uses poetic prose to describe Antia's past and creates a trance like atmosphere befitting the occasion. He writes:

"He (Antia) shut his eyes. Somewhere deep came the poisonous seep of memory, he felt it in his stomach like a living stream, and his mother was looking at him, her eyes unfocussed in a kind of daze" (*Ibidem* : 24).

Then we are told about Sohrab, Antia's brother who died young, and Antia's ancestry has been personalised. Haunted by the spirit of the boy, Jago Antia went to the roof and came face to face with it. Chandra depicts the whole scene in an accurate way, in a matter of fact tone:

"When Jago Antia stirred weakly on the roof, when he looked up, it was dawn. He held himself up and said, "Are you still here? Tell me what you want". Then he saw at the parapet, very dim and shifting in the grey light, the shape of a small body, a boy looking down over the edge towards the ocean. As Jago Antia watched, the boy turned slowly, and in the weak light he saw that the boy was wearing a uniform of olive green, and he asked, "Where shall I go?" Jago Antia began to speak, but then his voice caught, because he was remembering his next and seventh birthday, the first party without Soli, and his parents holding him between them, soothing him, saying you must want something, and he looking up at their faces, at the lines in his father's face, the exhaustion in his mother's eyes. Burjor Mama sits on the carpet behind him with head down, and Amir Khan stands behind, and Jehangir shakes his head nothing. His mother's eyes fill with tears, and she kisses him on the forehead, "Baba, it's all right, let us give you a present," and his heart breaks beneath a surging weight, but he stands up straight, and looking at her and his father, he says, "I want a uniform." So Jago Antia looked at the boy as he came closer, and he saw the small letters above the pocket, J. ANTIA, and the sun came up, and he saw the boy clearly, he saw the enormous dark eyes, and in the eyes he saw his vicious and ravenous strength, his courage and his devotion, his silence and his pain, his whole misshapen and magnificent life, and Jago Antia said, "Jehangir, Jehangir, you're already at home" (*Ibidem* : 30-31).

The story comes to a close with Thappa and Amir Khan offering Jago Antia a cup of tea in order to bring him back to reality. Chandra concluded the story with a note of relief.

"'Thank you', Jago Antia said. Then they drank the tea together".

The second story in this collection, "Shakti" is about two rival business families whose women Sheila (Bijlani) and Dolly (Boatwalla) are ill disposed to each other. The club culture of Bombay life with its so-called sophistication has been exposed thoroughly in this story. Sheila, a beautiful Air Hostess married the U.S.A.-returned Bijlani (T.T.) for money and started a business. In their neighbourhood lived Dolly Boatwalla in her Boatwalla mansion. There was a Lunch Club in Bombay, dominated by Dolly. Sheila in spite of the former's objection finally succeeded in joining the Lunch Club. Chandra gives a vivid description of the club in the following words:

The women in the Lunch Club met once a month for lunch at one of the members' houses. After lunch they played cards. Then they had tea and went home. That was it, nothing very exciting on the face of it, but if you knew anything you knew that was where marriages were arranged and sometimes destroyed, deals were made, casually business was felt out, talk went on about this minister in Delhi and So-and-So's son who was school captain at Mayo. It was the real stuff, you know, masala-grinding, how the world works (*Ibidem* : 37).

The Lunch Club had met next at Sheila's house for lunch. The dish was served and during the lunch Sheila's son Sanjeev was introduced to the members. Mani Mennon, Sheila's friend liked the boy. 'Isn't he so cute?' Mani said, but Dolly was offensive. Sheila turned and saw 'the look on Dolly's face, a kind of absurd pursuing of the nostrils, an unmistakable look of offense, as if she had just begun to smell something bad'. The bitterness between the two, Sheila and Dolly took a new turn. Chandra brings a contrast between the two in a simple but forceful language:

"Dolly was not perfect, she was long everywhere, she was sallow, she wore old jewellery sometimes missing a link here and there, today she wore a tatty green scarf over her shirt, and that was just it. Sheila was perfect, and she knew that, however, hard she tried she could never achieve the level of careless imperfection that Dolly flaunted. It had nothing to do with perseverance or intelligence and it took generations. It couldn't be learnt, only grown with the bone. It was absolutely confident and sure of itself and easy. Dolly had it and she didn't: looking at it honestly, Sheila knew this. She knew it and she was absolutely determined that if it took her the rest of her life she would defeat Dolly that it had come to open conflict she knew, and she would not stand losing" (*Ibidem* : 41-42).

Sheila launched a new club called the Shanghai Club with the help of Mr. Fong. Dolly was invited to join it. The war between the two — Sheila and Dolly continued for a long time. The feud between the two can be taken as a symbol for the conflict between women of the high society who can do anything for the sake of their vanity. False sense of dignity and vulgar display of wealth are taken as a distinguishing mark of new culture in the present-day society. The desire to show up oneself and look down upon others becomes a way of life with the so-called upper class woman in the metropolis of our country. No wonder that both Sheila and Dolly fell a prey to this kind of modern malaise and continued their war to the bitter end. Chandra has rightly observed:

"Sheila and Dolly had conducted a ruthless but fiercely polite war for years, in which the victories were counted in receptions given and famous writers annexed and huge sums collected for causes and the casualties were bruised egos of partisans of either side, who cut each other in Derby boxes and flicked razar-sharp looks over shoulders at openings. But there were some rulers, a certain code of conduct that kept it all civilized until the incident of the blackball" (*Ibidem* : 49).

The story took a dramatic turn when Sheila's son Sanjeev fell in love with Dolly's third daughter, Roxanne and expressed his desire before his mother to marry the girl. Sheila was shocked but she kept her cool. Dolly took Roxanne to London. Sanjeev's agony for not being united with Roxanne shattered him and made his mother realise the futility of her feud with Dolly. At Asha's (Ganga's daughter) wedding Sheila observed that her relatives and Dolly's relatives had gathered under the same Shamiana to bless the newly-wed couple, and children of both the families, Roxanne's second cousin and her niece played there. This made her change her mind. Perhaps, she was willing to make amends by asking Dolly to marry her daughter to Sanjeev. The story ends with a hope, 'May be I'll tell you about that another evening'.

Apart from exposing the hollowness of the feud in upper-class society and the hypocrisy of high people to whom 'the rest of the world is invisible', Chandra has made references to living personalities like Amitabh Bachchan and Tiger Pataudi in his effort to create new myths around them. This is certainly a daring act to mythicize the living heroes in the field of art and sports. Raja Rao made such an attempt in *Kanthapura* to create a myth around Gandhi, the father of the nation. Chandra has also made references to several films of Amitabh Bachchan like *Coolie, Dewar, Sholay* and *Muquddar Ka Sikandar.* He has also used a lot of Indian words without making an attempt at translation. The success of the story lies in the fact that he has successfully re-created his characters in their own situation.

The third story in the collection, 'Kama' dives deep into the intricacies of the life as lived upon in the city of Bombay and exposes the hypocrisy of the so-called sophisticated people. The Police Inspector, Sartaj Singh while investing into the murder case of Chetanbhai Ghanshyam Patel gets drawn into the 'spiralling layers of corruption and deceit' prevalent in the society. As the irony of fate would have it, he also reflects upon his discontented married life that ultimately terminates in divorce. In course of investigation, he got pressurised by senior officers like Paralkar and local M.L.A. Shantilal Nayak not to pursue the case too far. "These are delicate times" said Parulkar. "Pushing too hard, without sufficient reason, on that family could lead to, let us say, sensitivities" (*Ibidem* : 110). Sartaj Singh arrested a man called Ghorpada, who not only died in detention but proved to be not guilty in the end. Kshitiji, Patel's son seemed to be innocent in the beginning but in the end turned out to be a member of an association which is given to violence and lawlessness. The members of the association called themselves 'Rakhaks'. The murdered man, Patel had connection with a racket that used to exploit women sexually and run a flesh trade. After sex act, nude photographs were taken for blackmail afterwards.

What is worse, he has not spared his own wife, Ashaben. Chandra makes reference to several people who were given to crime, sex and violence in love.

Sartaj Singh, the investigating Police Officer was also a victim of failed married life. His wife, Megha who married him for love in their college days, decided to marry some one called Raj Sanghi. The worse is that Megha came personally to Sartaj to inform him about her decision, 'I am getting married' (*Ibidem* : 116). What is most surprising is that the wife (Megha) who came to inform the husband (Sartaj) of her decision to marry, someone (Raj) enters into an elaborate sex act for hours together and Vikram Chandra takes nearly ten pages (pp. 116-25) to describe the love-play between them. This is how he describes:

"He felt Megha's hands on his shoulders, and her breath on his forehead as she whispered, "Sartaj, Sartaj," and he turned away from her, from his own embarrassment, but his strength was gone, and she pulled his head back, into the solid curve of her shoulder. He shook again and she held him tight, hard, and he felt with piercing awareness the pain of her forearm against the back of his neck. He was gone, then, vanished into the familiar fragrance of her perfume, unknown for so long, with its flowers and underlying tinge of salt. He was perfectly still. Her lips moved against his cheek, murmuring, something that he couldn't quite hear, and then he felt the brush on his mouth, a gift of softness and then the shifting suppleness, what he always experienced as a question. He kissed her desperately, afraid to stop or pause because then she would stop. But she wasn't stopping, she held his face in her hands, her long palms strongly on cheeks and chin, and sipped at him with little murmurs. Despite himself, Sartaj curved against her, an arm up and around, and he felt the weight of her breasts against his side, and she laughed into his mouth, not here, not here" (*Ibidem* : 118).

The scene, then shifts to the bed room.

"Finally she drew him up and kissed him, licking his mouth and fingers. This time he put the condom on himself. They moved together and the bed creaked under them. His body bent over her and he looked back over his shoulder at their tangled shadows, rising and falling, and then down at her and at their hair mingling. He bent down to kiss her, and when he came away she was crying. With a groan he touched her cheek but she put a hand on his wrist. "Don't stop," she said. "Don't stop. Don't stop." And so he went on. In the twilight she raised a hand to his mouth and he could see her tears. And so then a moment when everything was lost, but her" (*Ibidem* : 124-25).

Sartaj's own married life (rather the failure of it) made him understand the murdered Patel's wedded life, who did everything for money and pleasure and, 'under his hands there was Chetanbhai's case file, closed. It was over, according to the file, and there was a murderer who had died in the hospital' (*Ibidem* : 159).

The story comes to an end not only with the closure of the murder case but with Sartaj's divorce of his wife, Megha. The wheel has turned a full circle. Chandra does not offer solutions to the problems presented in the story. There are only hints and guesses, and it is for the discerning readers to read meanings into it. Like Keats' Odes, Chandra's stories, particularly 'Kama' 'Whispers results'.

The fourth story in the collection, 'Artha' is about gangsters. Here the narrator, Subramaniam tells us a story told to him by a stranger on the train, Rajdhani when the former was travelling from Delhi to Bombay. The main characters in the story are two — Sandhya and the protagonist, Iqbal Akbar but other minor characters are Anubhav, the painter with whom Sandhya is in love, Latif, Sandhya's son, Vasant, Sandhya's ex-husband, Ratmani, a builder, Rajesh, Iqbal's friend, the missing postal clerk and a few others. Rajesh and Iqbal met Anubhav, the painter in Sandhya's house. At that time Anubhav was painting something against the backdrop of Amitabh Bachchan in Colie's rope in his film *Deewar.* Gradually the story unfolds that Sandhya has a son called Latif, an ex-husband, Vasant and a mother. She is drawn towards the painter, Anubhav who works for *The Times of India*. Iqbal saw them 'standing nearby with their heads close together'.

As the story proceeds, we are told that Rajesh, who worked in the post office, was missing. Iqbal searches for him and in the process encountered the gangsters, the underworld people and was beaten by them. The 'bhai log' (the underworld people whose leader was Govardhan bhai) played tricks on Iqbal. Iqbal describes a scene in the underworld when he was tortured by them in a matter of fact tone:

"When I managed to focus my eyes I saw three uniformed guards with lathis in their hands standing over me. To the left there was a man in plain clothes, with hair cut short and a very straight back. In his hands he held a sten gun, the muzzle pointed directly at me.

And stepping through the gate there was the man with the clipped moustache from the Atreya Lane gym" (*Ibidem* : 209).

In the story there is a reference to communal riot which created havoc. People belonging to different communities who lived together for ages turned enemies in no time. Iqbal came to know that Rajesh worked with some 'bhai log' and one of them was Ratmani. Iqbal lost a friend, Rajesh to the people of the underworld. The Sub-inspector's cryptic reply 'in this life some people just vanish' explains the deplorable state of life in the modern metropolis. Painting turns out to be more lively than life. So Iqbal concludes the story by imagining what Rajesh would look like in painting (because Rajesh the person is lost for ever):

"I will lie in my long narrow room and look at the strong fingers holding the white cigarette and wonder what it is in the shapes that is Rajesh" (*Ibidem* : 228).

The last story in this collection, "Shanti" is written in a different vein. It is here that teller enters the tale and the story gets a personal touch. Subramaniam, the teller of the stories invites the narrator to his house to say how he met Shanti and married her. Characters in his story are very few but they are convincing as human beings. Frankil Furtado, the assistant station master at Leharia puts Mrs. Shanti Chauhan, a second class passenger in first class because 'she is very beautiful'. Frankie has taken interest in Shanti, as she used to come to that station in every two or three months. When Subramaniam asked him about Shanti's destination, "Going where?", Frankie replied in the negative.

"I don't know. She catches a tonga outside the station. I think to the cantonment. Her attaché has stencilling on it" (*Ibidem* : 237).

She is a married woman who is in search of her missing pilot husband. On being asked about her husband she said:

"He was in the first batch of Indian fighter pilots in the RIAF. He was flying a Hurricane over Burma in 1942. They were protecting transports. They were attacked by Japanese fighters. The last his wingman saw of his was the plane losing height over the jungle. The plane was smoking. That was all they saw" (*Ibidem* : 243).

She was hopeful of her husband's return but gradually the hope receded with the passage of time. In the meanwhile Shiv Subramaniam took interest in her and tried to win over her. At this point the author introduces story within story technique and makes Shanti to tell stories to Subramaniam. She told him how she met the man with the bluest eyes, who was also the 'most evil man in the world'. Then she told another story about Zingu who died because he thought 'all men are equal' and asked for equality of status with other upper caste people. For showing this kind of courage, he was killed along with his son. Then Shanti tells stories about ghosts as to how they had cast their spell on Janamohini and makes us aware of nuclear warfare as it affected Amma. These stories are told to build a kind of intimacy between Shiv and Shanti. At long last Shiv proposed himself to Shanti which she accepted and happily they became man and wife. The story comes to a close with the narrator being introduced to Shanti, Subramaniam's wife. The fitting conclusion to the series of five stories comes when the narrator feels like asking Ayesha to marry him, so that they can get into life. The narrator concludes the story with an assertion of life. ·

"I know I am looking for Ayesha. I will stand before her building and when it is morning I will call up to her. I might ask her to go for a walk. I might ask her to marry me. If we search together, I think, we may find in Andheri, in Colaba, in Bhuleshwar, perhaps not heaven or its opposite, but only life itself" (*Ibidem* : 267-68).

In *Love and Longing in Bombay,* Vikram Chandra has adopted a new technique of storytelling. The five stories in this collection are told by the same person and are interlocked with a dozen of shorter narratives, fused together as it were, by a 'story within story' technique. To read these stories is to see Bombay inside out. Violence, Crime, activities in the underworld, club-culture, witch-hunting — all the negative qualities that dehumanize the modern man are highlighted in these stories with consummate skill. What seems to me to be more important in this collection of stories, is the use of Indian words by way of code mixing, that successfully recreates, the characters in our own situation. The use of Indian words like *thali, diya, massala, dupatta, shamiana, jira, paan, bidis, tamasha, daroga, dusserimango, besan, Karhais, bhajiyas, puris, haveli, takath, durbans, safas, pranam, rakshaks, kurta, pyjamas, panchnama, agarbattis, saukeen, pattn, regada-patis, patta, peripauna, jite rhaobeta, janaab, kaisehai, (pati) parameswar,* and swear words like *bhenchod, maderchod, bhai log, dada, bewda, kalua, musalta, kattu,* etc. evoke an atmosphere in which the characters live and interact with each other. Apart from using Indian words in his attempt at creating an Indian English idiom, Chandra also takes recourse to transliteration to re-create a familiar scene in his stories. Here, are a few examples:

(i) 'maine Shayad tumhe pahale bhi kahin dekha hai' (p. 26).
(ii) 'voh jo ham me tum me karaav tha, tumhe yaad ho ke ya na yaad ho ...' (p. 104).
(iii) 'baat karni mujhe khabi muskil aisi to na thi' (p. 105).
(iv) 'Stop Phenoko-ing, yaar' (p. 163).
(v) 'dandi mein current hai?' (p. 198).

Love and Longing in Bombay depicts the 'horror and boredom' of the city of Bombay in our time. The book successfully fictionalizes some aspects of modern life as it is lived upon in our metropolis and therefore, makes an absorbing reading.

WORK CITED

Chandra, Vikram. *Love and Longing in Bombay.* New Delhi: Penguin Books India (P) Ltd., 1997.

13

Short Story as Autobiography: A Study of Ruskin Bond's *Our Trees Still Grow in Dehra*

Ruskin Bond is a front ranking fiction writer of Indian English Literature. In course of a writing career spanning over four decades he has written more than a hundred short stories, two full length novels, three novellas and a number of essays. His collection of short-stories include *The Night Train at Deoli, Time Stops at Shamli* and *Our Tress Still Grow in Dehra,* his latest collection of stories which won him the Central Sahitya Akademi Award in 1992. Besides, he has edited two anthologies of short stories, *The Penguin Book of Indian Ghost Stories* and *The Penguin Book of Indian Railway Stories.* Ruskin Bond's stories dive deep into human psyche and unfolds human mind in relation to nature and environment. The incidents and situation depicted in his stories are not wholly fictional. He projects a part of his personality into his stories to make them authentic and interesting. *Our Trees Still Grow in Dehra,* as the blurb of the book says, is 'Semi-autobiographical in nature' and therefore, can be read as a disguised autobiography.

In his opening remarks "Maplewood: An Introduction" Ruskin Bond harks back to the past, when he came to live in the Maplewood cottage, resigning his job in Delhi. He writes:

"It was all done on an impulse — the decision to give up my job in Delhi, find a cheap house in a hill-station, and return to freelance writing. It was a dream I'd had for some time, lack of money had made it difficult to realize. But then, I knew that if I was going to wait for money to come, I might have to wait until I was old and grey and full of sleep. I was thirty-five — still young enough to take a few risks. If the dream was to become reality, this was the time to do something about it" (1991 : X).

Most of the stories of this collection, *Our Trees Still Grow in Dehra* were written here. Ruskin Bond was rooted in the place and became a part of it. He states, "Once you have lived with mountains, there is no escape. You belong to them".

Love of nature and concern for ecological imbalance in the Hills, make the writer sad as he sees the felling of trees and the rapid deforestation going on all around him. In some of his stories he makes a dig at the unwise decision of the authorities to cut trees and build roads and buildings in their place. In "Death of the Trees", Bond tells us how the felling of trees one by one, had broken his heart. What pains him more is our lack of understanding of the importance of the trees to maintain ecological balance. He writes with a tinge of irony.

"The peace and quiet of the Maplewood hillside disappeared for ever one winter. The powers that be decided to build another new road into the mountains, and the PWD saw fit to take it right past the cottage, about six feet from the large window which had overlooked the forest" (*OTSGID,* 1991 : 93).

On the surface level this story records the author's reaction to the felling of trees which makes the hill bare and forest birds homeless. 'Forest birds, all of them, they will now be in search of some other stretch of surviving forest. The only visitors will be the crows, who have learnt to live with, and off humans, and seem to multiply along with roads, houses and people', says Bond with a deep sign. Deforestation is closely followed by rapid urbanisation causing damage to the environment and creating ecological imbalance to the region. At the deep level, the author resents the mindless action of the power that be, in felling trees along the hill side. Bond concludes this story with an implicit warning: "Never mind. Men come and go; the mountains remain".

The opening story of this collection, *Our Trees Still Grow in Dehra,* titled "Escape from Java" sets the tone of the book. It is both adventurous and autobiographical. It deals with an event in the childhood of Bond when he ran for life along with his father from Jakarta to India. The Japanese attack on Batavia (now called Jakarta) had forced Bond and his father to leave the country and return to India. On the eve of Japanese bombing Bond and his father left for India. Bond describes the scene that was prevalent then in Batavia in a matter of fact tone.

"There were no anti-aircraft guns in Batavia — at least we never heard any — and the Jap bombers came over at will, dropping their bombs by daylight. Sometimes bombs fell in the town. One day the building next to my father's office received a direct hit and tumbled into the river. A number of office workers were killed" (*Ibidem* : 3).

The lack of security in that country forced Bond's father to leave the city. Who knows they might be killed. Hence, the preparation to leave the place. Bond recalls:

"We had to be up very early the next morning. Our bags had been packed late at night. We were taking a few clothes, some of my father's business papers, a pair of binoculars, one stamp album, and several bars of chocolate. I was pleased about the stamp album and the chocolate, but I had to give up several of my treasures — favourite books, and gramophone and records, an old Samurai Sword, a train set and a dartboard. The only consolation was that Sono, and not a stranger, would have them" (*Ibidem* : 6).

On Way to India, Bond and his father faced many difficulties. Their plane had engine failure and it hit the water. It came to a standstill and a few passengers including Bond and his father managed to climb into the dinghy. They had a very tough time in the dinghy. A fishing boat came to their rescue and then, they returned home. Finally they reached Bombay. Selling stamps Bond earned some money and with that Bond was sent to a school at Shimla. His father joined RAF. Bond writes:

"A week later I was on a small train which went chugging up the steep mountain track to Shimla. Several Indian, Anglo-Indian and English children tumbled around in the compartment. I felt quite out of place among them, as though I had grown out of their pranks. But I wasn't unhappy. I knew my father would be coming to see me soon. He'd promised me some books, a pair of roller-skates, and a cricket bat, just as soon as he got his first month's pay" (*Ibidem* : 16).

Later on Bond was shifted to New Delhi and stayed with his father when the latter was serving in the RAF. In 'Untouchable', Bond narrates his experience as a boy when he was asked not to mix with an untouchable boy. Here he makes a dig at the superstitions and prejudices prevalent in the society (Incidentally this is Bond's first short story written at the age of sixteen). When his father was admitted in the hospital for treatment of Malaria, he was left alone.

He was supposed to stay with neighbours but he did not. "I kept away. I did not like them and they did not like me", says Bond. He was left with a sweeper boy. But the woman in the neighbourhood warned him: "Don't play with the sweeper-boy, he is unclean. Don't touch him. Remember, he is a servant. You must come and play with my boys." Ironically, it is the sweeper boy to whom the writer turned to for emotional support when there was thunder and lightning. He writes:

"But at the next thunderclap, louder this time, louder than I had ever heard, I leapt from my bed. I could not stand it. I fled, blundering into the sweeper-boy's room.

> The boy sat on the bare floor.
> 'What is happening?' he asked.
> The lightning flashed, and his teeth and eyes flashed with it.
> Then he was a blur in the darkness.
> 'I am afraid', I said.
> I moved towards him and my hand touched a cold shoulder.
> 'Stay here', he said. 'I too am afraid'.

I sat down, my back against the wall, beside the untouchable, the outcaste ... and the thunder and lightning ceased, and the rain came down, swishing and drumming on the corrugated roof.

'The rainy season has started', observed the sweeper-boy, turning to me. His smile played with the darkness and he laughed. And I laughed too, but feebly.

But I was happy and safe. The scent of the wet earth blew in through the skylight and the rain fell harder (*Ibidem* : 27).

"Coming Home to Dehra", is a touching story about the author's return to Dehra after his father's death to find his mother's and stepfather's indifference glaring in the face. The memory of the father and the nostalgia, overwhelmed him. This story should be read in the context of the opening words (under the caption 'Return to Dehra') to the book.

> "So this is old Dehra of mangoes and lemons,
> Where I grew beside the jack fruit tree
> Planted by my father on the sunny side
> Of the house since sold to Major — General Mehra.

> The town's grown hard, none know me now or knew
> My mother's laughter. Most men come home as strangers.
> And yet, the trees my father planted here, these
> Trees — old family trees — are growing still in Dehra."
> (1991 : VIII)

At the age of eleven, Bond returned to Dehra after his father's death. His father died of Malaria and his class teacher broke the news to him. He looked for someone at the Dehra Station but in vain. His mother sent no one to the station to receive him. So he went to his Grandmother's house. Seeing him the Grandmother asked:

"Didn't any one meet you at the Station?" She asked. I shook my head. Grandmother said: "Your mother doesn't live here any more. You can come in an wait, but she may be worried about you, so I'd better take you to her place. Come on, help me up into the tonga. I might have known it would be a white horse. It always makes me nervous sitting in a tonga behind a white horse" (*Ibidem* : 42).

She took him to his mother's house. On reaching there Bond found that his mother and stepfather were absent. His six-months old half-brother was at home. The Grandmother was upset about the irresponsible behaviour of her former daughter-in-law. Leaving Bond there she returned home. After sometime his mother and step father came but they were cold to him. This made him feel miserable. He felt the absence of his father. Bond writes:

"Going home was something that I had always looked forward to. But going home had meant my father, and now he had vanished and I was left quite desolate.

I suppose if one is present when a loved one dies, or sees him dead and laid out and later buried, one is convinced of the finality of the thing and finds it easier to adapt to the changed circumstances. But when you hear of a death, a father's death, and have only the faintest idea of the manner of his dying, it is rather a lot for the imagination to cope with — especially when the imagination is a small boy's. There being no tangible evidence of my father's death, it was, for me, not a death but a vanishing. And although this enabled me to remember him as a living, smiling, breathing person, it meant that I was not wholly reconciled to his death, and subconsciously expected him to turn up (as he often did, when I most needed him) and deliver me from an unpleasant situation" (*Ibidem* : 44-45).

Bond concludes the story with a note of irony.

"I was fortunate in having my own room. I was as much desirous of my own privacy as my mother and step father were desirous of theirs ... I was even willing that my mother should leave me alone" (*Ibidem*).

Bond writes about his Grandfather and Grandmother with a note of fondness and nostalgia in stories like "All Creatures Great and Small", and "The Last Tonga Ride". His Grandfather was fond of animals and birds, and therefore, he kept a number of animals in his house. The writer like his Grandfather was also fond of animals and enjoyed their company in the latter's house. Bond writes:

"Instead of having brothers and sisters to grow up within India, I had as my companions an odd assortment of pets, which included a monkey, a tortoise, a python and a Great Indian Hornbill. The person responsible for all this wildlife in the home was my grandfather. As the house was his own, other members of the family could not prevent him from keeping a large variety of pets, though they could certainly voice their objections; and as most of the household consisted of women — my grandmother, visiting aunts and occasional in-laws (my parents were in Burma at that time) — Grandfather and I had to be alert and resourceful in dealing with them. We saw eye to eye on the subject of pets, and whenever Grandmother decided it was time to get rid of a tame white rat or a squirrel, I would conceal them in a hole in the jackfruit tree; but unlike my aunts, she was generally tolerant of Grandfather's hobby, and even took a liking to some of our pets" (*Ibidem* : 28).

The story reminds us of Nehru's *An Autobiography* in which he describes animals, lizards and pigeon in the prison. Bond describes how his Grandmother gradually tolerated birds and animals brought to their house by her husband. However, she was allergic to reptiles. Bond has hinted at, though implicitly, in this story that we should not be cruel to birds and animals and kill them unnecessarily.

In "The Last Tonga Ride" the writer describes his Grandmother's attitude to Tonga ride and his own friendship with Tongawalla, Bansi. He had his last Tonga ride with his Grandmother to the Railway Station. In this story Bond tells us of a superstition narrated to him by the Ayah. After reaching the station on a Tonga, he boarded the train with his Grandmother. And on the train he recalls:

"I remembered something that Ayah had once told me, that stars are the spirits of goodmen, and I wondered if that shooting star was a sign from my father that he was aware of our departure and would be with us on our journey. And I remembered something else that Ayah had said — that if one wishes on a shooting star, one's wish would be granted, provided of course that one thrust all five fingers into the mouth at the same time!

'What on earth are you doing?' asked Grandmother staring at me as I thrust my hand into my mouth.

'Making a wish', I said.

'Oh', said Grandmother.

She was preoccupied, and didn't ask me what I was wishing for; nor did I tell her" (*Ibidem* : 58).

The autobiographical note in "The Last Time I Saw Delhi" is unmistakable. It was in early August the writer reached New Delhi to see his ailing mother. In a tone imbued with pathos the writer records his conversation with his mother:

'How do you feel?' I ask.

'All right. They, say they will operate in the morning. They've stopped my smoking.'

'Can you drink? Your rum, I mean?'

'No. Not until a few days after the operation'.

She has a fair amount of grey in her hair, natural enough fifty-four. Otherwise she hasn't changed much; the same small chin and mouth, lively brown eyes. Her father's face, not her mother's.

The nurse has left us. I produce the photograph and hand it to my mother.

'The negative was lying with me all these years. I had it printed yesterday'.

'I can't see without my glasses'.

The glasses are lying on the locker near her bed. I had them to her. She puts them on and studies the photograph.

'Your grandmother was always very fond of you'.

'It was hard to tell. She wasn't a soft woman.'

'It was her money that got you to Jersey, when you finished school. It wasn't much, just enough for the ticket'.

'I didn't know that'.

'The only person who ever left you anything. I'm afraid. I've nothing to leave you, either'.

'You know very well that I've never cared a damn about money. My father taught me to write. That way inheritance enough'.

'And what did I teach you?'

'I'm not sure .... Perhaps you taught me how to enjoy myself now and then'.

She looked pleased at this. 'Yes I've enjoyed myself between troubles. But your father didn't know how to enjoy himself. That's why we quarrelled so much. And finally separated.'

'He was much older than you'.

'You've always blamed me for leaving him, haven't you?'

'I was very small at that time. You left us suddenly. My father had to look after me, and it wasn't easy for him.

He was very sick. Naturally I blamed you'.

'He wouldn't let me take you away.'

'Because you were going to marry someone else'.

I break off; we have been over this before. I am not there as my father's advocate, and the time for recrimination has passed (*Ibidem* : 65-66).

Apart from the autobiographical elements, one notices a note of didacticism in the short stories of Ruskin Bond. The desire to teach and preach is unmistakable.

"The Bent-Double Beggar" is replete with didacticism. Here are some of the teachings of the Bent-Double Beggar:

(i) "It is no use getting upset about delays in India: they come with unfailing punctuality".
(ii) "His favourite proverb: If you must eat dung, eat elephant's dung".
(iii) "One can forgive ignorance in a man who has had little or no education, but ignorance in a man who has been to college is unforgivable. Yet it is quite common."
(iv) "For democracy to succeed, the first requirement is that the majority of people should be honest."
(v) "Nietzsche was wrong; it isn't action but pleasure that binds us to existence."

"It is difficult to be miserable all the time. Human nature won't permit it. Even when we are burning or burying our dead, we are thinking of what we will eat or drink later in the day".

(vi) "Chance gives, and takes away, and gives again."

(vii) "I travelled a lot once (said Ganpat), but you can go on doing that and not get anywhere. Wherever you go or whatever you do, most of your life will have to happen in your mind. And there's no escape from that little room" (*Ibidem* : 22-23).

The above quotations remind us of Bacon's aphorism. It seems that Bond wants to preach through his stories. The moralising tone in his stories is unmistakable.

In another story, "What's your Dream?" in a conversation with an old beggar Bond hints at the cruelty of shattering other people's dreams and underlines the importance of freedom in one's life. This is how he puts it:

"Follow your own dream, but don't take other people's dreams, don't stand in anyone's way, don't take from another man his room or his faith or his son. And he turned and shuffled away, intoning the following verse, which I have never heard elsewhere, so it must have been his own.

Live long, my friend, Be wise and strong,
But do not take from any man his song.

I remained in the litchi tree, pondering his wisdom and wondering how a man so wise could be so poor. Perhaps he became wise afterwards. Anyway, he was free, and I was free, and I went back to the house and demanded (and got) a room of my own. Freedom, I was beginning to realize, is something you have to insist upon" (*Ibidem* : 47).

Ruskin Bond's stories reveal his love of nature and particularly his attachment to trees. They are firmly rooted in Dehra. The landscape of the place haunts him without end. Like Wordsworth's visit to Tintern Abbey, Bond's stay at Dehra helps him to build an intimate relationship with the hillside, trees, and birds, which becomes an integral part of his life. To live without them becomes painful for him. By doing violence to nature, man has caused ecological imbalance which ultimately harms him. Therefore, Bond warns mankind against this kind of violence to nature in a number of his stories. The rapid urbanisation and deforestation would spell disaster for mankind someday. He writes:

"In either side of the road are the houses of well-to-do Punjabis, who came to Delhi as refugees in 1947 and now make up more than half the capital's population. Industrious flashy, go-ahead people. Thirty years ago, fields extended on either side of this road, as far as the eye could see. The Ridge, an outcrop of the Aravallis, was scrub jungle, in which the black buck roamed. Feroz Shah's 14th century hunting lodge stood here in splendid isolation. It is still here, hidden by petrol pumps and lost within the sounds of buses, cars, trucks and scooter-rickshaws. The peacock has fled the forest, the black buck is extinct. Only the jackal remains. When a thousand years from now, the last human has left this contaminated planet for some other star, the jackal and the crow will remain, to survive for years on all the refuse we leave behind" (*Ibidem* : 64).

Bond's fondness for trees is evident to us when he describes the plantation of the Cherry tree in his story, "From Small Beginnings":

"One day I had this Cherry seed in my hand, and on an impulse I thrust it into the soft earth, and then went away and forgot all about it. A few months later I found a tiny cherry tree in the long grass. I did not expect it to survive. But the following year it was two feet tall. And then some goats ate its leaves, and a grass cutter's scythe injured the stem, and I was sure it would wither away. But it renewed itself, sprang up even faster; and within three years it was a healthy, growing tree, about five feet tall.

I left the hills for two years — forced by circumstances to make a living in Delhi — but this time I did not forget the cherry tree. I thought about it fairly often, sent telepathic messages of encouragement in its direction. And when, a couple of years ago, I returned in the autumn, my heart did a somersault when I found my tree sprinkled with pale pink blossom (The Himalaya cherry flowers in November). And later, when the fruit was ripe, the tree was visited by finches, tits, bulbuls and other small birds, all come to feast on the sour red cherries" (*Ibidem* : 84).

The first-person narrative in Bond's stories not only underlines the autobiographical elements in them but lends a sense of authenticity to them. He does not invent situations camouflaging them as real, to elicit readers' participation. The stories are based on his own experiences, 'felt in the blood, and felt along the heart' and that is why they are the successful in evoking the readers' participation. To read Ruskin Bond's stories is to see the Maplewood in Dehra and to transport one's self into the quiet realms of nature and Garhwall hills — there in lies his success as a story teller.

WORK CITED

Bond, Ruskin. *Our Trees Still Grow in Dehra.* New Delhi: Penguin, 1991.

14

A Critique of Nissim Ezekiel's *Don't Call it Suicide*

Indian English drama has no tradition to fall back upon. It did not seriously begin to exist till independence (i.e. 1947). Compared to the success of Indian English fiction writers and poets, the achievement of Indian English playwrights is insignificant and, therefore, it sinks into oblivion. In terms of number and in respect of quality, Indian English drama lags way behind Indian English fiction and poetry. The history of Indian English drama reveals that it is very small in number and what is more disturbing is that it is also poor in quality.

It is obvious that Nissim Ezekiel as a playwright has no tradition to fall back upon. His plays are new to Indian English Literature in post-independence period. He is in a sense one of the pioneers in the field of Indian English drama. Ezekiel's plays include *Three Plays* (1969) and *Don't Call it Suicide* (1993). He has published another dramatic text, *Song of Deprivation* (1969), which has not been published in book-form. Ezekiel's plays can be termed plays of ideas. The ironic undertone is unmistakable.

Ezekiel latest play, *Don't Call it Suicide* was published in 1993. It's a tragedy in two Acts. It centres round one family and is confirmed to a particular place. It is based on a real life incident. Ezekiel tells us about the background of the play in the following words:

"I was told about the event by an acquaintance of mine in an Indian city (not Bombay). It was about his son and family .... but I did not confine myself to his experience, relatives, etc." (*Don't Call it Suicide* : VIII).

It's a short play with an 'unusual' title. The plot of the play is based a dilemma — whether to call an unnatural death of a young man (which was neither an accident nor homicide), suicide or not. Mr. Nanda, the deceased's father refuses to call the death of the son, a suicide. The protagonist of the play is not Mr. Nanda but the dead son.

The play opens with the discussion between Nanda and Sathe on some business matters but soon it takes an inward turn when Mr. Nanda chooses to tell Sathe about the tragedy that has befallen on his family. The characters in the play could be divided into two groups: the sentimentalists and the pragmatists. Only Mr. Nanda belongs to the first group and the rest belongs to the second.

As persons Mr. Nanda and Mrs. Nanda can be taken as contrasts. The husband is a conscientious rather a sentimental person who is unable to reconcile to the unnatural death of his 25-year-old son 14 years ago. He broods over the death of his son and breaks down when he recalls the sad incident to his mind. In the first scene, in course of his discussion with Sathe, Nanda says,

"My eldest son ... at the age of 25 ... committed suicide"

(*Don't Call it Suicide* : I : I : 4)

He adds in the same breath that it is difficult to forget that tragedy. Emotion takes hold of him and he recalls the sad incident with nostalgia.

"It was about 14 years ago. My eldest son never did well in his exams. He never failed but he did not do well either. He was intelligent and very sensitive, yet somehow, he did not care at all about his school and college, we did not know why. He just wasn't happy there. He complained bitterly all the time. He did not like most of the teachers, and he didn't like most of the students, though he had two or three good friends" (Act I, Scene I : 14).

The above lines suggest that the eldest son was unhappy about the ways of the world. Though he was married for 2 years and his wife was not unhappy with him, he remained calm and silent. Nobody knew what he was upto. Getting a chance (when he was alone in the house), he hanged himself to death. His wife is given shelter by her in-laws. But she is made to work hard in the house. Mr. Nanda is sympathetic to her and wants her to be treated more kindlier by his wife. Mr. Nanda never gets over the incident of his son's death and, therefore, has a soft corner for his daughter-in-law, Meeta. Mrs. Nanda, on the other hand, is a pragmatic person who accepts life as it comes. She tells her husband to forget the past and accept life as it comes. She urges upon him to come to terms with life:

"Come on, we have to live a normal life, after all, whatever may have happened in the past. We have to think of our children and grand children. Life includes suffering but it is not all suffering.... Whatever happens, I will always do my duty. I am satisfied with my life as it is. Thank God for it" (Act I, Scene I : 7).

Contrary to this Mr. Nanda is not satisfied with his life. He counters her argument saying:

"I am not satisfied to be what I am. I am not satisfied with my life as it is" (Act I, Scene I : 7).

There is a major difference between the husband and the wife in their attitude to Meeta. Ezekiel brings out in a subtle way the intricate relationship between the mother-in-law and the daughter-in-law through the characters of Mrs. Nanda and Meeta. When Mr. Nanda wants Meeta to meet other members of the family over dinner, Mrs. Nanda puts her foot down and asks her not to come out of kitchen. When Mr. Nanda proposes to have a family gathering and wants Meeta to meet Sheila and Hari, Mrs. Nanda frowns upon him saying that there would be no time for her to do so. She asks Meeta to cook the food and clean the utensils and above all, she is to eat in the kitchen. When Mr. Nanda insists on saying that, why can't she eat with us and talk with us? Mrs. Nanda retorts: "Alright baba, have your way. I will do the cooking and I will do the serving, and I will do the washing up. Let Meeta eat with you and talk with you". This shows how unkind is Mrs. Nanda to Meeta. Not only that a little later in the play she says, "I allowed my eldest son's widow, Meeta to live with us, but that is only because she is helpful to me in the house."

Hari, Mr. Nanda's second son is pragmatic and dominating like his mother. He ill treats his wife, beats her and always tries to boss over others. He takes his brother to be a sentimental fool and has no sympathy with her sister-in-law. In what looks like a soliloquy Hari tells us about his opinion on his deceased elder brother.

"Why should any student be miserable because some teachers are bad or some students don't care about education? So what? Let them be what they are. Why should we be so sad about it that we actually want to die? Yes, you won't believe it, but my elder brother was like that, 'I feel like killing myself', he would say, as if someone had personally done him great wrong. That's foolish, isn't it? I mean, after all, we have got to survive, haven't we? .... I guess he just wasn't emotionally equipped to cope with life. He was a sensitive idealist. He wasn't-what's — the word? — pragmatic" (Act I, Sc III : 13).

It's really shocking that not only Mrs. Nanda is rude to Meeta, but all of them Hari and his wife, Malati, Sheila, and her husband, Gopal all ignore her. The only exception being Mr. Nanda who has a humanistic approach to life. All these people (Son, daughter-in-law, daughter and son-in-law) are self-centred and pragmatic in their approach to life.

Ezekiel makes a dig at certain conventions of the contemporary society through some of the characters. Dominating and beating the wife is prevalent in certain sections of the society. Innocent wives like Malati suffer at the hands of husbands like Hari. Malati states the condition of million of women in a matter of fact tone:

"The choice for all of, those millions of women in our country whom you mentioned, is between being a happy slave or an unhappy slave. There is no other choice" (Act I : IV : 19).

The inhumanity of higher ups in the society comes in for criticism through a conversion between Mr. Nanda and Gopal. When Mr. Nanda asks Gopal to explain what the latter means by "the inhumanity we see in ordinary, everyday life", Gopal answers:

"Like humiliating people, bossing over them, treating them badly because we are in a position to" (Act I : III : 15).

A little later in the play Gopal becomes explicit in saying that in our country officers misbehave and look down upon the subordinates. Gopal explains:

"A branch manager will always treat another branch manager politely, but he will not be polite to his executive assistants those who work under him, and of course, never to his head clerk or other subordinates" (Act I : V : 22).

The play moves to its end by explaining the doubts raised by Mr. Nanda in the beginning of the play regarding the cause of his son's suicide. Sathe seems to have the authorial voice when he says:

"It seems to me that some people are entirely different from the rest of us. I'm not thinking of exceptional people, like philosophers, poets, and artists. I mean ordinary people. That sounds odd, I know. We treat them in the same way. We take it for granted that they accept all those unpleasant and puzzling things in life which others accept, whether they are ordinary or extraordinary. The particular type I'm talking about is in a class by itself. They have the same good qualities and bad qualities as others have, but there is something else at the source, some essential power that causes non-adjustment to things as they are. It makes many persons in this group feel hopeless, and also sensitive to their own helplessness. Now, surprisingly, I've-come to the conclusion that we, the rest of us, have something to learn from them" (Act II : II : 29-30).

The failure on the part of a person makes him feel diffident. The attitude of the society towards people who have failed in life, is to say the least, deplorable. Hence, people like Mr. Nanda's eldest son who is touchy and sentimental, think to be odd men out and commit suicide. Lack of sympathy on the part of people and inability on their own part to come to terms with life, forces and sentimentalists or persons given to repugnance, as Ezekiel would have us say, to commit suicide.

Mr. Sathe's explanation convinced Mr. Nanda that he cannot absolve the blame for his son's death. He takes pills and puts an end to his life. Thus, the play which begins against the backdrop of the elder son's suicide ends with the father's suicide. Tragedy is being recreated against in the character of Mr. Nanda. This brings to our mind, Ezekiel's observation: "My view is that Indian Society, as a whole is implicated in that and similar situations. The individual way of life, independent, wholly unconventional, has no place among the fixed traditional options" (Raju, A.K.).

Mrs. Nanda now breaks down and her pragmatism gives way to fatalism. She bursts out:

"I lost a son. Now I've lost my husband. What have I done to deserve this?" (Act II : III : 33).

At that moment Meeta comes to her and comforts her. She could not help saying, 'Oh! my daughter'. The end reminds us of Shakespeare's play, 'Pericles' and T.S. Eliot's closing words of 'Mariana'. Like a drowning person catching at a straw, Mrs. Nanda turns to Meeta for support. Hence, the address · 'Oh! my daughter!'.

Don't Call it Suicide can be read as a criticism of the contemporary society which looks down upon the failed persons and discriminates against the weak. It exposes the ills of the society like unfair treatment given to women in general and widows in particular in our time. Though the ending of the play is ironic, the implicit message is unmistakable.

Ezekiel as a playwright cannot be dismissed as a mere entertainer, for he not only entertains us but informs us about contemporary reality. He educates us and in a way his plays both 'instruct and delight'. He re-creates characters in their situation. For example, the advertising executives like Bharat and Raj, painter like Nalini, house wife like Mala come alive in the plays. Most intricate relationship between mother-in-law and daughter-in-law in our society has been brought out through the characters of Meeta and Mrs. Sathe in *Don't Call it Suicide*. Ezekiel through his plays makes us aware of the contemporary society and the rot that has set in. As an artist he does not offer any suggestion how to overcome it but the hints and guesses given in the plays are enough for the discerning readers to see. Ezekiel has established himself as a social critic and his plays bear testimony to it.

WORKS CITED

Ezekiel, Nissim. *Don't Call it Suicide*. Madras: Macmillan 1993, (All page references are to these editions).

Raju, A.K. (Quoted) "Introduction", *Don't Call it Suicide*: X, 1993.

15

Orissan Contribution to Post-Colonial Indian English Literature

In the post-colonial era we encounter a paradoxical situation in our country in regard to the status of Indian Literature. Oriya literature, Bengali literature, Telugu literature, Tamil literature, Hindi literature (in spite of the fact that Hindi is our national language) are regional literatures. And in the post-colonial age we hardly get literature written in Sanskrit (Sanskrit has become the language of our rituals). So, the only pan Indian literature we have in the post-colonial era, is paradoxically Indian English literature. Orissa has contributed immensely to the growth of Indian English literature in the last thirty years. We have a number of poets, fiction writers and critics who can be counted among the leading Indian English writers and critics of our country.

Post-colonial Indian English poetry is a new term for Post-Independence Indian English poetry, the same way as Post-colonial Literature is a new term for Commonwealth Literature outside Anglo-American tradition. It is different from Colonial Indian English poetry (i.e., Pre-Independence Indian English Poetry) in its treatment of themes, choice of imagery and creation of a new idiom. The Indian English poetic movement of the fifties and the sixties, which denounced the Pre-Independence Indian English poets (Toru Dutt, Sarojini Naidu and Sri Aurobindo) for being imitative and derivative of the English Romantics and Victorians, unfortunately followed the genteel English poets or the confessing Americans. It is only in the seventies, the earlier influence of Eliot, Pound, later Yeats. Wallace Stevens, Dylan Thomas, Ted Hughes, Robert Lowell, Sylvia Plath and Roethke has been overcome and post-colonial Indian English poetry has proved increasingly robust, varied, responsive to the times and enjoyable. Orissa has made a significant contribution to the growth and development of post-colonial Indian English poetry in the last three decades of the twentieth century.

The first Oriya who made a mark in Indian English Literature is Jayanta Mahapatra. Like Nissim Ezekiel and A.K. Ramanujan, he is widely read and discussed both at home and abroad. But unlike Ezekiel and Ramanujan, Mahapatra is difficult to read for obscurity, complexity and allusiveness in his poetry. He is rather in the company of Shiv K. Kumar and Keki N. Daruwalla, in creating contrived images and learned vocabulary that immediately set him a class apart from most of his contemporaries. At the same time, in his desire to acclimatize an indigenous tradition to English language, and create a new Indian English idiom, he shares some of the concerns of the well-known Indian English poets of our time. Therefore, to study Jayanta Mahapatra in isolation seems to be a difficult task, especially when he has influenced a number of contemporary Indian English poets and brought recognition to this new poetry by winning the first ever award by the National Academy of Letters for his book of verse, *Relationship* in 1981.

Mahapatra is a prolific poet. Though he began writing poetry rather late (he has not published poems before he was forty) he has not looked back since he published his first book of verse, *Close the Sky Ten by Ten* in 1971. His other volumes came in quick succession. *Svayamvara and Other Poems* (1971), *A Father's Hours* (1976), *A Rain of Rites* (1976), *Waiting* (1979), *The False Start* (1980), *Relationship* (1980), *Life Signs* (1983), *Dispossessed Nests* (1986), *Selected Poems* (1987), *Burden of Waves and Fruit* (1988), *Temple* (1989), *A Whiteness of Bone* (1992), *The Best of Jayanta Mahapatra* (1995) and *Shadow Space* (1997). His poetry shows a continuous development both in theme and technique. Mahapatra is a conscious poet who looks 'before and after' and endlessly revises his poems in order to make them more effective and meaningful.

Mahapatra began writing poetry echoing T.S. Eliot and Nissim Ezekiel in his early forties. His first book of verse, *Close the Sky Ten by Ten* begins with quotations from both Eliot and Ezekiel. Like R. Parthasarathy, he was infatuated with the English language in the beginning of his poetic career. He states:

"I started writing poetry late.... When I began, I suppose I was more carried away by what the English language could do; I was so much obsessed by the feel for words, their sound qualities. It was a wrong thing perhaps, this craze for language, and hence, my first poems were in a way, attempts in which the language left the ideas of the poems behind them, lost in the depths of words. But as the years went by and I went on to publish more, finding out what my contemporaries in other countries were writing, my notions of poetry kept changing. Today I see that the idea behind the poem (or in the poem) is slowly beginning to surface, and my poems are perhaps being more direct ones. But I am in no position to talk about my poems. The poems, the poetry remain exploratory, as I try to find out the person within myself, as I try to face this stranger that comes out of my poetry" (Simms : 33-34).

As he went writing poems volumes after volumes, he discovered his voice and outgrew the Anglo-American influence. He tries to look within and realise the world. He writes:

"For poetry is voice — 'Vaak' and it is a voice forged from those elements which constitute the world both within and without a voice which carried with it, its unusual power of survival" (Das : 65).

Mahapatra's poetic exploration of the places to which he belongs turns out to be a search for the self. A sense of belonging to the places of his land of birth and to the landscape of his state urges upon the poet to relate it to his poetic craft as is shown in the following lines:

> A man does not mean anything
> But the place
> Sitting on the river bank throwing pebbles
> into the muddy current,
> a man becomes the place.
>
> (*Somewhere, My Man*)

Jayanta Mahapatra is firmly rooted in the Orissan soil. Puri, Konark, Cuttack and Bhubaneswar form as it were, a quadrangle in the landscape of Mahapatra's poetry. Legends, history and myths associated with these places immensely interest Mahapatra and become the nerve centre of his poetry. He wrote a number of poems on Puri (the great place of Lord Jagannath, the presiding deity of Orissa) one of the four great sacred places of pilgrimage for the Hindus of India.

In these two poems titled, "Dawn at Puri" and "Main Temple Street, Puri" Mahapatra underlines the importance of Puri and what it means to Hindus in our country. Widows long for breathing their last at Puri lest they should attain salvation. As the poet puts it:

her last wish to be cremated here
twisting uncertainly like light
on the shifting sands.

(*Dawn at Puri*)

Since the temple of Lord Jagannath at Puri points to unending rhythm, dying in this place will take one to Silence, the ultimate desire of a human being which will enable him to attain *Nirvana.* In another poem titled *The Temple Road, Puri,* Mahapatra describes the stream of common men on the road to the temple and the form of their prayer. Thus, the poet says:

Later,
as the shrines of light
slowly close their eyes,
something reaching into them
from that place they learn to bear
the lame lamp post
to the huge temple door,
the sacred beads in their hands
gaping
at the human ground.

(*The Temple Road, Puri*)

The devotion to the deity makes the devotees transformed as if they seem to hear his message and begin to understand it. A sense of universal brotherhood overwhelms them and their hearts get purified. Mahapatra's poetic exploration of the places to which he belongs turns out to be a search for the self as well as identity. A sense of belonging to the places of his land of birth and to the landscape of his state urges upon the poet to relate them to his poetic craft, too, a point of his poetic contour.

Places like Puri, Konark, Bhubaneswar and Cuttack are important for Mahapatra as they embody the tradition of ancient Orissa and her heroic past. Poems like *Indian Summer Poem, Evening in an Orissa Village, The Orissa Poems, The Indian Poems, The Indian Way* reveal his typical indigenous sensibility. Mahapatra has rightly stated his view while receiving the National Academy of Letters Award in the following words:

"To Orissa, to this land in which my roots lie and lies my past and in which lies my beginning and my end, where the wind knees over the grief of the River Daya and where the waves of Bay of Bengal fail to real out today to the twilight soul of Konark, I acknowledge my debt and my relationship."

The search for roots is a trend in modern Indian English poetry which Mahapatra shares with A.K. Ramanujan and R. Parthasarathy. Mahapatra's Central Sahitya Akademi Award Winning book, *Relationship* is, in a way, a quest for Mahapatra's roots. "This poem is no collection of mere observation, a place here, a character there, an unstrenuous meditation or two, inevitable landscapes, but a determined integrated set of selections built into the theme. For the poet of Orissan landscape is the objective setting of his mental evolution, the phases of which get mixed up with the lyrical vocabulary of a humanist creed. The poem being set in Orissa embodies the myth and history of the land. As the conflicting principles of man and nature, history and autobiography and faith and suffering interact against the vast panorama of Orissan landscape, the poem shows a dialectical progression where every synthesis in further analysis turns into a thesis" *(Ibidem* : 9-10).

The heroic Oriya past is vividly remembered and recalled with a sense of nostalgia. The glory and pride of our ancestors exhibited in the climatic *Kalinga War* in 261 B.C. which turned Ashoka the Great into a deeply religious man, is now a long-lost trait in our racial character. The river Daya is a witness to our ancestor's heroic effort which has become a sort of myth for us. Once a heroic and a militant race is no more than a mere memory now for its successors proved to be unworthy of keeping the glory of their ancestors afloat and drifted away from their ideals. Thus, Mahapatra notices a sharp contrast in the descending order between the past and the present marking an overwhelming decline in values of life in our time. The following passage makes it amply clear:

It is hard to tell now
What opened the anxious skies
how the age old proud stones
lost their strength and fell
and how the waters of Daya
Stank with the bodies of my ancestors
my eyes close now
because of the fear that moves my skin.

(*Relationship*)

The poet's life is integrated with the heroic tradition of the land of his birth and as he becomes conscious of it, his heart throbs and a kind of unknown fear engulfs him. The landscape of Orissa moves him when he observes the annual migrating birds from far North

Siberia to the warm waters of Chilika, a beautiful lake in Orissa. The agony of the poet springs from the fact that while the birds and animals react naturally to the seasons of the year, he is cut off as it were from the heroic traditions of his ancestors. He tells that 'I can never come alive/if I refuse to consecrate at the altar of my Origins' and thus 'a prayer to draw my body out of a thousand years'. There is a sense of nostalgia which pervades the atmosphere of the poem. Cuttack, a city of historical importance, which had the great Barabati Fort, is now a symbol of 'vanquished dynasties'. A sense of belonging overwhelms the poet, and in a voice charged with emotion, he tells us:

> Now I stand among these ruins
> waiting for the cry of a night bird
> from the river's far side
> to drift through my weariness listening
> to the voices of my friends
> who have become the friends of others
> writing poems, object and anxious
> in rooms which reek of old folk,
> of their sloth and arthritis and neglect,
> like state cupboards which are going black
> with the smells of a rancid fat of the past.
>
> (*Relationship*)

If this long poem, *Relationship* is an amalgam of history, myth and vision, there are quite a few poems in which the poet turns to his private history like his own family to make an inward journey to establish his link with the past. It is, in this aspect, he resembles three outstanding contemporary Indian English poets namely A.K. Ramanujan, R. Parthasarathy and Kamala Das. Like Kamala Das's Grandmother, Jayanta Mahapatra's Grandfather is a dominant figure in his family poems. In a poem called *Grandfather,* Mahapatra dives deep into his family history and reflects the basic issues of life including change of religion. Driven by hunger, the poet's grandfather, Chintamani Mahapatra embraced Christianity during the devastating famine that struck Orissa in 1866. With a sense of agony and disgust, the poet directs his volley of questions to his grandfather, only to regret it in the end. Thus, the past comes alive for a moment to remind us of the misfortune that befell on our people to choose the path they did. We may now 'Change and smile but the agony abides', the poet rightly asks:

What did faith matter?
What Hindu World so ancient and true for you to hold?

When we analyse the consequences of that great famine our conscience pricks us. What remains between our ancestors and us is 'a conscience of years'. The poet rightly feels that it is no use to hold our ancestors responsible for the change of faith and regrets:

We wish we knew you more,
we wish we knew what it was to be, against dying,
to know the dignity...

(*Grandfather*)

In another poem called *The Hour Before Dawn,* the poet records his concern for his ailing father. The poem is imbued with a sense of pathos when the poet apprehends his father's death:

My father, sad-faced father (How very far you are
from this empty room filled only with myself)
without a sound the dark tree out there struggles with
its
death in my life. The silent world floats beside me;
tomorrow may be I will here my father is dead
but he might bear the face of my son.

(*The Hour Before Dawn*)

This is a significant poem for it embodies the Hindu faith that parents are born to their children as their children, which Mahapatra shares with other Indians. This prompts the poet to look within and to know his own self. As he puts it:

This evening I look at that part of myself
which remains with me, but I do not know
what it is, hard to recognize it anymore.

(*Of This Evening*)

In some of Mahapatra's poems Indian landscape, seasons and environment become the starting point giving his imagination a free play to reflect on his private moments of desire, despair, guilt and illumination.

Mahapatra is a humanistic poet. Hunger in Kalahandi district of Orissa, Bhopal gas tragedy, terrorism in Punjab or the tragedy in Nicaragua all attract his attention. Though most of his poems are set in Orissa, it is unfair to say 'Jayanta Mahapatra is an Orissan poet writing in English' (Paniker, 15). Mahapatra speaks to us of an indigenous tradition in his poetry particularly in *Relationship*

(1980) and tries to extend it by his individual talent. Again Paniker harks on this point when he observes: "Mahapatra resorts to local colour and cultural echoes while Daruwalla uses the open air both as cultural theme and backdrop" (*Ibidem* : 18). But Mahapatra has overcome his local obsession and native cultural preoccupation by using national myths in Temple and writing patriotic poems concerning the nation and on the Father of the nation in his latest book of verse, *A Whiteness of Bone*. Mahapatra seems to have transcended the place (Cuttack, Puri, Bhubaneswar the golden triangle) by writing about the country as a whole. Mahapatra writes about Bhopal (in Dispossessed Nests) Independence Day, Gandhiji and quite a few subjects concerning the whole of India. Like Ezekiel, he tries to identify himself with modern India so that he can speak with confidence and reach many a readers all through the country. Mahapatra broadens his thematic range here. Some of the poems strike us most by evoking contemporary situation. India's recent past which seems to be a little disturbing, attracts the attention of the poet. Mahapatra writes about it in 'Of Independence Day', 'The Fifteenth of August', 'A Sullen Balance', 'Red Roses for Gandhi' and 'Seeing Things in the Dark'. He writes:

Everywhere one looks,
One is stirred by skies
that protects a bourgeois order ...
Or sees the child-skeleton from Kalahandi
Whose neck cannot support
the weight of its head
Or the death by bullets
that any government calls a natural death.

(*Seeing Things in the Dark*)

It is incorrect to say that 'Jayanta Mahapatra is an Orissan Poet writing in English' for that would amount to saying Nissim Ezekiel is a Maharashtrian Poet writing in English, or Parthasarathy is a Tamil Poet writing in English, or Kamala Das is a Keralite poet writing in English. These poets write about India and express Indian sensibility in their poetry and create a new Indian English idiom. Consider, for example, the following lines from Mahapatra:

When we learn to let
Our minds leave us, we do not care where
true feeling lies, or for a country's
national anthem floating around in counterfeit freedom

its time moves to echo the rain-voice
lying too deep for our nerves' reach, besieging
in vain the poet's lonely walls.

(*Dispossessed Nests*)

Only an Indian English poet could express his feelings in such a situation in this typical coinage like 'Counterfeit freedom', 'rain voice', and 'nerves' reach'. Typical imagery, simile and collocation of words in Mahapatra's Poetry go a long way to create distinct Indian English idiom.

No matter where an Indian English poet lives, he writes India in his bones. So it would be more appropriate to say that Jayanta Mahapatra is an Indian English poet living in Orissa.

Jayanta Mahapatra has come a long way from *Close the Sky Ten by Ten* and with the publication of his latest book of verse, *Shadow Space* (1997) he has come to terms with reality. The phase of nostalgic harking back to the past is over and he has realized the world and felt it in his pulses. Poetry, becomes a medium to interpret life and source of sustenance for him. Hence, he makes a bold attempt in a poem called "The Stories in Poetry" to present the reality in this harsh world which tends to engulf us.

The world plots on
And poetry stumbles and falls
Everything is called sacred
in my land. Even poems. And children
Who are sold and bought everyday
in the streets of Bombay and Calcutta

He further adds:

It's the world again
that must not take one unawares
a world where hundreds die
of hunger in Somalia and elsewhere
where poetry is no mystery
even the most tender embrace says
there is no heroism for us to live on.

The poet urges upon us to know ourselves and move with the time. He says:

This time is not an easy one
for those who forget themselves.

(*The Waiting*)

Apart from Jayanta Mahapatra, a host of other poets from Orissa are writing in English. They are Deba Patnaik, Bibhu Padhi, Biswakesh Tripathy, Niranjan Mohanty, Niranjana Mishra, Chinmay Jena, Shanta Acharaya, Sulekha Samantray, Raju Samal, Khirod Mallik, Jayaram Panda, M.K. Ahmed, L.N. Mohapatra, Rishi Agarwal, Snakarshan Parida, Sailendra Tripathy, Simachal Patnaik, P.K. Jagdeb, Saroj Padhi, Sarbeswar Samal and Prasanjit Mukherjee. Some of these poets have brought out collection of their poems in a book or two and others are contributing to poetry magazines and in the process of collecting their poems in the form of a book. This writer Bijay Kumar Das after contributing to different poetry magazines has brought out a collection of his poems titled *Quondam Beloved* in 1989, which was well received by critics like Shiv K. Kumar and Shyamala A. Narayan. Of these poets three stand out — they are Deba Patnaik, Bibhu Padhi and Niranjan Mohanty. Deba Patnaik belongs to older generation (he published his poems before Jayanta Mahapatra) and has now become an expatriate poet (he now lives in U.S.A.). So also Shanta Acharya, an Indian English poet of our State who now lives in London.

Bibhu Padhi is the most promising poet after Jayanta Mahapatra and it's a pity that he has not got the attention he deserves. He has brought out three volumes of poems in English — the most important and matured volume is his *A Wound Elsewhere*. The thematic range is very wide. Padhi is with A.K. Ramanujan. Most of his family poems remind us of Ramanujan's family poems. He makes a 'voyage within' and describes situations, and incidents of day today life which are not only real but authentic. He makes us see into reality of joint-family life and secures the readers' participation. Important poems in this mode which deserve special mention are 'The House', 'Letter to my Wife' and 'Grand mother'. In 'The House' Padhi tells us, how he is bound to it when his brothers have left for other places.

> I've been here since the time
> I learnt to know one house from another
> There've been times when I thought
> of leaving it altogether, for ever.
> Perhaps I'll never be able to do so.

This poem is reminiscent of A.K. Ramanujan's family poem, "Small Scale-reflections on a Great House". In the same way Padhi writes:

> Nothing moves here as though chained
> to ancestral blemishes never forgiven.

No one visits us, not even my brothers.
They now live in large cities,
in rented buildings, government quarters.
I don't blame my father, who put
all that he had saved into this house
in the hope his children wouldn't have to seek
Other houses.

This poem evokes a sentiment which is genuine, and authentic. The observation is very apt and the tone is conversational befitting the theme. 'Grandmother' reminds us of Kamala Das' "My Grandmother's House". The memory of the grandmother is very poignant and it is associated with events in life, one can never forget. Concern of a grandmother for the grand-children and other members of the family and children's love for her evoke the atmosphere of a family in its realistic terms. Her warning:

"Take care of your child
You will never get another like him"

and the poet's son's affection for her has been described in an authentic manner.

... I watch my son
kiss her cold breathless hands
in his own small, childish way;

Padhi's title poems *Going to the Temple* (that is his first collection of poems) and *A Wound Elsewhere* are both evocative and suggestive in nature. While going to the temple, Padhi says,

Let us wash our hands clean
of the cruel day light
wipe the acquired and inherited
meanings off our tired faces.

The deep meaning of these lines is a dig at the way people worship mechanically or perform rituals. The transferred epithet 'cruel day light' is ironical of our outward show of love and devotion to the deity. Padhi makes an attempt at new collocation of words like 'rooted grief' ('Hamlet's Song'), 'Crowless silence' ('Crow'), 'nightly dreams' ('Konarka') in his first books of verse. The title poem of *A Wound Elsewhere* is reminiscent of Eliot's 'Burnt Norton' in its use of words and lines ('Not here, not here, not this, not here') and partly autobiographical (should we way, confessional?). The poetic persona seeks to find the wound that hurts him and brings to his mind the causes that might have created it — migraine, death of the father, nervous breakdown of 'still young mother', erstwhile friends, son, brothers, losing faith — but to no avail. Then he concludes:

> No one knows, no one need know.
> It is always some other lace —
> the hurt stealing into the might from there.

Is it not Eliot who said 'People may change and smile but the agony abides?' Eliot's shadow looms large.

Padhi's poetry is evocative in nature. The language is polished, neat, chiselled. In his use of language Padhi is with Ezekiel, Ramanujan and Parthasarathy. He is successful in acclimatizing an indigenous tradition to English language. Therein lies the strength of his poetry.

Niranjan Mohanty is a prolific poet. He has not looked back since he published his first book of verse, *Silencing the Words* in 1977. He writes poetry in the ironic mode. His poem sequence, "Prayers to Lord Jagannath" seeks to evoke the myth in modern terms and ends with a prayer to Lord Jagannath:

> Strengthen my bosom to bear the burden
> the World shall plant: strengthen
> my fingers to hold a pen.

Mohanty's later collection of poems, *Oh This Bloody Game!* contains 52 poems. Here he has written a number of poems on the art of writing poetry. Creating poems out of diverse elements (an amalgam of disparate experience) seems to be his approach to poetry writing. He writes:

> All else is false
> but this single act of the mind
> wherein a tiger, a rose, a river
> a snake, an apple appear
> simultaneously and form
> a world and sky of love hangs
> over it, poised.
> I know
> this sky only melters.

Niranjana Mishra writes poetry in ironic mode. With his first collection of poems (and only one, so far) he has attracted the attention of critics both at home and abroad. This volume of poems titled, *The Stoneman and Other Poems* (1994) contains a number of poems on contemporary life. In 'A New Year Poem, 1991', Mishra ridicules the way we take things for granted and express our feelings in clichés. If there is any violence anywhere in the country, the authorities will say, 'the situation is tense/but under control' and try to explain away things. Like Ezekiel, Mishra is an ironist and also a parodist.

Shanta Acharya, though began as a romantic poet, writing poems of human love in all its aspects in the early eighties, now she seems to have come to terms with life. In a recent poem 'perhaps' (The Indian PEN April-June 1997: 14), she has shown a mature understanding of life by pleading for an acceptance it 'as it comes'. She writes:

> Perhaps, we were never meant
> to be like other creatures:
> more at home in their environment,
> driven by instincts, their natures.
>
> We pine for what we are not,
> and cannot be; .....
> Who can tell what this need to be at home
> will deliver to us, as we pursue self-discovery
> through our myriad desires' satisfaction?

Indian English poets of Orissa like their counterparts elsewhere in India write in both the modes — one, by turning inward, going on one's 'voyage within' and two, by making an ironic observation of reality, in "voyage without". Our poets have lived up to the expectation of a Bruce King or an Anniah Gowda who had earlier expressed the hope that Orissa would contribute substantially to Indian English poetry. Time had justified it. To conclude, I should say, no anthology of Indian English poetry would be complete today without giving an adequate representation to the Indian English poets of our state.

Turning to fiction writing, I should state at the outset, that there is only one name from Orissa who has made a significant contribution to Indian English fiction and short fiction and, he is Manoj Das. As a short story writer Manoj Das has few peers but not many equals in post-colonial Indian English Literature. As a story teller he is with R.K. Narayan. His short fiction is Indian in sensibility and the idiom in which it is written is Indian English. The originality in themes is matched by the felicity of expression in an idiom that is shared by all the English-speaking Indians and above all, his writing is intelligible to the English-speaking world outside India. His stories are deeply rooted in the native soil i.e. the birthplace of the writer, in Orissa and they evoke the landscape of the place in unmistakable terms. Manoj Das' important collection of short stories include *The Crocodiles Lady* (1975), *Fables and Fantasies for Adults* (1978), *The Vengeance and Other Stories* (1980), *The Submerged Valley and Other Stories* (1986), *The Miracle and Other Stories* (1993), *Farewell to a Ghost* (1994) and *Mystery of the Missing Cap and Other Stories* (1995). His stories dive deep into human psyche and present characters as they are, not as they should have been. Das exposes the characters who preach one thing and practise the other, by unmasking them. His characters are real persons whom we encounter in our daily life; only names have been changed. Let us take a story like, *Mystery of The Missing Cap*. Two important characters here are Sri Maharana, a well-to-do villager who "nurtured an ambition to be elected to the State Legislature" and Babu Virkishore, Minister for Fisheries and Fine Arts. Virkishore was invited to the village by Maharana to create field for the latter's entry into the Legislature. Ministers are good at speech making. They advise people to practise simple living and high thinking but they do the reverse in their private life. Here, Das gives an illustration of how Ministers are treated in our country.

At Shri Moharana's house the Minister and his entourage were treated to tender-coconut juice, followed by the most luxurious lunch I had ever seen, with about twenty dishes around the sweetened ghee-baked rice mixed with nuts, cloves, etc.

Irony is implicit in most of the stories of Das. In our society it has become a habit with the people of one profession to look down upon the people of another profession. In *Encounters* Das presents two characters, a school teacher and another chauffeur. The writer tells us that both of them were class mates and they used to sip tea in the same canteen after years of their schooling, they recognise each other but don't talk because each one thinks he is superior to the other. Das presents this awkward scene perfectly well in this story.

In another story named *The Vengeance* Das shows how a man burning with rage to take revenge is stupefied by the quick turn of fate. Vilas Singh who swore revenge on Bahadur was finally defeated when he found that his enemy was born as his son. Vilas wanted to kill Bahadur for the latter had taken away his would-be wife and hurt him in the head. But he could not kill Bahadur as the latter died earlier than expected. Vilas Singh was stupefied to realise that the astrologer's prediction had come true when he saw a wound in the forehead of his son. Das ends the story skillfully:

Hidamba Baba, the tantrik-astrologer, had assured him that Bahadur's soul would creep into an infant that was about to be born in the village situated to the North-East of the forest. Further, with a meaningful snicker he had whispered to him that it should not be difficult for him to recognise Bahadur in that infant, for, the new born soul would reveal his identity by sporting a mark which Vilas Singh cannot miss.

Vilas Singh looked at the infant's forehead for the third time. The mark was a delicate miniature of the wound he had once Inflicted on Bahadur.

He tried to retreat into a room, but could not. He collapsed while the women were tickling the infant to make it smile.

The Submerged Valley is the remarkable title story of the collection of short stories, *The Submerged Valley and Other Stories,* shows how children appreciate their parents when they find them doing their duty to the best of their ability by helping the needy. It also shows how rustic people are deeply touched when they have to leave their place of birth. A dam was to be constructed in a particular area. The people of that area approached an engineer, the narrator's father, to stop the construction of the dam at any cost. This reasonable man listened to them and persuaded them not to obstruct the construction of the dam.

But the same engineer risked his life to save the life of *Abolakara* (literally, disobedient) when the latter refused to leave the place in the face of an immediate flood. When the villagers went to see their ancestral place which was temporarily visible in summer, the water level began to rise and all of them left the place by boats and launch except *Abolakara.* This engineer risking his life went to him once again and brought him in his launch. This made the narrator's younger sister to say, "Father is wonderful, isn't he?" The narrator quipped, "Fool, how long you take to realise things that are obvious!"

In his later collection of stories, *The Miracle and Other Stories* (1993) and *Farewell to a Ghost* (1994) (which contains a novelette), Das has come to terms with reality. The charging scenes of villages come out well in stories like *The Gold Medal, The Jackals, The Strategy, The Miracle* and *The Centenarian.* He sees life 'steadily and sees it whole'. His themes in short fiction are vast-ranging from ghosts, animals, human and demons. His world is warm, palpable, and his characters are known by their chief intensity as the author himself. There are hints and guesses, pathos and humour, subdued irony and gentle mockery that go well with the plot and the situation. He never spares people of dubious nature and reputation. While dealing with contemporary situation, he comes down heavily on those who corrupt the society and hoodwink the public. Stories dealing with contemporary life and society where parents are cast away by children as in *Trespassers* or friends disown each other as in *Encounters* have atmosphere surcharged with subdued irony and the tone becomes potentially mocking. Although Das does not create another Malgudi like R.K. Narayan, the locale of most of his stories is the same, i.e. a small place in Balasore District of Orissa. The landscape of the place with a nostalgia for the writer's past comes alive in most of his stories. His two novels *Cyclones* and *A Tiger at Twilight* make good reading but compared to his snort fiction, they are not widely read. But it must be said that Manoj Das ranks among the tallest short-fiction writers of Indian English Literature.

With the publication of *The Green Gardener,* India's leading poet in English, Jayanta Mahapatra (to be precise, the first Indian English' poet to have been honoured by the Sahitya Akademi for his book of verse, *Relationship* in 1981) has triumphantly arrived at the field of a distinct literary genre called the short story. Though he was writing short stories sporadically, the book under review is his first collection of stories. It contains 18 stories, written and published at different point of time and in different magazines.

Mahapatra's stories are different from the conventional stories in the sense that they focus not so much on the thematic content as on the subtlety of form and expression. Mahapatra explores many grey areas of human existence in the contemporary world and gives vent to the feelings of individuals in trying situations. What is important in his stories is the evocation of human agony in a dehumanized world. In *The Mango Tree,* the tree planted by the husband becomes a symbol of life for the woman. She reflects:

The Mango Tree, there in the yard beyond, looks in through my window into my life. There it stands, sharp-sighted and alert, pressing against the dark firm earth, its roots somewhere deep inside the darkness of the dead. It is not hard for me to imagine those roots-twisted, lonely explorings, turning away here and there, growing into silence, into the slime of both my past and my future.

The tree for this woman is 'the centre of my (her) life' and it is her 'my mango tree'. But the members of the family fail to understand her sentimental attachment with this mango tree. That broke her heart. With a heavy heart and deep agony she asked:

> 'What have you done to my tree?
>
> Why have you cut it down'?

The agony of an oldman for being neglected in the family and ill-treated by his daughter-in-law, abides. In *Old Man in the Dark* Mahapatra depicts the plight of an oldman in such a subtle way that this 'old man' becomes all oldmen and the daughter-in-law becomes all daughters-in-law in this harsh world where purblind men enact hell. The oldman bitterly complains:

"Everyone else comes first in this house. And it is I who am responsible for that husband of hers! Ungrateful Wretches".

Finally, the harsh behaviour of the daughter-in-law compels the oldman to commit suicide.

Mahapatra probes deep into the dark recess of the human heart and sees not only the agony but the desire to gratify the senses. In An *Afternoon of Doctor Das,* Doctor Das a sixty-two years oldman, (Sixty two is a grandfather's age), deflowers a fifteen year old girl in a lonely afternoon. The story exposes the hypocrisy of the so-called civilized men who can be savage in their lonely moments.

Jealousy, poverty, greed and revenge motifs can lead a man to force his wife into another man's arms, as we find in *Turn left for Happiness.* Appa Rao, the rickshaw puller, driven by poverty and being suspicious of his wife, Malati's character and her relation with liquor dealer, Kasi Biswal, forced her to sleep with another man for rupees thirty only. In another story, *Ringing Silences,* a suspicious wife watches the telephone call of her husband. This situation was saved by the husband's reassuring tone 'I Love you too' in reply to her 'I love you'. She came to her senses and said, "What was wrong with me? In 'Eyes' we get the picture of an anguished husband because of the failing eye-sight of his wife."

"I looked at her then, now disappearing into the darkness behind a bank of cloud. Soon, very soon, she would not be able to see anything at all.... And looking at her then, I seemed to hear night-bird's cry: a place where time stood still, and hours sank into the horizon of pity".

The Hostel Room exposes the hollowness of the so-called modern sophisticated people who run away from their wives to gratify their lust in hotel rooms. In a highly emotional tone, Mahapatra describes a scene in poetic-prose how a man and a woman make love in an act of deception and self-deception.

"Night, so very foetal, by itself beside a strange woman I sacrifice my proverbial neutrality, even artistic ambitions. Far, far way I am a poet. She never knows who I am.... This earth is you and I, assembled by black blood. Her name is Gina.... She tells you glibly tonight's name. Tomorrow who knows?"

In *Red* we find how fear complex affects the characters of individuals. The protagonist's fear for the red eye of Habib Khan, makes him afraid of anything that looks red. Mahapatra's observations: "Each one's secrets are his or hers alone" seems to explain the protagonist's predicament of life. Habib Khan reflects:

"It led me to believe too that there could be nothing concrete between birth and dying, the wall of years totally meaningless".

Mahapatra's stories tell us about human condition and helplessness resulting in pain, agony and loneliness. The language is adequate to the thematic content and above all there is felicity of expression. There is a kind of poetic touch, that heightens the memorables and appeal of his stories. The stories of Mahapatra sing, for the rhythm of poetic-prose is highly commendable. It is an irony of fate that when most of his poems are prosaic, his prose is poetic. The short, crisp and thought-provoking sentences written in conversational and simple language attract the attention of the readers and make the stories interesting and lively. It seems that the poet in Mahapatra, never leaves Mahapatra, the story-teller. Like the endings of his poems, the ending of his stories (at least, most of them) is intricate but there are hints and guesses that 'whisper results'. His technique remains the same. So it will not be wrong to say that his stories are an extension of his poetry.

Some of our writers have also contributed to Indian English literary criticism. Mention may be made of Niranjan Mohanty, Rabindra Kumar Swain and Bibhu Padhi who have written critical essays on Indian English poets and poetry. Niranjan Mohanty has edited a critical anthology on O.P. Bhatnagar's poetry. The writer of this paper (Bijay Kumar Das) has contributed in his humble way to Indian English Criticism. Apart from his critical essays on Raja Rao's

Kanthapura, Anita Desai's *Fire on the Mountain,* Shashi Deshpande's *That Long Silence, Indian English Fiction,* and stories of Manoj Das, he has published full length books on Indian English poetry, poets and criticism. His works include, *Modern Indian English Poetry, Trends in Indian English Poetry Criticism, The Poetry of Jayanta Mahapatra, The Horizon of Nissim Ezekiel's Poetry, Critical Essays on Poetry and Aspects of Commonwealth Literature.* He has also edited two critical anthologies titled *Contemporary Indo-English Poetry* and *Perspectives on the Poetry* of R. Parthasarathy.

To conclude, I should say that the contribution of Orissa writers to Indian English literature is substantial.

WORKS CITED

Das, Bijay Kumar, quoted. *The Poetry of Jayanta Mahapatra,* New Delhi: Atlantic Publishers, 1995.

Panikar, K. Ayyappa, ed. *Modern Indian Poetry in English,* New Delhi: Sahitya Akademi, 1991.

Simms, Norman, quoted. *The Poetry of Jayanta Mahapatra* ed., Madhusudan Prasad, New Delhi: Sterling Publishers, 1986.

16

Post-Colonial English Studies: The Indian Context

Let me, at the outset, make my stand clear *vis-a-vis* the status and position of English Studies in India in the present context. English studies all over the world have undergone a sea change in the post-colonial era. I will briefly touch the issue of post-colonial attitude to English studies in the global context; for that will give us a clue to English studies in India in our time.

The history of the nineteenth century and a few decades of the early twentieth century can be conveniently summed up by the word, "Colonialism". The decolonization which followed the Second World War is reflected in the rapid evolution of literature in the erstwhile Colonies and the Third World as an expression of new local realities and the new international political order. The situation is that at present English is now the main language or an important alternative language of about fifty countries and of more than five hundred million people. It is different (and bound to be so) in those different countries each with its own culture, and literary and social background. Each lay claim to be language *sui generis*. Frankly speaking each is a 'dialect' of English but unfortunately (or, fortunately?) there is no longer a norm against which they can be appraised. In the second half of the present century the language of the educated people in the South of England (Standard English) has lost its prestige and it is no more than a 'dialect' of English 'accepted' for its region. Scottish, Welsh and Irish English have gained independent status as valid forms of English.

In the absence of 'Standard English', how does one account for literatures written in English language all over the world. Where can one place writers such as Chinua Achebe, Wole Soyinka, Nadine Gordimer, A.D. Hope, Margaret Atwood, Derek Walcott, Patrick White, V.S. Naipaul, R.K. Narayan, Salman Rushdie, Raja Rao,

Nissim Ezekiel, Vikram Seth and a host of other writers? Third World, Commonwealth, New English Literatures, New Literatures, and Post-Colonial Literature — the names multiply because there is a basic problem in drawing the boundaries. A literature written in a language is usually named after that language. But when literature is written in a language that is in use in several countries and continents, the problem arises as to how to name it. Moreover, all the new World literatures in English are not extensions of English literature — they are African Literature, Australian Literature, Canadian Literature, Indian English Literature and so on. Thus, we have come a long way from English literature to literatures in English (i.e., English Studies).

This brings to my mind Sarla Palkar's apt observation on this issue:

"The colonial discourse had cast English literature in the role of a Promethean hero, who had undertaken the mission of spreading light and sweetness to all the dark corners of the earth, carrying thereby the message of (Western) civilization to the people still living in a state of degeneration or ignorance. The post-colonial discourse now regards English literature as a sort of hypocritical villain or as an agent of the Western imperialism who under the pretext of civilizing the colonized people suppressed and to a great extent destroyed the native traditions and cultures" ("Where are We Going From Here?" : 160).

At this point I would like to make it clear that in the Third World countries, or Commonwealth countries, outside Anglo-American tradition, all the teachers and scholars in the English departments were brought up on the tradition of English (i.e., British English) Studies. Indian teachers of English are no exception.

A close look into the past reveals that the Syllabi of English Studies remained fairly static from mid-nineteenth to mid-twentieth century. I am inclined to agree with Meenakshi Mukherjee when she says that "the great tradition of English literature (the standard canon being from Chaucer and Shakespeare, through Milton, Dryden, Pope, the Romantics to major Victorians, and to which by our time Shaw, Yeats and Eliot were added) and its elevating and purifying function remained unquestioned for generations. The first fissures in the monolith came with the introduction of American literature in certain universities in the early sixties, followed some years later by the grudging acceptance of Indian Writing in English and Commonwealth Literature. But some of the premier institutions in India — like Calcutta University or Delhi University — even to this day refuse to 'dilute' their courses of study by introducing texts from outside Anglo/American Canon" ("Indian English Literature in the Global Context", 67).

It is clear that the English studies in India in the colonial era meant the study of English literature proper and nothing else. In the 1960s, we have broadened our area of English Studies by including American Literature as a special paper at M.A. level. The establishment of A.S.R.C. at Hyderabad and the introduction of American Literature as a course at Osmania University, Hyderabad and Ravenshaw College, Cuttack in the sixties revolutionalized English studies in India. Olive I. Reddick, William Mulder, C.D. Narasimhaiah, P.K. Pati and a few others have done Yeoman service to the cause of American Studies in our country.

In 1958, Leeds University introduced a course in Commonwealth Literature — thanks to the effort of Norman Jeffares. K.R.S. Iyengar was invited to deliver a series of lectures on what was then called 'Indian Writing in English' (now termed Indian English Literature). Out of his series of lectures at Leeds, grew Iyengar's book *Indian Writing in English*. It is Iyengar who was instrumental in introducing Indian English Literature as a course in Indian Universities in the 1970s. Iyengar was supported by three able scholar-critics. V.K. Gokak, C.D. Narasimhaiah and M.K. Naik in his great endeavour to bring recognition to Indian English literature as an independent subject. In our state, a fine scholar and brilliant teacher, Sarbeswar Dash espoused the cause of Indian English Literature and introduced it as a special paper in M.A. in 1972-73 academic session. Mention may be made here that Indian University Professors who would not touch Indian English Literature with a barge pole in the seventies, now hail it as an integral part of Post-colonial Literature. It is gratifying to note that nearly sixty per cent of Ph.D. theses written at Indian Universities now are on Indian English Literature.

Closely on the heels of American Literature and Indian English Literature came Commonwealth Literature (now termed Post-colonial Literature). It is introduced as a course in Indian Universities in the late seventies and eighties — thanks to the efforts of C.D. Narasimhaiah, H.H. Anniah Gowda, M.K. Naik, Meenakshi Mukherjee and a few others. Some of the Indian Universities have also introduced Translation (i.e., Translation of European Classics into English and translation of classics in Indian regional languages into English) as a course at M.A. level. Utkal University has done a significant work in this direction. Translation seems to be the only solution to acquainting Indians with various classics of India and abroad. V.K. Gokak makes a point when he says:

"Until we have our own translations of world classics in our languages in larger numbers, we shall also have to study Greek, Roman, French, German, Italian and Scandinavian classics in English translation for purposes of comparative criticism" (Pathak : 24).

The study of Translation as a course paved the way for the study of Comparative Literature in our country. Some English Departments of Indian Universities like Delhi, Aligarh (A.M.U.), Banaras (B.H.U.), Agra, Jadavpur, Sambalpur, Visva Bharati and Allahabad have introduced it as a course.

In the nineties some of the English Departments of the Indian universities have broaden their base by introducing Canadian Literature and Australian Literature as a course at M.A. level. Our own Utkal University has introduced a full paper on World Literature in English at M.A. level. With the shifting of emphasis from English Literature to Literatures in English in the Post-Colonial era in Indian Universities, the English Studies in the nineties have come full circle. So much so, that two Indian Universities namely J.N.U., New Delhi, and M.S. University, Baroda have introduced a Course in English Studies in our country. In the words of Meenakshi Mukherjee, J.N.U. introduced, "a course called 'English in India' that attempts an overview of the rise and spread of English studies in our country from nineteenth century taking into consideration the complex historical and ideological factors that conditioned its discursive formation" (Provocations, 29). The Department of English, M.S. University, Baroda has also been teaching a similar kind of core course, "Politics, Ideology and the Teaching of English" to its M.A. students for the last eight years. Keeping in mind, the changes that have taken place in the field of English Studies in our country, Karnatak University, Dharward has renamed its Department of English as Department of English Studies.

Having stated the changes that took place in the Syllabi of English Studies in our country, let me focus on the plan and approach, the teachers of English adopt in literature classes. It's a truth widely acknowledged that mostly we teach others' views and ideas in the class. Our critical values have not been shaped by our own tradition, much less to our immediate context. First Saintsbury, then Eliot, Richards, Leavis, Cleanth Brooks, R.P. Blackmur, Trilling, later Derrida, Culler, Foucault and Stephen Greenblatt have done the thinking for us. T.S. Eliot, F.R. Leavis, and I.A. Richards were formative influences on Indian teachers of English right from the late forties. In course of reviewing C.D. Narasimhaiah's autobiography, *N. For Nobody: Autobiography of an English Teacher,* in *Indian Literature,* Bidhubhusan Das underlines Leavis' influence on Indian teachers in no uncertain terms:

"It may, however, be pointed out here that in regard to the influence of Leavis on English studies in India both Rajan and Narasimhaiah are not correctly informed. The influence began at Patna college in the late 1930's under the leadership of F. Rahman from London and K. Ahmed with a double Tripos in English and French from Cambridge. Ahmed was a pupil of Leavis. The modernisation of the syllabus had been initiated by J.L. Hill, who was from Oxford but it was Rahman and K. Ahmed who established the Leavisian tradition in almost all the colleges and universities in Bihar and Orissa through their students. The late Sisirkumar Ghose carried it to Viswabharati. But Ahmed's contribution is of a wider dimension in that he, for the first time, introduced Leavisian criticism into Urdu Literature making a radical 'revaluation' of its poetry, fiction and literary criticism by his writings and also by publishing an influential journal modelled after Scrutiny. So when Narasimhaiah visited Ravenshaw College and was pleasantly surprised to see the important English journals in Kanika Library he could have learnt, if he had cared to enquire, that the modernisation of English studies in Orissa had been introduced in the mid 40's. What is more, J.M. Mohanty, after his critical training in English has 'revalued' Oriya literature in the same manner as Ahmed. As such Narasimhaiah's pioneering effort in the same direction embraces the Southern Universities at a later date. Here one might not forget the contribution of Shiv K. Kumar, who, also from Cambridge, taught at Osmania, Sita Chari, who taught at Presidency College, Madras. There were others, too, in other parts of the country" (Insight into Human Life : 172-73).

I should hasten to add that Bidhubhusan Das himself has made a significant contribution to English Studies by carrying forward the Eliot-Leavis tradition to the classroom. As the Professor and Head of the Department of English, Ravenshaw College, Cuttack and as the Editor of *The Indian Journal of English Studies*, B. Das has done a lot to help the Eliot-Leavis Critical tradition set it roots in our country.

If Eliot, Richards and Leavis have influenced our teachers in the fifties, the New Critics of U.S.A. have attracted the attention of our teachers in the sixties. Rajnath has taken a lead in this direction. We mostly apply the method of New Criticism in our classroom situation. Explication of the text becomes the sole burden of the teacher in the classroom — so much so that we have introduced practical criticism as a core course at B.A. (Hons) and even at M.A. level.

In the closing decades the twentieth century, with the advent of structuralism, post-structuralism, Reader-Response criticism, Deconstruction and New Historicism, the nature of literature has become suspect. With the structuralists and post-structuralists, the meaning itself began to disappear. The structuralists' rejection of authorial intention and advocacy of polysemy is an extention of the New Critical position. The structuralist, having done away with the author and his intention, tried to show that it is language which speaks in literature and meaning is made possible by the existence of the underlying systems of convention which enable the elements to function individually as signs. The most outstanding essay proclaiming the death of the author comes from the pen of Ronald Barthes under the title, *The Death of the Author* (1968).

The absence of the author leads us to the proposition that the text does not have a fixed meaning but a plurality of meanings. Derrida argues that language is not anything stable and, therefore, no reading can take us to the meaning, for all meaning is fiction. A word has several meanings and each meaning becomes a signifier in its turn leading to more signifieds. Derrida would even go further and say that there is no transcendental signifier or reality principle behind any text or word and hence all our hunt for meaning is only a wild goose chase. All that is obtained is free play. Needless to say that the Deconstructionists deny the author. Prior to them, the New Critics, by emphasizing that the poem is on the printed page, had banished the empirical author from the text. Now by saying that the meaning is not in the text but in the mind of the reader, the Reader-Response critics indirectly subscribe to the idea of the death of the author. Taking cue from Barthes, Jonathan Culler argues that the author is dead and that the text is produced by the reader.

I would like to state that the above-mentioned schools of criticism are read and discussed in the seminars, and classrooms in our country only theoritically. These schools have been popularized in the pages of influential journals like Rajnath's *Journal of Literary Criticism* and Narasimhaiah's *The Literary Criterion* and *The Indian Journal of English Studies* and a few others. But we have not made any of these schools of criticism as a tool for evaluation of literature in classrooms. Some Indian teachers of English also questioned the basis of Deconstruction. Hiren Gohain remarks:

"The reader's delight in the craft of literature thus springs not only from the play of meaning, or from play with meaning, but also from a 'wisdom' beyond plain sense. To attempt a deconstruction of something so elusive is to destroy literature itself. Urgent voices speak to us from the texts, that would neither be silenced nor accept reduction to the terms of a binary opposition. Deconstruction only unearths in every text the same montonous message — that construction is impossible, and that meaning is a delusion. Is not that as much an ideological compulsion as the 'closures' it condemns? To be sure, there is no going back to the innocence of the myth and the folk-tale. But to dream that analysis may deliver us from the guilt of symbolic action is to suffer from an ultra-modern delusion" (Some Reflections on English Studies in India Now : 158).

Derrida's attempt to include Literature under the cover term 'Human Sciences' (Literature Plus Social Sciences) to underline the importance of Culture and New Historicists' idea to 're-historicise' the text by emphasizing on history and culture, created problems for the Indian teachers of English.

The study of literature through culture creates a problem. Literatures in English (i.e., English Literature and Post-Colonial Literature with the exception of Indian English Literature) being rooted in alien cultures create a difficult problem for Indian teachers of English. This prompted the Indian scholars to Ponder: Could we study Literatures in English outside our tradition from the Rasa-Dhvani angle? Scholars like Krishna Rayan, P.S. Shastri, C.D. Narasimhaiah, R.S. Pathak and a few others have pleaded for indigenous approach to English studies. R.S. Pathak in his books, *Oblique Poetry in Indian and Western Poetics, Vakrokti and Stylistic Concepts* and *The Poetics of Encounter* and Krishna Rayan in his books like *The Burning Bush*, and *Sahitya: A Theory* and V.S. Seturaman in his edited work *Indian Poetics* have pleaded for

Eastern approach to English Studies. But we have not yet adopted such an approach to our classroom situation.

It will not be out of place to say that though we are mostly applying new critical approach to classroom studies of English, we are slowly incorporating stylistic, deconstructive and new historicism approaches to English Studies in our country. I am sure, the familiarity of our teachers with these new approaches will grow soon and we will be able to adopt the methods of the latest schools of criticism in our classroom situation. About Rasa-Dhvani approach, I should say, that it would be possible only when we acquire a sound knowledge of Sanskrit and Comparative Poetics.

Our approach to English Studies will be incomplete without making a reference to the research done in this field. Now more and more teachers and young scholars are doing research in the field of English Studies — English Literature, American Literature, Post-Colonial Literature including Indian English Literature and Literary Criticism. Many senior teachers of English express their dissatisfaction with the standard of Ph.D. theses in our country and rightly so. Research has been reduced to the stage of knowing more and more about less and less. But it is not easy to define the proper subject for research in the field of English studies. There is nothing inherently low or high in the type of theme one may choose for this study for there can be an excellence appropriate to each kind which he may try to achieve. V.Y. Kantak makes a pertinent point on this subject.

"There is, of course, no blue-print to define for us the proper field for 'literary' research, the methods that may be employed and the means of securing high quality in the work produced. The nature of the theme itself would decide for us the most suitable approach. One can, for the sake of convenience, divide the entire field of research as far as literature is concerned under two broad heads. Firstly, there is the kind of theme which though connected with literature has a strong historical, linguistic or sociological side to it and hence would require to some extent a scientific approach and the employment of techniques appropriate to the social sciences. The emphasis in such an inquiry would not be on literary appreciation and the power of responding sensitivity to artistic work. Though this may be necessary in some measure, the issues that are raised would require a predominantly scientific treatment. Secondly, there are themes which depend chiefly on literary appreciation and critical judgment of a high order. The mode of inquiry here would be properly speaking 'literary criticism' as commonly understood, one in which literature is valued primarily for those artistic qualities it has in common with the fine arts." (Whither 'Literary' Research? 148).

Nowadays Ph.D. theses are written on new subjects and new approaches are made to old authors. For example, Shakespeare is now being studied from the stand point of New Historicism and women writers like Margaret Atwood, Anita Desai and a few others are being studied from the point of Eco-feminism. Authors are being studied from new angle and what is more, Ph.D. theses are being published for the dissemination of knowledge. It's a welcome venture for it enables the readers to know what goes on in the name of research. Here, we can only demand excellence in the field of research and a proper inquiry into the subject under study and investigation.

To conclude, I should say that the concept of English Studies in our country in the post-colonial era has widened to include Creative Literatures in English outside Anglo-American tradition. Now the need of the hour is to develop an indigenous approach to our English Studies along with the Anglo-American Critical tradition.

WORKS CITED

Das, Bidhubhusan. "Insight into Human life", *Indian Literature,* 35 : 3 (1992), 165-75).

Gohain, Hiren. "Some Reflections on English Studies in India Now", *Journal of Contemporary Thought* (1993), 153-58.

Kantak, V.Y. Whither. "Literary Research?", *The Indian Journal of English Studies,* 4: 1 (1963), 146-153.

Mukherjee, Meenakshi. "Indian English Literature in the Global Context", *University News,* 32 : 6, 7 Feb. 1994.

——. "Certain Long-Simmering Questions", *Provocations: The Teaching of English Literature in India* (eds.). Sudhakar Maratha et. al. Madras: Orient Longman, 1993.

Palkar, Sarla. "Where are we going from Here?: A Note on the Dilemmas and Uncertainties of an English Teacher in an Indian University Today", *Journal of Contemporary Thought* (1993), 159-65.

Pathak, R.S. quoted, *The Poetics of Encounter,* Delhi: Ajanta Publications, 1998.

17

Nissim Ezekiel's Humanistic Poetry: An Overview

Do not be satisfied with the world that God created. Create your own.
"Advice to a Painter"

The epigraph to the paper is a pointer to Ezekiel's attitude to life and poetry. Not only has he created a body of poetry that can stand comparison with poetry written in English elsewhere in the world in the second half of the twentieth century, but he has laid the foundation of Modern Indian English Poetry. And rightly he has been hailed as 'the founding father' of Modern Indian English Poetry and eulogized as a poet-critic, who gave a new direction to it in the Post-Independence (or Post-colonial) era. His poetic career spans over a period of 37 years — starting with A *Time to Change* (1952), and ending with *Collected Poems 1952-88* (1989). In between he has published six volumes of poetry such as *Sixty Poems* (1953), *The Third* (1959), *The Unfinished Man* (1960), *The Exact Name* (1965), *Hymns in Darkness* (1976) and *Latter-Day Psalms* (1982), for which he received the Sahitya Akademi Award in 1983. Ezekiel is both a modernist and post-modernist poet, whose two volumes of poetry, *A Time to Change* and *Latter-Day Psalms* herald modernism and post-modernism respectively in Indian English Poetry. No discussion of post-Independence Indian English Poetry can begin without making reference to Ezekiel's poetry. There are two distinct phases in Ezekiel's poetry: the first phase coinciding with the publication of *Hymns in Darkness* marks Ezekiel's quest for coming to terms with contemporary reality and landscape of the place to which he belongs. With his moving away from modernism to post-modernism, comes the change in his stance from individualism to humanism. In this paper, an attempt has been made to evaluate Ezekiel as a humanistic poet in the light of his humanistic poetry.

Ezekiel has shifted emphasis from nationalism to individualism. The question of identity became central to Indian English Poetry in 1950s and 1960s. Poets like Ezekiel, Ramanujan and Kamala Das made an attempt to relate themselves to India and asserted their individual right to write poetry in English.

Ezekiel in a number of his early poems made an attempt to relate himself to India disregarding his past (his ancestors came to India from Israel two thousand years ago). Poems like "Background, Casually" and "Island" bear testimony to it. Since "Background, Casually" is a commissioned poem about the life of the poet, Ezekiel tells us swiftly beginning with his childhood, then school days, his stay abroad and return home and then his marriage and finally his change of jobs. 'The song of my experience sung', says Ezekiel, and then goes on to personalize his ancestry. In the course of an interview with Adil Jussawalla, Ezekiel states emphatically:

> I am an Indian national. I was born in India, my tribe of the Jewish community has lived in India for 2,000 years. If I had rejected my Indianness, which some Indian writers obviously have done, and if I had decided that I am so much of an outsider that I have to settle down in London or New York, and then if I did write about India, I do not know if I could be regarded as an Indo-English Writer (*Selected Prose,* 167-168).

Ezekiel towards the close of "Background, Casually" overcomes his Jewish heredity and gets reconciled to Indian environment. Hence comes the resolution:

> The Indian landscape sears my eyes.
> I have become a part of it
> To be observed by foreigners....
> I have made my commitments now,
> This is one: to stay where I am.
>
> (*Collected Poems, 1952-88*, 181)

What makes a poet belong to a particular country necessarily involves nationality, and his identity is to be found in being rooted in the soil. A poet's response to the landscape of his country, his sense of tradition and culture of the land of his birth and many factors go together to make him assume an identity of his own. Nissim Ezekiel is right when he says that "There is no single Indian flavour which alone can claim the designation ('Indianness') and that its value too depends on a host of generative factors which should never be simplified for purposes of praise or blame" (*OJES*, 50).

Ezekiel is deeply rooted in the Indian soil. His 'growth of mind' is helped by unhabitable condition of the city. If Wordsworth could measure his life with 'mountains and valleys', and Eliot with 'coffee spoons', then Ezekiel does so with 'slums and skycrapers'. Therein, comes his resolution:

> I cannot leave this island
> I was born here and belong.
>
> (*Collected Poems, 1952-88*, 182)

Having established his identity and made his mark as an Indian English Poet, Ezekiel turned to his inner life for inspiration. In "Poster Prayers-III", Ezekiel says:

> I have to sing
> The song of my experience.

In the course of an interview given to *Gentleman,* Ezekiel says:

> To start with, my own inspiration is and always was 'my inner life'. And writing is, for me a way of coping with tension between my inner life and the outer life. Looking back, this from the earliest days seems to be the main source of my writing. Every other source is somehow related to it, even the experiences of people. My poems are often introspective and therefore express self-criticism and self-doubt. I also write about my relationship with other people: love, sex, the individual in society, etc. (97)

Ezekiel believes in humanism. In poem after poem he expresses his concern for humanity and tries to find out what ails mankind and how to get out of it. Ezekiel being a conscious artist, the centre of poetic interest in him, lies in the process of adjustment between the knowledge derived from experience or personal feelings and the knowledge which imposes a pattern. That is why, his poetry is a veritable apotheosis and dramatization of personality through passion and affirmation. His characters — Miss Pushpa T.S., the Railway Clerk, the Professor, the English teacher, Ganga, the maidservant, Guru, the beggars in the railway station, and a host of others — appear life-like. He recreates the characters in their own situations. His characters like the characters in Chaucer's *The Prologue to Canterbury Tales* are both individuals as well as types. That is because he consciously cultivated the language of the people and related the people to their situations. Ezekiel says,

Language
Is our conspicuous gift: the Word
Made flesh, is sought again
We make it as we make our lives.

Ezekiel is aware of the injustice meted out to people at various levels of the society and therefore he uses irony and parody as a mode to expose the people who are responsible for this. He knows that 'Life is not as simple/as morality.' The agony of a railway clerk who lives in poverty and does not get promotion is brought out in the following lines:

I am never neglecting my responsibility,
I am discharging it properly,
I am doing my duty
But who is appreciating?
Nobody, I am telling you.

("The Railway Clerk")

The discrimination between man and man on the basis of knowledge and power in society pains the poet. What is important is not man's designation or marital status but humanity to understand people, the poet seems to say. Whether a man is a professor or a journalist, tall or short, handsome or 'Crabbed-looking' is immaterial as long as 'he is simply man/and his speech is human'. In this world both the oppressor and the oppressed suffer and become victims of different man-made institutions. Here is an apt observation:

The oppressor who worships God
And the oppressed who worship God
Are victims of the Enemy.
They rot in families, in castes,
In community, in clubs
In political Parties.

("Hymns in Darkness")

Ezekiel has insight into human nature and is aware of man's predicament in the world. He tells us about man's helplessness and suggests a way out of it. He says:

You are master
neither of death nor of life
Belief will not save you
nor unbelief.
All you have
is the sense of reality.

("Hymns is Darkness")

Ezekiel believes in creating one's own life and all human beings should make an effort in that direction. Thus he says,

May you be
poet, painter, scholar
thinker, musician
even if you create nothing that matters
except your life, which too
has to be created

("Blessings")

In a poem titled, "An Atheist Speaks" Ezekiel lays the blame on God for making man part fool and part wise — a kind of concept that brings him closer to W.B. Yeats. He wants to do some human good to alleviate man's condition on earth. Ezekiel, the poet who began his poetic career by trying to define his own identity, comes to the end of his poetic life by wishing to do something for mankind. In "At 62", he makes a Confession:

I want my hands
to learn how to heal
myself and others
before I hear
my last song.

This is a kind of conclusion which reminds us of the closing section of *Four Quartets* in which Eliot wishes mankind well, "All shall be well/ All manner of things shall be well."

Ezekiel will be remembered for three things: one, for bringing everyday conversational language into the realms of poetry; two, re-creating characters from all walks of life in their situations; and three, for giving a human touch to his characters — real or imaginary. To read his poetry is to watch an actor enacting his tragic-comic play on the stage. It is to see him inside out. That is because, the humanistic note in his poetry is unmistakable.

WORKS CITED

Ezekiel, Nissim. "What is Indian in Indo-English Poetry," *Osmania Journal of English Studies*, 1983.

——. "Interview," *Gentleman*, July 1994.

——. *Collected Poems, 1952-1988*. New Delhi: Oxford University Press, 1989.

18

How Difficult is *Difficult Daughters*!

Manju Kapur's *Difficult Daughters* won the Best First Book Commonwealth Writers Prize for 1999. Needless to say that this book gained wide publicity both at home and abroad. Opinions have been formed about the book before the reader has gone through it between the lines. The question is: what is the intrinsic merit of the book? The book as it turns out to be, is not about partition, though it is set around the time of partition. Thus, it does not belong to the galaxy of Indian English novels like Khushwant Singh's *Train to Pakistan*, Raj Gill's *The Rape*, Attia Hossain's *Sunlight on a Broken Column*, B. Rajan's *The Dark Dancer*, Manohar Malgonkar's *A Bend in the Ganges*, Chaman Nahal's *Azadi* and Shiv K. Kumar's *A River with Three Banks*. To my mind, *Difficult Daughters* can be read profitably as a post-colonial and feminist novel.

The plot of the novel is simple and the story is fascinating. It is the story of a woman Virmati who was hooked on with her Professor Harish at the latter's insistence. The eldest daughter of Suraj Prakash and Kasturi (the eldest of their eleven children), Virmati had an ambition to be highly educated. As chance would have it, she came in contact with Professor Harish who came to stay in her aunt's house as a tenant.

This married Professor Harish was not happy with his illiterate wife. He felt attracted towards Virmati and gradually came closer to her. Virmati though initially resisted his love subsequently gave in. Their affair led to Virmati's refusal to marry Inderjit, an engineer, arranged by her family and then to abortion, while she was still in the college. The whole family turned against her and she went through harrowing experiences. Finally, the professor took her home as his second wife. Virmati won the love of the professor but lost both the families. Then came the partition and they moved to Delhi and Ida, a daughter was born. The novel almost comes to an end except the epilogue. In the epilogue, we are told about Ida, whose marriage was disastrous like her mother's leading to her divorce. She was 'husbandless, childless'. Both Harish and Virmati pass away. The novel begins with the death of Virmati and her cremation and the story is unfolded to us by Ida, her daughter who learnt all about her mother's past from her aunt. The narrative with an assertion by Ida that, "The one thing I had wanted was not to be like my mother" and ends with her request to the dead mother, that: "Do not haunt me any more".

The story is not very startling though a little unconventional. That a married Professor with wife and children should fall in love with a student and eventually take her as his second wife, without divorcing the first wife, seems to be outrageous. But the merit of the novel lies elsewhere. That is, in the fashioning of a new language (i.e. Indian English). Post-colonial theory presupposes that post-colonial literature must be written in English (not Queen's English) but other 'englishes'. And it is these 'englishes' that give rise to African English, Australian English, Canadian English, Caribbean English. In the light of this theory Manju Kapur's *Difficult Daughters* has been successful in creating a new Indian English idiom (sometimes by code-mixing) that at once distinguishes it from Queen's English and other 'englishes'.

Manju Kapur uses English in a new way. For example, when Virmati was not allowed to go out, she writes to the Professor to explain her position in the following way:

> The evening is coming. The light in the *angan* grows dimmer and more mellow. You have taught me to notice such things. Before, I saw without any eyes. With my food will come a lantern, and then shadows will cover the walls. I go to sleep early, and get up with the Sun. The first thing I do is my *Sandhya*, slowly, and with great concentration." (*Difficult Daughters*, 81)

On another occasion Virmati feels sorry for the ordeal that she has to undergo and reflects:

> For a long time Virmati lay on the damp coolness of the thick *Khadi* sheets, surrounded by the white net cocoon that once used to make her feel so safe. The moon was bright and made her ache with sadness for herself, for that thing inside her that she couldn't name for fear of making it more real. Tears started sliding down her cheeks, and she cried, letting her breath out in small gasps in order not to wake Paro. From the gardens

> below she could hear crickets chirping in their thousands. The scent of the *raat-ki-rani*, so strong on moonlit nights, came floating up to her. The beauty added to her pain. She wishes it were hot and uncomfortable and ugly. Eventually her tears stopped, and she lay drained and corpselike. The other sleepers had long since come and settled down. She was the only one awake. Like Lady Macbeth, she had murdered sleep. How Harish's face had glowed as he murmured, tasted almost, 'the multitudinous seas incarnadine/making the green one red', so that the stretched-out vowel sounds one red', so that the stretched-out vowel sounds seemed to contain the mysteries of life. Given all that, she might as well wander around like Lady Macbeth. (*Difficult Daughters*, 149)

Even after her marriage to Harish, she could not overcome her restlessness. Manju Kapur describes her sleepless night against the backdrop of landscape in lucid prose in the following way:

> Virmati was not sleeping. Her lids were shut and her thoughts were wandering. How much cooler it would be in the *kothi* now, how inviting in summer were the large gardens and sprawling orchards. And then the mangoes, litchis and loquats, the juicy mornings and evenings when they glutted themselves on fruit fresh from their own trees, and on the melons and watermelons brought home by their father everyday. She could almost feel the taste in her mouth, almost hear the laughing and quarrelling of her brothers and sisters that accompanied these marathon eating sessions. Unconsciously her mouth half opened when Harish put his tongue in it and clamped it shut again.
>
> Afterwards they lay together, hotter than ever. (*Difficult Daughters*, 209)

Difficult Daughters, is written in live Indian English idiom (i.e. the way Indians actually use English, not as they should do) and re-creates characters in their own situation. There is a lot of code mixing — i.e. Indian words used as such without being translated into English. This gives a kind of authenticity to the novel. The 'locale' of the novel is North India and the time is partition and independence — i.e. the beginning of post-colonial era. Apart from the medium in which it is written, historically speaking, it is a post-colonial novel. But we can also read it as a feminist novel.

Feminism is an ideology which seeks not only to understand the world but to change it to the advantage of women. Simone de Beauvoir's phrase 'the second sex' with reference to woman cut ice. He opines that woman's idea of herself as inferior to man and dependent on him springs from her realisation that 'the world is masculine on the whole, those who fashioned it, ruled it and still dominate it today are men'. Though the biological distinction between male and female is an accepted fact, the notion that women is inferior to man is no longer acceptable to women in general and feminists in particular. No wonder that Helene Cixous has reiterated the demand for self-assertion by woman writers and leaders of the feminist movement in unequivocal terms: "Woman must put herself into the text — as into the world and into history — by her own movement." (Pravakar, 5). Manju Kapur portrays Virmati is a progressive women who would not forsake her desire to acquire a higher academic degree in life. To continue her higher studies, she is prepared to sacrifice her family and all norms of male dominated society. Not only that, her decision to marry a man with a wife and children is a clear defiance of the conventions of the society to which she belongs. A woman's right to love and choose her mate cannot be questioned. That is the message Manju Kapur seems to convey through the character of Virmati. And again, Virmati is also against the observance of the rituals like funerals in our religion and society. Ida tells us about her mother's wishes in the following words:

> I stared again at my mother's ashes and wondered what memorial I could give her. She, who had not wanted to be mourned in anyway. When I die she said to me, I want my body donated. My eyes, my heart, my kidneys, any organ that can be of use. That way someone will value me after I have gone. I glared at her as pain began to gnaw at me. And she went on, when I die I want no *shor-sharr*. I don't want a *chauth*, I don't want an *uthala*, I want no one called, no one informed. (*Difficult Daughters*, 1)

Implicit in this extract is the desire of the protagonist to defy the rituals of the society. This can also be taken as a feminine assertion of individual identity that refuses to submit to the dictates of male dominant society. Not only Virmati but her daughter Ida also protests against the male chauvinism. When Virmati took her to task by saying, "you are disappointing your father", Ida retorted, "Why is it so important to please him?" (*Difficult Daughters*, 257).

Ida felt herself hovering like a 'pencil notation on the margins of society' (*Difficult Daughters*) and she had no regrets. Her defiance is an assertion of feminine sensibility. The title of the novel is more than justified for both Virmati and daughter Ida, became difficult daughters for their parents.

WORKS CITED

Kapur, Manju. *Difficult Daughters*. New Delhi: Penguin Books India (P.) Ltd., 1998.

Pravakar, M. Quoted. "Pen as 'Weapon' in Margaret Atwood's Bodily Harm." *The Commonwealth Review*, 6 : 2 (1994-1995).

19

Post-Independence Indian English Fiction

Post-Independence Indian English fiction is virtually synonymous with Post-colonial Indian English fiction. The visibility of Indian English fiction dates back to the fourth decade of the twentieth century when Mulk Raj Anand, R.K. Narayan and Raja Rao published their novels in English. Anand's *Untouchable* (1935) and *Coolie* (1936), Narayan's *Swami and Friends* (1935) and *Bachelor of Arts* (1936) and Raja Rao's *Kanthapura* (1938) are the pioneering Indian English novels based on socio-political realism. Then came the partition of the sub-continent and a number of significant novels on the theme of partition were published. They include Khushwant Singh's *Train to Pakistan* (1956), B. Rajan's *The Dark Dancer* (1959), Attia Hosain's *Sunlight on a Broken Column* (1961) and Manohar Malgonkar's *A Bend in the Ganges* (1964). These novels deal with the outcome of partition and the resultant communal tension and frenzy. Of all branches of Indian English literature in the post-Independence period fiction is the most developed and widely acclaimed (both nationally and internationally) genre. Central Sahitya Akademi, New Delhi has chosen sixteen Indian English novels beginning with R.K. Narayan's *The Guide* in 1960 for its Annual Award till date. R.P. Jhabvala (married to an Indian), Salman Rushdie and Kiran Desai, Indian born immigrant writers and Arundhati Roy have won Booker Prize for their novels. Apart from them Vikram Seth, Shashi Tharoor, Vikram Chandra, Upamanyu Chatterjee, Anita Desai, Kamala Markandaya, Manju Kapur, Amitav Ghosh, Amit Chaudhuri and a host of others have won international recognition for their fiction. (It may be mentioned here that the great trio, Anand, Narayan and Raja Rao are international celebrities who continued to write till 1990s.)

If we take a look at the trends in Indian English fiction, we will be struck by realism that underlies this genre in the post-Independence period. We come across five broad types of realism — social realism, psychological realism, historical realism, mythical realism and magic realism in Indian English fiction. Women novelists like Kamala Markandaya, Nayantara Sahgal and Shashi Deshpande lay emphasis on social realism and family relationship. Markandaya's *Nectar in a Sieve* and *A Handful of Rice* deal with stark social realism depicting how the transition in the society affects family relationship. The woman in women's fiction seeks an identify of her own, independent of her husband. Shiv K. Kumar has rightly observed this with reference to Shashi Deshpande's *That Long Silence*:

> In *That Long Silence*, Jaya the protagonist, resents the image of a wife 'yoked' to her husband — 'a pair of bullocks yoked together'. This is the image that haunts her all the time. So married to Mohan — a sedate, well-placed business executive — she secretly wishes to savour existential freedom through some disaster befalling him. So she feels 'relieved' when he is charged with embezzlement and they have to live in a sort of hide-out. She now feels redeemed as a woman with an identity of her own, seeing her husband rudderless and pathetically dependent upon her — this man whose 'fastidiousness, passion for neatness and order had amazed me when we got married' (23).

Nayantara Sahgal writes about the political situation in the country and politics becomes a metaphor for her fiction. Anita Desai, on the other hand, dives deep into human psyche and writes about psychological realism. In course of an article, "The Indian Writer's Problems", Anita Desai says,

> By writing novels that have been catalogued by critics as psychological and that are purely subjective, I have been left free to employ simply, the language of the interior. Even when two characters meet, they use this particular type of language — the language of their thoughts, their interior selves — which has nothing to do with geography and can be written in any language (*Explorations in Modern Indo-English Fiction*, 225).

Anita Desai experiments this in her Sahitya Akademi Award winning novel, *Fire on the Mountain.* The novel depicts the predicament of women in a society that fails to satisfy their desire and fulfil their hope. There is a need for women to understand each other. That is why Desai brings a kind of reconciliation between Nanda Kaul, the protagonist and her great-granddaughter, Raka towards the end of the novel.

Mythic realism we find in the fiction of Shashi Tharoor's *The Great Indian Novel and* Kiran Nagarkar's *Cuckold.* Tharoor by borrowing names from the *Mahabharata* for his characters makes an effort to give the myth contemporary relevance. Nagarkar's *Cuckold* won him the Central Sahitya Akademi Award for 2000. *Cuckold* is a different kind of novel, the like of which we don't find in Indian English literature. It is a culmination of history and legend, artistically woven into the framework of fiction. Nagarkar has done a good deal of research in Rajput history to write the novel. The time of the novel is the sixteenth century India and the locale is the Rajput Kingdom of Mewar. The novelist has made an attempt to resituate the text in the historical context. The protagonist is Bhojraj, Meerabai's husband and the novel is depicted from his point of view in the first-person narrative. The canvas of the novel is vast — it encompasses four kingdoms: Rajput Kingdom of Mewar (Capital : Chittor), Muslim Kingdom of Gujarat (Capital : Ahmedabad), Muslim Kingdom of Malwa (Capital : Mandu), Muslim Kingdom of Delhi (Capital : Delhi) — and the characters of the novel are drawn from history. It contains 49 chapters with an 'Epilogue', 'Afterword' culminating in the closing 'Historical Note'.

This is one of the finest novels written in English in our time. Based on history and myth, the novel acclimatizes our tradition and heritage to English language. It gives a lie to the critics who denigrate Indian English novelists and writers for what they call, the lack of 'authenticity' in their works. It is a novel about India's past which combines the historicity of fiction with fictionality of history. It richly deserves the Sahitya Akademi Award and perhaps, much more.

Vikram Seth created history by writing a novel, *The Golden Gate* in verse for which he won Central Sahitya Akademi Award in 1988. This novel and *An Equal Music* are set in U.S.A. and characters are drawn from that society. Seth has proved that Indian novelist do not write about India only, they also write about other countries and the world. In that respect, Indian English fiction can stand comparison with fiction written in English anywhere in the world outside Anglo-American tradition. Upamanyu Chatterjee has contributed substantially to Indian English fiction. His novels *English August* and *The Last Burden* depict family relationship in contemporary society.

Indian English novelists have experimented with magic realism following Salman Rushdie's *Midnight's Children* (1980). Amitav Ghosh is very successful in handling magic realism in his fiction.

His best known novel *Shadow Lines* (which won Sahitya Akademi Award in 1989) re-creates history in fictional terms. For him 'History is Textuality/ Textuality is History'. His *Glass Palace* and *The Hungry Tide* are well known novels. Githa Hariharan makes use of magic realism in her novel, *The Thousand Faces of Night* (1992) and *When Dreams Travel* (1999).

Novelists like Amit Chaudhuri who won Sahitya Akademi Award for his novel *A New World* for the year 2002 and Allan Sealy who won the Sahitya Akademi Award for his novel, *The Trotter-Nama* for the year 1992 have contributed to the growth of Indian English fiction and popularized it abroad. Vikram Chandra's *Red Earth and The Pouring Rain* brought a new kind of experimentation with myths of the land. His re-creation of myths in fictional terms is very successful.

Feminist criticism and gender studies have emboldened women writers the world over to write freely about love and sex and above all about a woman's right to consummate love the way she likes. This gave rise to the description of lesbian relationship in fiction as Manju Kapur has done in *A Married Woman.* A woman's right to choose a lover and have a love child became favourite themes with women novelists as we find in R.P. Jhabvala's *Heat and Dust* and Margaret Atwood's *Surfacing*. Manju Kapur depicts love relationship between woman-student and a married professor resulting in marriage in *Difficult Daughters*. Arundhati Roy depicts love and sex boldly in *The God of Small Things*. Here, Ammu chooses her low caste lover Velutha against all odds of the society.

Indian English fiction faces two challenges — one, at home posed by Bhasa literature novels and two, abroad posed by English language novels written the world over. Indian English novelists belong to three groups — one group of writers like Shashi Deshpande and Kiran Nagarkar and many others who stay in the country and write in English, the second group of writers like Vikram Seth, Amitav Ghosh and many others who divide their time between the country and abroad and write about their country and also other countries, and the third group of immigrant writers (or writers of Indian origin) like Bharathi Mukherjee, Rohinton Mistry, Salman Rushdie and many others also write about India and the Indian sub-continent. Here it may be mentioned that some academic novelists like Shiv K. Kumar and Manju Kapur who have gone abroad and lived there for some time also write about their own country and draw their characters from contemporary society. Shiv K. Kumar's

A River with Three Banks (1998), is a brilliant novel on communal hatred and tension between different communities in our country. It portrays the communal holocaust in the aftermath of partition in 1947. It can be read as a sequel to Khushwant Singh's *Train to Pakistan*. It is a novel about love and hate, marriage and divorce, revenge and forgiveness against the backdrop of partition. Mulk Raj Anand makes a pertinent comment on this novel:

> Shiv K. Kumar's novel has both beauty and power. It recreates in a language that glows with fragrance and colour, not only the trauma that one associates with partition, but also love, compassion and forgiveness that it evoked even in the midst of communal frenzy. Here is a poet's visualization of the India of 1947 — its brutality and romance, its agony and ecstasy (blurb, *A River with Three Banks*).

Indian English novelists writing in India or abroad or those who write both in India and abroad are essentially writing in the same way and producing national literature in the English language. This new national literature in English is not very much different from Bhasa literatures written in different regional languages of our country. Bruce King emphasizes this point when he says that, "just as there is no clear dividing line between the new national literatures in English and their overseas branches in the United States or England, so there is no clear division between the new national literatures in English and in local languages" (14).

Post-Independence Indian English fiction is post-colonial Indian English fiction because it continues to evoke colonial legacies in the contemporary society and seeks to compete with English language fiction for international prizes like the Commonwealth Fiction Prize, and the Booker Prize, etc. In sum, post-Independence Indian English fiction is rich in thematic content and it has acquired an idiom of its own which can be called, 'Indian English idiom'. It is immensely readable.

WORKS CITED

Desai, Anita. "The Indian Writer's Problems." *Explorations in Modern Indo-English Fiction*. Ed. R.K. Dhawan. New Delhi: Bahri Publications, 1992.

King, Bruce. "New Centres of Consciousness: New Post-colonial and International English Literature." *New National and Post-colonial Literatures*. Ed. Bruce King. New York: OUP, 1996 rpt. 2002.

Kumar, Shiv K. *Contemporary Indian Literature in English*. Shimla: Indian Institute of Advanced Study, 1992.

20

The Politics of Identity: The Emigrants Write Back

English language writers from the erstwhile British and French colonies in the last thirty years (1980 onwards) have become migratory birds flying away from their homeland to UK or USA for occupation, international recognition and fame. More often than not they choose not to return home for one reason or the other. As a result, they face the problem of identity both for themselves and their writings. How are they to be labelled as writers — African, Indian, Caribbean, Sri Lankan, Pakistani and so on or African American, Indian American, Black British, etc.? Again what should be the nomenclature of their writings? Indian English literature, African literature, Caribbean literature, Sri Lankan literature and so on.

The title of this paper, "The Emigrants Write Back" is foregrounded in Salman Rushdie's article, "The Empire Writes Back With a Vengeance" (*The Times,* London, 3 July 1982, p. 8) and a Volume called, *The Empire Strikes Back* (1982) published by the Centre for Contemporary Cultural Studies in Birmingham (the full title is *The Empire Strikes Back: Race and Racism in 70's Britain* (London: Hutchinson, 1982). C.L. Innes suggests that Rushdie's above-mentioned article, "plays with the title of the contemporary film, *The Empire Strikes Back,* the sequel to *Star Wars*" (214). The title of Bill Ashcroft, Gareth Griffiths and Helen Tiffin's influential and much publicized book, *The Empire Writes Back* (1989) is also modelled on the above-mentioned article and book. The title of my paper is double bind — that is, because of the concern of the emigrants to reach out to "a double audience, one existing as an immediate community within or identified with a colonized people, the other an outside or metropolitan readership, often connected with the colonizer" (Innes 201).

The postcolonial terms — expatriate, emigrant, exile, immigrant, diasporic are often overlapping and confusing. Expatriate writer is one who voluntarily leaves the country to promote his/her career and keeps the option open to return home. A.K. Ramanujan, R. Parthasarathy, Meena Alexander, Raja Rao, Kiran Desai belong to this category. Bapsi Sidhwa, Bharati Mukherjee, Rohinton Mistry, Salman Rushdie, V.S. Naipaul, Ben Okri, Ngugi wa Thiong'o, Michael Ondaatje belong to the category of emigrant or immigrant writers. V.S. Naipaul for us is a diasporic writer but for Caribbeans an emigrant writer. The diasporic writers are those whose ancestors have left for another country. Salman Rushdie can also be treated as a writer in exile for almost a decade. The boundaries of literatures in English by these English language writers of all varieties (expatriate, exile, emigrant, immigrant and diasporic) are blurring. Moreover, there are some writers who divide their time between UK, USA and their homeland. To this category belong many African, Caribbean and Indian writers. Names of Anita Desai, Vikram Seth, Vikram Chandra, Amitav Ghosh, George Lamming, Chinua Achebe and Derek Walcott can be cited in this context.

The question is what the themes are, the emigrant writers work on, in spite of their living in a different country? It is mostly about their former homeland and its culture. Ramanujan wrote more about India (Tamil and Kannada literary tradition and culture) remaining in USA, than what he had done when he was in India. R. Parthasarathy now writes more about India invoking Tamil and Sanskrit literary traditions than what he has done in India before 1982. Both of them have done excellent translation of Tamil, Kannada and Sanskrit literatures into English. Ramanujan felt more about India while living outside it. Kiran Desai writes about Darjeeling in her Man Booker Prize Award Winning novel, *The Inheritance of Loss*.

The Emigrant writers are always conscious of their identity. What Chinua Achebe said in an interview to Kwame Anthony Appiah in 1982, seems to be valid for all categories of English language writers (exiles, emigrants, expatriates and diasporans):

> I'm an Ibo writer because this is my basic culture; Nigerian, African and a writer...no, black first, then a writer. Each of these identities does call for a certain kind of commitment on my part. I must see what it is to be black — and this means being sufficiently intelligent to know how the world is moving and how the black people fare in this world. This is what it means to be black. Or an African — what does Africa mean to the world? What you see an African, what does it mean to a white man. (qtd. in Innes 208)

What Achebe says here, Raja Rao said the same thing in a different language in his foreword to *Kanthapura* in 1938.

> There is no village in India, however mean, that has not a rich *sthala purana* or legendary history of its own.... One such story from the contemporary annals of a village I have tried to tell. (p. vii)

In "The Novelist as Teacher" Achebe states that his wife,

> who teaches English in a boys' school, asked a pupil why he wrote about winter when he means the harmattan. He said the other boys would call him a bushman if he did such a thing.... I think it is part of my business to teach that boy that there is nothing disgraceful about the African weather, that the palm-tree is a fit subject for poetry (qtd. in Walder 10).

As Robert Fraser rightly observes, it is,

> an early attempt, in Homi Bhabha's words, to "write the nation": to depict in vivid outlines the writings, the jostlings and the uneasy birth pangs of the Indian collective consciousness. (53)

The question of identity of the English language writers from former colonies becomes imperative in the face of the former colonizers trying to neo-colonize them through prizes and awards. C.L. Innes makes a valid observation in the following passage:

> As journalists and critics have been quick to point out, literary prizes provide welcome publicity not only for their sponsors but also for the publishers of these authors, and the Man Booker Prize is conducted in such a way as to maximize publicity and book sales through advertising the shortlisted writers and encouraging speculation and participation by readers before the televised announcement of the winner. Many critics, including myself, would agree with Richard Todd's argument that the Booker Prize awards have encouraged a greater awareness of Britain as a pluralist society and welcome its recognition of writers from 'the Commonwealth'. However, the very success of postcolonial writers in these and other awards has given rise to cynicism, a suspicion among certain critics that the metropolitan centre has appropriated postcolonial writing for its own ends, and has sought to control which ones should be given the seal of approval. Thus some African and African American critics claimed that the award of the Nobel Prize for Literature to

> Wole Soyinka and Derek Walcott (and also Toni Morrison) indicated that their writing was more European and 'elitist' than 'authentically' African or Caribbean. The fact that the Booker McConnell company had originally been based in Guyana, and had derived its income from the Demerara sugar plantations, and that one of the criteria for the award is that the book must have been published in Britain, added to the suspicion that its sponsorship of the literary awards was another form of neocolonialism. (197-98)

English language writers from former colonies of Britain and France, move across the world and prefer to study and write mostly in England or USA. Some of them choose to live either in UK, USA or Canada permanently like Salman Rushdie, V.S. Naipaul, Bharati Mukherjee and Michael Ondaatje. They are known as immigrant writers. But others like Chinua Achebe, R. Parthasarathy, A.K. Ramanujan (who is no more) Vikram Seth, Derek Walcott live in a foreign territory and write about their homeland and keep the option open to return home. They are called emigrant writers (expats). Both these groups mostly write about their origin and their tradition. Some of them translate their ancient literature into English as R. Parthasarathy and A.K. Ramanujan have done.

There is, it seems to me, a design in the emigrant writer's writing about the land of their birth or the birth of their ancestors. They deliberately keep the term 'postcolonial' to describe their writings, so that they can appeal to the readers of both the worlds (the old country) which they left behind and the new country of domicile. V.S. Naipaul in his Nobel Prize acceptance speech declared that this Prize was a tribute to the country of his living (U.K.) and 'the country of my ancestors' (India). This is a clear example of a writer seeking a double audience. Rushdie and a host of other emigrant writers do the same thing.

Postcolonial literature is international in dimension — a literature without borders but it is foregrounded in 'colonial' countries.

Bruce King suggests a new nomenclature for the English language writers' literature. He says,

> 'English literature' now meant such writers as Wole Soyinka, Chinua Achebe, Nadine Gordimer, J.M. Coetzee, Derek Walcott, V.S. Naipaul, Margaret Atwood, Michael Ondaatje, Les Murray, Salman Rushdie, Vikram Seth, Anita Desai and Janet Frame, none of whom was British, American, or even Irish. As English was the main international language of

> business, science, politics, travel, education and social change, even nations that were not former English colonies produced English-language writers. The new national literatures, national multicultural literatures and International English literature were parts of a developing urban global culture, produced by international politics, communications and a world-wide economy, which included a heightened awareness of difference partly to assert identity. (3)

It seems to me an oversimplification and the term 'International English Literature' is an umbrella term. Literature presupposes a land, a language, and above all nationality. Derek Walcott makes it clear in "The Schooner Flight".

> I'm just a red nigger who love the sea,
> I had a sound colonial education,
> I have Dutch, nigger, and English in me,
> And either I'm nobody, or I'm a nation. (qtd. in Walder 123)

Some Caribbean writers and poets feel that the island is not good enough to fulfil their aspirations, and that is why they have chosen to live abroad in UK, France and USA. Novelists like Samuel Selvon, George Lamming, Wilson Harris and V.S. Naipaul realized in the words of Naipaul the, "threat of failure, the need to escape.... Living in a borrowed culture, the West Indian, more than most, needs writers to tell him who he is, where he stands" (Naipaul 45, 73). Referring to E.A. Markham's anthology titled, *Hinterland: Caribbean Poetry from the West Indies and Britain* (1989), Dennis Walder writes:

> I focus upon two contrasting giants of the current generation of Caribbean poets — (Edward) Kamau Brathwaite and Derek Walcott — and three self-confessedly 'Black British' poets, Linton Kwesi Johnson, James Berry and Grace Nichols. Brathwaite was born in Barbados in 1930, educated at Cambridge and Sussex Universities, and worked as an Education Officer in Ghana for eight years, before becoming a Professor of History at the University of the West Indies in Jamaica (he moved to New York in 1990). Walcott, born in St. Lucia in 1930 and educated at the University College of the West Indies (as it then was), worked as a journalist in Trinidad, where he founded the Theatre Workshop, before taking on a succession of visiting professorship in America, where he now teaches 'creative writing' for half the year,

> returning to his home island other half. James Berry was born in 1924 in Jamaica, and arrived in Britain in 1948, becoming a full-time writer after more than two decades as a telegraphist. Like Nichols, who was born in Guyana in 1950, where she was educated at the University and worked as a school teacher and journalist before emigrating in 1977, and Johnson, who was born in Jamaica in 1952 and went to a Brixton comprehensive on his arrival in London in 1963, Berry has long been settled in the U.K.
>
> Most Caribbean collections include 'Black British' poetry; but the term usually refers to African and Asian as well as Caribbean communities in contemporary Britain. (119)

Most Postcolonial writers are under the spell of migration. The emigrant writers seem to corroborate what Iska, the central character of a novel, *Iska* by Cyprian Ekwensi, the Nigerian novelist says,

> What I want is to go away from Nigeria — to England, France, America, anywhere at all. As long as it's away!... From there I can read all about Nigeria from a distance. It will all be like fiction and won't hurt much. (199-200)

Emigrant writers feel that one has to be away from one's own country to understand it better from outside and at the same time, to understand other territories anew. Andrew Smith cites one incident from Ben Okri, an emigrant writer's life to explain migrancy:

> Okri is on a voyage somewhere in the mid-Atlantic and together with his fellow passengers he is watching a magician perform. He tells us that the scene brings to his mind another image, that of the traditional oral African storyteller. A realization dawns on him that "the old storytellers were the first real explorers and frontiers people of the abyss". They were, in other words, the first to expand and challenge the horizons of their communities, imaginatively and conceptually. Okri, the modern-day novelist, summons up this ancestral figure precisely because he believes that we live in a world in which there are no longer set centers, definite horizons, or clear limits on things. By settling his readers with him on-board ship, mid-ocean, Okri places us as common dwellers in this in between space. He goes on to argue, quite deliberately, that it falls to the contemporary migrant writer to rediscover the role of the cultural frontier's person. Now more than ever, he suggests, we need the individual who can explore, in writing and art, what life is like in a world where everything

> is becoming border space. For Okri, and for many who work in postcolonial studies, this fluid cultural landscape seems an inviting prospect. He goes as far as to discern in it the glimmerings of a "first universal golden age". Here *migrancy* becomes the name for the condition of human beings *as such*, a name for how we exist and understand ourselves in the twenty-first century. (qtd. in Lazarus 246-247)

In course of an interview of A.L. Becker and Keith Taylor (included in *Uncollected Poems and Prose of A.K. Ramanujan* edited by Molly Daniels-Ramanujan and Keith Harrison. OUP), Ramanujan denied being a writer in exile, even, an expatriate writer:

> I don't even call myself an expatriate, because I have done a lot of work on India since coming to this country (USA). I have done it more comfortably here than I could have done it in India. (52)

So, it is clear that the emigrants write back to the homeland. They too write back to the centre (i.e., former colonizers and neo-colonizers). In the same interview Ramanujan opines that if colonization of our country affected our own indigenous language, culture and literature, English has helped us fight against the colonizers and taught us to be self-critical:

> It might be good that English is so widespread as a second language. English has distorted our traditions, but it has also made us look at our traditions. It's not enough to say that it is all colonialism and has done nothing but distort. This whole question of colonial distortion has been formulated in English. It requires a dialogue with English. English has been the 'other' through which we have returned to ourselves. English has become a part of us. To say we want to return to a pre-English state is chimerical. The anti-colonial discourse is all done in English. Nobody's writing this in Kannada. In India, there is a wonderful group of new historians called the Subalterns, who are looking at all the distortions of the colonial intellectual practices. But all their work is done in English. Isn't the English in which they are writing distorting what they are writing about? English has made us self-critical and made us critical of English itself. (79)

There is a good deal of debates over the status of the emigrant writings. It is not like the mythical Shakuntala disowned by both the parents. On the contrary, the emigrants have endeared themselves both to the natives of their former homeland and the country of their new home. They live in the west and write about the country they have left behind. Metaphorically speaking the emigrant write back to the centre and the homeland.

The emigrant writers travel frequently across the world including the former colonized countries. They not only migrate to UK or USA but to former colonies. For example, Ondaatje migrated from Sri Lanka to Canada via UK and J.M. Coetzee from South Africa to Australia and Uma Parameswaran from India to Canada. Yann Martel travelled to India and wrote the Man Booker Prize Award Winning Novel, *Life of Pi.* Martel makes references to the Indian political scene and personalities in the above-mentioned novel. The use of Indian myths reinforces Martel's desire to recreate an atmosphere that immediately would attract the imagination of the people. References to the *Ramayana* and the *Mahabharata* to recreate the myth in the contemporary post-colonial situation, are examples of intertextualities. Thus writes Martel about Lord Krishna:

> "Tut! Tut! Open your mouth," orders Yashoda, Krishna does as he is told. He opens his mouth. Yashoda gasps. She sees in Krishna's mouth the whole complete entire timeless universe, all the stars and planets of space and the distance between them, all the lands and seas of the earth and the life in them; she sees all the days of yesterday and all the days of tomorrow; she sees all ideas and all emotions, all pity and all hope, and the three strands of matter; not a pebble, candle, creature village or galaxy is missing, including herself and every bit of dirt in its truthful place. "My Lord, you can close your mouth," she says reverently. (55)

As Bill Ashcroft, Gareth Griffiths and Helen Tiffin have rightly stressed in their most widely known and circulated book, *The Empire Writes Back,* the migrant writers from former colonies have "rewritten particular works from the English 'canon'" (32):

> Writers such as J.M. Coetzee, Wilson Harris, V.S. Naipaul, George Lamming, Patrick White, Chinua Achebe, Margaret Atwood, and Jean Rhys have all rewritten particular works from the English 'Canon' with a view to restructuring European 'realities' to postcolonial terms, not simply by reversing the hierarchical order but by interrogating the philosophical assumptions on which that order was based. (32)

Elleke Boehmer brings to our notice Coetzee's *Foe* which is re-written on the Robinson Crusoe story in the following words:

> J.M. Coetzee's *Foe* (1986), a postmodern rewriting of the Robinson Crusoe story, gives a neat symbolic shorthand for this process of self-articulation by the colonized. In this novel, the Friday character, who lacks a tongue, mutely represents the colonized problem of making meaning. He dances in a circle, he plays one tune on the flute, he writes one character only, o, the empty set, the empty mouth. In a situation where there is no access to the media of cultural authority — the voice, the pen, the book — the forms of expression available to Friday are either silent, repetitive, or both. Yet, by enacting his own exclusion, by tracing the circles of interpretation which shut him out — by writing o — Friday begins to signify. (172)

Similarly Jean Rhys' *Wide Sargasso Sea* (1966) is made on Charlotte Bronte's *Jane Eyre* (1847) and George Lamming's *Water With Berries* is a 'Coda to *The Tempest*' (W.H. New's remark), (King 109).

Apart from the themes, the emigrant writers have brought a sea change in the use of English language in their texts. They have made the use of English language flexible in their fiction. One instance, from Rushdie's *Midnight's Children* will suffice. The novel begins with the first person narrative:

> I was born in the city of Bombay...on the stroke of midnight, as a matter of fact. Clock-hands joined palms in respectful greeting as I came. Oh, spell it out, spell it out, at the precise instant of India's arrival at independence. I tumbled forth into the world.... And there are so many stories to tell, too many, such an excess of intertwined lives events miracles places rumours, so dense a commingling of the improbable and the mundane! (9)

Rushdie writes with his own generation in India in his bones. The emigrant writers wherever they live they do one of the two things: one, they write about the country of their origin or birth, two they write about their adopted country. In either case they write back (to the centre or periphery — is a matter of debate). Finally, a word about the nomenclature of the literature written by the emigrant writers. How long can we go an calling the literature written by the people of former colonies in English, Postcolonial literature? Which is the limit — the sky? How long can we continue to call the writings of the people in English from former colonies 'Literature in English'? It's time for us to make amends. Literature needs a geographical territory and people for its identity. By people, I mean common readers (not the elite class or academics), who read that literature and speak that language in which it is written. Even when that language is the second language of the people, the literature should be named after their country and nationality.

We have already lived a decade of the twenty-first century. Let's do away with the nomenclatures 'Postcolonial literature', 'Literatures in English' and name the literatures after the countries where the writers live in. In order to distinguish those writers who are new to the country of their domicile, from the natives of that country, we can call them Black British writers, Indian American writers, African American writers and so on. Alternatively we can call them Indian emigrant writers, African emigrant writers, Caribbean emigrant writers and their writings should be termed Indian emigrant literature, African emigrant literature, and Caribbean emigrant literature and so on.

WORKS CITED

Ashcroft, Bill, Gareth Griffiths and Helen Tiffin. *The Empire Writes Back*. New York: Routledge, 2002.

Boehmer, Elleke. *Colonial and Postcolonial Literature*. Oxford: OUP, 1998.

Ekwensi, Cyprian. *Iska*. London: Hutchinson and Co., 1966.

Fraser, Robert. *Lifting the Sentence: A Poetics of Postcolonial Fiction*. Manchester: Manchester University Press, 2000.

Innes, C.L. *The Cambridge Introduction to Postcolonial Literatures in English*. New Delhi: Cambridge University Press. 2008.

King, Bruce. *New National and Post-Colonial Literatures: An Introduction*. New York: OUP, 1996, rpt 2002.

Lazarus, Neil, ed. *The Cambridge Companion to Postcolonial Literary Studies*. New York: CUP, 2004.

Martel, Yann. *Life of Pi*. New Delhi: Penguin Books, 2002.

Naipaul, V.S. *The Middle Passage*. New York: Penguin Books, 1962.

New, W.H. "Colonial Literatures". *New National and Postcolonial Literatures: An Introduction*. Ed. Bruce King, New York: OUP, 1996, rpt 2002.

Ramanujan, A.K. *Uncollected Poems and Prose*. Eds. Molly Daniels-Ramanujan and Keith Harrison. New Delhi: OUP, 2005.

Rao, Raja. *Kanthapura*. New York: Grove Press, 1963.

Rushdie, Salman. *Midnight's Children*. Great Britain: Vintage, 1995.

Smith, Andrew. "Migrancy, Hybridity, and Postcolonial Literary Studies". *The Cambridge Companion to Postcolonial Literary Studies*. Ed. Neil Lazarus. New York: CUP, 2004.

Walder, Dennis. *Post-colonial Literatures in English: History, Languages, Theory*. New Delhi: Atlantic Publishers, 2005.

21

Contrapuntal Reading of Yann Martel's *Life of Pi*

The reading of literature is an open question, for no reading could be definitive. That is, because literature as a subject is elusive. It could be read with or without theories. Even when it is read without any particular theory it falls into the terrain of one of the practicing theories. On the other hand, when it is read according to a particular theory, it brings an ideology to the text and distorts it. Reading of literature turns out to be a dialectic of the personal and the impersonal. We know that an individual's approach to the literary text is personal and the reading convention is impersonal. The question that needs to be addressed is that whether the text has an identity of its own or merely it basks in the reflected opinion of the reader. This is more applicable to postcolonial literature. Terms like 'the empire writes back to the centre' and 'the centre strikes back' make the relationship between the former colonizers and the colonized complicated (I would refrain from using the postcolonial buzz word 'Problematic'). To read a work of literature written by an ex-colonized writer brings to our mind the question of 'imperialism', 'colonialism', 'postcolonialism' and what is more, 'neo-colonialism'. Here in comes the scope of contrapuntal reading. (Edward Said's term).

As Said puts it:

> "As we look back at the cultural achieve, we begin to reread it not univocally but *contrapuntally*", with a simultaneous awareness both of the metropolitan history that is narrated and of those other histories against which (and together with which) the dominating discourse acts. In the counterpoint of Western classical music, various themes play off one another, with only a provisional privilege being given to any particular one; yet in the resulting polyphony there is concert and order, an organized interplay that derives from the themes, not from

> a rigorous melodic or formal principle outside the work. In the same way, I believe, we can read and interpret English novels, for example, whose engagement (usually suppressed for the most part) with the West Indies or India, say, is shaped and perhaps even determined by the specific history of colonization, resistance, and finally native nationalism. At this point alternative or new narratives emerge, and they become institutionalized or discursively stable entities. (59-60)

Bill Ashcroft, Gareth Griffiths and Helen Tiffin explain the term contrapuntal reading in the following words: "A term coined by Edward Said to describe a way of reading the texts of English literature so as to reveal their deep implication in imperialism and the colonial process. Borrowed from music, the term suggests a responsive reading that provides a counter point to the text, thus enabling the emergence of colonial implications that might otherwise remain hidden" (55-56).

According to K.M. Newton "Post-colonial criticism tends to have a double focus: it concentrates either on the representation of the non-European in Western canonic literature or on writing from non-European cultural traditions, particularly writing from countries that have been colonised by Western nations.... He (Edward Said) advocates what he calls a contrapuntal reading that plays of the Western and non-Western against one another" (283).

Yann Martel's Man Booker Prize Award Winning novel, *Life of Pi* for the year 2002, a highly imaginative work of fiction on shipwreck deals with man's faith in God and trust in animals. In his 'preface' to the novel Martel states that on having arrived in Pondicherry, he met an elderly man named Francis Adirubasamy, who told him that, "I have a story that will make you believe in God.... It starts right here in Pondicherry just a few years back, and it ends, I am delighted to tell you, in the very country you come from" (X). That is the story of Mr. Patel, which Martel tells in this novel with imaginative skill in a lucid language.

On the art of giving an imaginative shape to reality Yann Martel tells Subash Jeyan in course of an interview in the following words:

> Reality is a 100 million details.... The forte of the arts, the forte of the imagination is that it can take some of those details and give them immortality. A painting, a story, a song can float across the ocean of time like a life boat. (*The Hindu Literary Review Sunday*, 2 May 2010 : 1)

The blurb of the book makes the story line of the novel crystal clear:

> Pi Patel lives in Pondicherry, where his father owns a zoo. When he is sixteen, his parents decide to emigrate to Canada, taking their large family with them, but tragedy strikes when the cargo ship carrying them sinks during a storm. One solitary lifeboat remains bobbing on the wild blue Pacific. In it are five survivors: Pi, a hyena, a zebra (with a broken leg), a female orangutan, and a 450-pound Royal Bengal Tiger. The scene is set for an extraordinary adventure.

In *Life of Pi* at the surface level we find the portrayal of animals, and if we stick to it, we would lose the deep meaning of the novel. The novel is about man's faith in God and therefore, in a subtle way Martel examines the three important religions of the world — Hinduism, Islam and Christianity. This reminds us of E.M. Forster's *A Passage to India* where all these three religions come under review. The protagonist, Pi (Piscine Molitor Patel) believes in all the three major religions: Hinduism, Christianity and Islam and tells that "They didn't know that I was a practising Hindu, Christian and Muslim" (64). But the priests of all these religions made claims on him. Thus, Pi says,

> After the "Hellos" and the "Good days", there was an awkward silence. The priest broke it when he said, with pride in his voice, "Piscine is a good Christian boy. I hope to see him join our choir soon".
>
> My parents, the pandit and the imam looked surprised.
>
> "You must be mistaken. He's good Muslim boy. He comes without fail to Friday prayer, and his knowledge of the Holy Qur'an is coming along nicely." So said the imam.
>
> My parents, the priest and the pandit looked incredulous.
>
> The pandit spoke. "You're both wrong. He's good Hindu boy. I see him all the time at the temple coming for darshan and performing puja."
>
> My parents, the imam and the priest looked astounded.
>
> "There is no mistake", said the priest. "I know this boy. He is Piscine Molitor Patel and he's a Christian".
>
> "I know him too, and tell you he's a Muslim," asserted the imam.
>
> "Nonsense!" cried the pandit. "Piscine was born a Hindu, lives a Hindu and will die a Hindu!" (66)

What is common to all religions is non-violence. But it seems that the priests of all religions have closed minds. They praise their own religions and see nothing good in other religions. That is the root of all conflicts. And that is the contrapuntal reading of Martel's description of Pi's attachment to all the religions. Pi by accepting all the faiths disapproves of the conflict and violence that issue out of biased interpretation of religions. That is the deep meaning of the novel. The protagonist's faith in God served him from being killed in the sea. Martel describes Pi's feelings in lucid prose in the following passage.

> I was alone and orphaned, in the middle of the Pacific, hanging on to an oar, an adult tiger in front of me, sharks beneath me, a storm raging about me. Had I considered my prospects in the light of reason, I surely would have given up and let go of the oar, hoping that I might drown before being eaten. But I don't recall that I had a single thought during those first minutes of relative safety. I didn't even notice daybreak. I held on to the oar, I just held on, God only knows why. (107)

In course of the novel, Martel describes Pi's experiences with hyena, zebra, a female orangutan, and a 450 pound Royal Bengal tiger with an insight into animal behaviour. Pi recalls their sailing in the ship with delight. "We sailed from Madras across the Bay of Bengal, down through the Strait of Malacca, around Singapore and up to Manila. I loved every minute of it. It was a thrill to be on a ship" (100). When the ship sank the hyena jumped over the Zebra and came to the life boat. Pi was surprised to see a 450-Pound Royal Bengal tiger in a life boat twenty-six feet long. Then he describes how he survived the attack of the Royal Bengal tiger:

> Four times he struck at me with his right paw and sent me overboard, and four times I lost my shield. I was terrified before, during and after each attack, and I spent a long time shivering with fear on the raft. Eventually I learned to read the signals he was sending me. I found that with his ears, his eyes, his whiskers, his teeth, his tail and his throat, he spoke a simple, forcefully punctuated language that told me what his next move might be. I learned to back down before he lifted his paw in the air. (207)

The agony of Pi is described with an analogy to Arjun's plight in *The Mahabharata*. Martel writes:

> My (Pi's) greatest wish — other than salvation — was to have a book. A long book with a never-ending story. One I could

> read again and again, with new eyes and a fresh understanding each time. Alas, there was no scripture in the lifeboat. I was a disconsolate Arjuna in a battered chariot without the benefit of Krishna's words. (207)

Finally, Pi reached Mexico in the life boat. Here the story takes a new turn. Pi got a new lease of life. He says,

> I was overwhelmed by the generosity of those who rescued me. Poor people gave me clothes and food. Doctors and nurses cared for me as if I were a premature baby. Mexican and Canadian officials opened all doors for me so that from the beach in Mexico to the home of my foster mother to the classrooms of the University of Toronto, there was only one long, easy corridor I had to walk down. To all these people I would like to extend my heartfelt thanks. (286)

In Part III of the novel, the officers came and interrogated Pi, the lone survivor of the Japanese cargo ship Tsimtsum. Pi told them what has happened during the shipwreck and how he swam for life boat and survived. Martel brings out the conversation between investigating officers and Pi with a touch of pathos:

"The weather was bad enough to scare me witless, that's all I know for sure".

"You said the weather improved quickly. The ship sank and right after it was a beautiful day, isn't that what you said?"

"Yes."

"Sounds like no more than a passing squall".

"It sank the ship."

"That's what we're wondering"

"My whole family died."

"We're sorry about that."

"Not as much as I am."

"So what happened, Mr. Patel? We're puzzled. Everything was normal and then....?"

"Then normal sank."

"Why?"

"I don't know. You should be telling me. You're the experts. Apply your science."

"We don't understand." (315)

Martel ends the novel with an apt comment:

> As an aside, story of sole survivor. Mr. Piscine Molitor Patel, Indian citizen, is an astounding story of courage and endurance in the face of extraordinarily difficult and tragic circumstances. In the experience of this investigator, his story is unparalleled in the history of shipwrecks. Very few castaways can claim to have survived so long at sea as Mr. Patel, and none in the company of an adult Bengal tiger. (319)

The novel tells a tale of human adventure in the midst of natural calamity that caused shipwreck. The story deals with man's belief in God in the midst of difficulties. And again, it brings man and animals face to face, in which the tiger and the protagonist, Pi survive, miraculously. We know that miracles do sometimes happen. The novelist imagines the situation camouflaging as real to elicit reader's participation. But this text, like any other text exists with the author's interior signature attested by his nationality.

Reading the novel contrapuntally brings to our mind Martel's references to the Indian political scene and personalities, which means how colonization has deeply affected our mind. The use of Indian myths reinforces Martel's desire to re-create an atmosphere that immediately would attract the imagination of the people. References to the *Ramayana* and the *Mahabharata* to re-create the myth in the contemporary post-colonial situation, are examples of intertextualities. Thus writes Martel about Lord Krishna:

> "Tut! Tut! Open your mouth," orders Yashoda. Krishna does as he is told. He opens his mouth. Yashoda gasps. She sees in Krishna's mouth the whole complete entire timeless universe, all the stars and planets of space and the distance between them, all the lands an seas of the earth and the life in them; she sees all the days of yesterday and all the days of tomorrow; she sees all ideas and all emotions, all pity and all hope, and the three strands of matter; not a pebble, candle, creature village or galaxy is missing, including herself and every bit of dirt in its truthful place. "My Lord, you can close your mouth," she says reverently. (55)

The novel affirms man's faith in God. This is the colonial belief which Martel as a post-colonial writer wants to believe in. Thus, the says, "That is God as God should be. With shine and power and might. Such as can rescue and save and put down evil" (55).

The hallmark of post-colonial literature is that it brings out successfully the colonial experiences of different countries that have affinities with each other. Not only people migrate from their countries to other countries but they let their stories travel with them. It is the story of a shipwreck that travelled from India to Canada. *Life of Pi* is a successful novel of memory and remembrance, with an irresistible appeal.

WORKS CITED

Ashcroft, Bill, Gareth Griffiths and Helen Tiffin. *Postcolonial Studies: The Key Concepts*. New York: Routledge, 2004.

Jeyan, Subash (Interviewing Yann Martel). "*Against the Tyranny of Facts*." *The Hindu Literary Review*, Sunday May 2, 2010.

Martel, Yann. *Life of Pi*. New Delhi: Penguin Books, 2002.

Newton K.M., ed. *Twentieth-Century Literary Theory: A Reader*. London: Macmillan Press Ltd., 1997.

Said, Edward. *Culture and Imperialism*. London: Vintage, 1994.

22

Remembering the Founding Fathers of Indian English Fiction

Though historically Indian English Fiction owes its origin to Bankim Chandra Chatterjee's *Rajmohan's Wife* (1864), its foundation was laid by Mulk Raj Anand when he published his *Untouchable* in 1935. R.K. Narayan and Raja Rao joined him in giving, as it were, 'a local habitation and a name' to Indian English fiction in the nineteen thirties. Anand's *Untouchable* and *Coolie,* Narayan's *Swami and Friends* and *The Bachelor of Arts.* Raja Rao's *Kanthapura* mark the beginning of Indian English fiction. And these three novelists continued to write till the end of the twentieth century.

Now we live in the age of fiction when poetry and drama have taken a back seat. Thanks to the prizes given exclusively to fiction (such as The Man Booker Prize) and several other prizes, researchers and critics turn to fiction and espouse its cause at the cost of other genres of literature. If poetry had its heyday in nineteen seventies and early eighties, when R. Parthasarathy as the Poetry Editor of Oxford University Press, issued a series called "New Poetry from India" with poets like Nissim Ezekiel, Jayanta Mahapatra, Shiv K. Kumar, A.K. Ramanujan, R. Parthasarathy, Keki N. Daruwalla publishing their collections of poems, in the late eighties, thereafter with the publication of Salman Rushdie's *Midnights Children* (1980), fiction has taken the center stage. Novelists like Amitav Ghosh, Vikram Seth, Shashi Tharoor, Upamanyu — Chatterjee, Shashi Deshpande, Arundhati Roy, Vikram Chandra, Manju Kapur and a host of others came to limelight in the last twenty-five years following Salman Rushdie's instant success with his *Midnights Children* winning the Booker Prize in 1981. Researchers and critics became so enamoured of the new authors that they have completely ignored the contribution of Anand, R.K. Narayan and Raja Rao. The purpose of the paper is to highlight and emphasize the real merit of these three novelists and their contribution to Indian English fiction.

Critics like William Walsh, Alastair, Niven, K.R.S. Iyengar, C.D. Narasimhaiah and M.K. Naik have evaluated the works of Anand, Narayan and Rao and appreciated them. "If Anand is the novelist as reformer, Raja Rao the novelist as metaphysical poet, Narayan is simply the novelist as novelist", says William Walsh (*R.K. Narayan* 6). And later on Walsh calls R.K. Narayan, "the novelist as moral analyst" (*Indian Literature in English* 96). C.D. Narasimhaiah says, "Where distinctions are made they fell into neat categories of Anand the Marxist, progressive or committed writer; Narayan the comic genius or writer pure and simple; and Raja Rao the religious, or philosophical novelist (148). These three novelists have broken new grounds in Indian English fiction, in terms of making innovations, in themes, and techniques. They have re-created their characters in their own situations social, as well as psychological. If Anand is known for humanism, Narayan is known for social and psychological realism and Rao for metaphysical ideas. It is interesting to know that our pioneering novelists, Anand and Narayan published their first novels with the help of British novelists, E.M. Forster and Graham Greene respectively and Rao, published his first novel sitting in Paris. Having said so let me discuss their works.

Right from his childhood, Anand was a rebel. He was against the injustice done to the inferior and socially low — placed people. In course of an article he wrote:

> Sensing the contempt of the superior whites for the inferior browns, hearing the big officers abuse the recruits, the literates ignoring the illiterates, my learned father turning away from the villager brothers of my mother and from the soiled clothes copper-smiths of our home town Amritsar. I became a rebel against the heavy voices, the heavy hands and the cocked head. (JLA 8)

In the same article recalling how he published his first novel *Untouchable* with E.M. Forster's help, Anand wrote:

> He (Forster) wrote a preface. A small publisher issued the novel. It was warmly received. All my novels, then, have come from self-actualising in the confessional, which is the source of my protests against religion reduced to ritual, against lakir *ki fakhir* to or customs, against the impositions of the Superiors or Inferiors, as against cruelties to the new young, against all bondage and for the many freedoms implicit in political freedom. (JLA 10)

Anand's "Cultural discovery of India and Asia through the 136-volumes of *Marg* that he founded in 1945 and edited till the early eighties is by itself an achievement that will immortalize him ..." (Kohli 32-33). No wonder that he was elected Fellow of Sahitya Akademi, Lalit Kala Akademi and Sangeet Natak Akademi, a rare distinction yet to be surpassed by any one in our country.

Anand was always for highlighting indigenous culture, art and creating literature out of our own environment. In course of a meeting with the present author during All India English Teacher's Conference in 1996 he told: "You, Oriyas you never write on Konarka and your own culture." (He was referring to contemporary writings in English from Orissa). Anand's important novels include *Untouchable* (1935), *Coolie* (1936), *Two Leaves and a Bud* (1937), *The Village* (1939), *Across the Blackwaters* (1941), *The Big Heart* (1945), *Seven Summers* (1951), *The Private Life of an Indian Prince* (1953), *Gauri* (1960), *Morning Face* (1968), *Confessions of a Lover* (1976), *The Bubble* (1984), *Little Plays of Mahatma Gandhi* (1991) and *Nine Moods of Bharata: Novel of a Pilgrimage* (1998).

Social realism is the major concern in his works. He has brought innovations in fiction by making an untouchable the hero or anti-hero of his first novel, Untouchable. As Marlene Fisher rightly put it:

> The heart of Untouchable, however, is not in its manifest social plea for the abolition of untouchability. It lies, rather, in the kind of person Bakha is. It lies in trustingness, in his naivete, and in his still unquenchable wonder at life. (29)

Anand takes characters from contemporary life web have been deprived of their rights by the oppressors. His Marxist learnings are unmistakable. A person who lived more than twenty years abroad during his youth, unlike the contemporary diasporic writers was never in search of "home". 'Home' was uppermost in his mind and deeply engraved in his heart. Hence, he never lost touch with Indian reality and social conditions. His characters are life like and they remind us of our own social environment which victimizes them. Of Anand's fiction, Anna Rutherford writes:

> Anand's characters invariably fail into three classes: the victims who are usually the protagonists; the oppressors, those who oppose change and progress, and the goodmen. Under the last category fall the social workers, the labour leaders, all those who believe in progress and can see how modern science can

> improve the lot of sufferers and help bring out the quality of all men. (qtd. in Walsh 64)

R.K. Narayan published his first novel, *Swami and Friends* in 1935, the same year as Anand published his *Untouchable*. Thereafter, Narayan published a number of novels such as *The Bachelor of Arts* (1937), *The English Teacher* (1945), *Mr. Sampath* (1949), *The Financial Expert* (1952), *Waiting for Mahatma* (1955), *The Guide* (1958), *The Man Eater of Malgudi* (1962). *The Vender of Tweets* (1967), *The Painter of Signs* (1977), *The Tiger of Malgudi* (1983), *Talkative Man* (1983), *The World of Nagaraj* (1990) and *Grandmother's Tale* (1992).

Narayan created history by creating an imaginary town, Malgudi (somewhere near the boundary of Tamil Nadu and Karnataka) the locale of his fictional world. If Anand concentrates on contemporary Indian reality, Narayan dives deep into Indian tradition and his characters are rooted in that tradition. William, Walsh makes a pertinent comment on this aspect.

Again, one must say that there is deeply in Narayan the profound Hindu conviction, or instinct for, the fundamental oneness of existence... The tension between the one and the many, a sustaining theme of Hinduism, operates quietly and unpretentiously throughout Narayan's fiction, (*R.K. Narayan* 167).

In Narayan's fiction was come across the comic relief sprinkled with humour. The art of storytelling is superb. For the art of narration and evocation of Indian myths, Narayan's fiction assumes a special significance for Indian readers. Take the character of Raju, the protagonist in *The Guide*, who wins the trust of people in spite of himself. That is where we find by the manipulation of the gods. Raju transforms his character and makes himself acceptable to the credulous Indians.

Raja Rao, the youngest of the trio, dives deep into Indian metaphysics and gets at the roots of Indian tradition. He tells his stories by referring to the great epics like the *Ramayan* and the *Mahabharata*. H.M. Williams make a pertinent observation in this regard:

> By choosing to develop the character of an Indian village Raja Rao moves from realism to symbolism. Helped by the parataxis of the sentence structure and the flow of the Indian narrator's stream of consciousness, the novel conveys an uncanny impression of the immense longevity into the

> twentieth century, of aeons of customs dating back to a time before the arrival in India of the Aryans. This makes inevitable the conflation of *Ramayan* and *Mahabharata* with the Swaraj movement; but it does more, it makes us aware of the timeless and eternal quality of the Hindu consciousness beyond the contingency of the political struggle. (48-49)

Raja Rao like Chinua Achebe is a forerunner of postcolonial criticism. If Achebe has emphasized his African idiom to write novels in his famous work, "Novelist as Teacher", Rao has done so admirably in his "Preface" to *Kanthapura*. If Edward Said, Gayatri Spivak Chakravorty and Homi K. Bhabha are credited with giving the theory of post-colonialism and Bill Ashcroft, Gareth Griffiths, and Helen Tiffin are eulogized for popularizing Postcolonial Theory (Courtesy: *The Empire Writes Back)*, then Raja Rao and Chinua Achebe should be given the credit of writing fiction in English with new idioms and new themes based on the stories of their own nations. Here is Raja Rao's clarion call to write fiction in English in our own way:

> One has to convey in a language that is not one's own the spirit that is one's own. One has to convey the various shades and omissions of a certain thought-movement that looks maltreated in an alien language. I use the word 'alien', yet English is not an alien language to us. It is the language of our intellectual make-up-like Sanskrit or Persian was before — but not of our emotional make-up. We are all instinctively bilingual, many of us writing in our own language and in English. We cannot write like the English. We should not. We cannot write only as Indians. We have grown to look at the large world as part of us. Our method of expression therefore has to be a dialect which will some day prove to be as distinctive and colourful as the Irish or the American. Time alone will justify it. ('Preface' to *Kanthapura*).

Raja Rao's important novels include *Kanthapura* (1938), *The Serpent and the Rope* (1962), *Cat and Shakespeare* (1965) and *The Chessmaster and His Moves* (1988). In *Kanthapura,* Rao has been able to create a living Gandhi myth through the struggle for independence. The Kenchamma myth has been dovetailed into the structure of the novel to show the belief of the villagers in rituals. The idioms befit the characters and they are recreated like Nissim Ezekiel's characters in their own situations. Expressions like "as honest as an elephant", "the pumpkin moon", "so you are a traitor to your salt givers", "your humble servant, "lick your feet" "son of a concubine", "son of a widow", "you donkey's husband", "you son of my woman", "sour-milk", "dung-eating cars", "a cow and sparrow story", "to stitch up one's mouth", "to eat mud", "every squirrel has his day", "not a mosquito moved", "my right eye winks", "heart-it beat like a drum", "heats squeezed like a wet cloth" and so on are good examples of code-switching. Here, Rao makes an attempt to create a new Indian English idiom based on our expressions. Raja Rao gives an account of his work in, the following words:

Starting from the humanitarian and romantic aspect of man in *Kanthapura* and *The Cow and the Barricades* (his early volume of short stories) — both deeply influenced by Mahatma Gandhi's philosophy of non-violence — I soon came to the metaphysical novel, *The Serpent and the Rope* and *The Cat and Shakespeare* based on the vedantic conceptions of illusion and reality. My main interest increasingly is in showing the complexity of the human condition (that is, the reality of man is beyond his person), and in showing the symbolic construed of one human expression. All words are hierarchic symbols, almost mathematical in precision, one and; of the unknown (qtd. in Walsh *Indian Literature in English* 73).

The Serpent and the Rope is a metaphysical novel written in the puranic tradition (say, *The Mahabharata* of our country). C.D. Narasimhaiah makes a pertinent comment in the following words:

> There is 'plot', 'character' and 'situation' and abundant 'life' — as it is actually lived in India, in Paris, in Southern France, in London and Cambridge. There are numerous beautiful 'stories' within the central story in the style of the *Mahabharata* — of Bhagyanagar that was Hyderabad, of Lakpati of Lahore, of Iswara Bhatta and his family, of Radha, Krishna and Durvasa; of Jagannath Bhatta and Shajehan's daughter; of Tristram and Iseult; of Buddha and Vassita with her dead son in her arms, not to speak of Buddha riding in a chariot to a place of no return, leaving his wife and child behind, their shades hovering for ever in the background; of the poor Brahmin of Benares carrying his own dead child on his shoulder to float in the Ganga; of Kabir and Ramananda; of *Budumeltayl* and the Prince, of Yajnyavalkya and Maitreyi — each of the stories delightful, poignant and elevating, hut having a value and a significance seen against the main theme of *The Serpent and the Rope,* itself a popular myth but most artistically elucidated in the course of the novel.

'The world is either unreal or real' — the serpent or the rope. There is no in-between-the-two — and all that's in-between is poetry, is sainthood. You might go on saying all the time, 'No, no, it's the rope', and stand in the serpent. And looking at the rope from the serpent is to see paradise, saints, avataras, gods, heroes, universe. For wheresoever you go, you see only with the serpent's eyes. Whether you can it duality or modified duality, you invest a belvedere to heaven, you look, at the rope from the posture of the serpent, you feel you are the serpent — you are — the rope is. But in true fact, with whatever eyes you see there is no serpent, there never was a serpent. You gave your own eyes to the falling evening and cried. *Ayyo! Oh!* It's the serpent'! You run, and roll and lament, and have compassion for fear of pain, others', or your own. You see the serpent and in fear you feel you are it, the serpent, the saint. One — the Guru — brings you the lantern; the road is seen, the long, white road, going with the statutory stars, 'It's only die rope'. He shows it to you. And you touch your eyes and know there never was a serpent. Where was it, where, I ask you? The poet who saw the rope as serpent became the serpent, and so a saint: Now, the saint is shown that his sainthood was identification, not realization. The actual, the real has no name. The rope is no rope to itself (232-33).

And, Narayan and Rao have many things in common. All these three 'the Big Three' as William Walsh called them, were influenced by Gandhi and tried to make a myth around Gandhi in their novels. All these three lived abroad, and were exposed to western life and culture. Unlike diasporic writers they never thought of 'imaginary homeland' — they were firmly rooted in India. All of them won Sahitya Akademi Award for their novels — R.K. Narayan for *The Guide* in 1960, Raja Rao for *The Serpent and the Rope* in 1963 and Mulk Raj Anand for *Morning Face* in 1971. They also won many other awards at home and abroad. For example, Raja Rao got the prestigious Neustadt Literary Prize in U.S.A. for his novel, *The Chessmaster and His Moves.*

If we compare Anand, Narayan and Raja Rao with the novelists of nineteen eighties and nineties say, Vikram Seth, Vikram Chandra, Shashi Tharoor, Arundhati Roy, Kiran Nagarkar, Upamanyu Chatterjee, and Amitav Ghosh, we find that the great trio have nothing to fear. If these new novelists have made innovations in terms of themes and techniques, the great trio have done that in their own way. The work of the new novelists is marked with social realism, psychological realism, mythic realism, East-West encounter, immigration and magic realism, Arundhati Roy's experiment with language in terms of new coinages and code mixing is admirable. Here, we should recall Anand's use of Indian words (Punjabi words) by way of code mixing is no mean achievement. R.K. Narayan's humour is missing in the contemporary Indian English novel, and who can surpass Raja Rao's metaphysical ideas embodied in Indian tradition? Shashi Tharoor's *The Great Indian Novel* based on *The Mahabharata* pales into insignificance when placed by the side of *The Serpent and the Rope*.

This paper has a two-fold objective: one, it seeks to establish that Indian English fiction began not with the anxiety of Indianness but with an assertion of it and two, the attempts to win attention to the founding fathers of Indian English fiction — Mulk Raj Anand, R.K. Narayan and Raja Rao — who deserve to be canonized. The greatness of Raja Rao will become explicit if his statements are read alongside Chinua Achebe. Let us recall Raja Rao's 'preface' to *Kanthapura* cited in the paper earlier, and read it with Achebe's statement made in course of interview with Kwame Anthony Appiah in the following words:

> I'm an Ibo writer because this is my basic culture; Nigerian, African and a writer...no, black first, then a writer. Each of these identities does call for a certain kind of commitment on my part. I must see what it is to be black — and this means being sufficiently intelligent to know how the world is moving, and how the black people fare in this world. This is what it means to be black. Or an African — the same: what does Africa mean to the world? When you see an African, what does it mean to a white man? (73). (qtd. in C.L. Innes, *The Cambridge Introduction to Postcolonial Literature in English*, 208)

Ania Loomba makes an apt observation on Achebe's assertion of his African identity in the following words:

> Achebe invokes the creative hybridity of African writers who moulded English to their experience rather than the other way round,

and concludes that

> I feel that the English language will be able to carry the weight of my African experience. But it will have to be a new English, still in full communion with its ancestral home but altered to suit its new African surroundings. (qtd. in Loomba 91)

It is clear that both Rao and Achebe have asserted their national identity while writing novels in the colonial period (*Kanthapura* in 1938 and *Things Fall Apart* in 1958, nine years before Indian Independence and two years before Nigerian Independence respectively) these novelists were not apologetic about writing in English. They wrote their nation and asserted their nationality boldly and proudly. C.L. Innes makes an apt observation on Rao's attempt to create an Indian consciousness through writings in English in the following passage:

> The Indian novelist Raja Rao declares in the foreword to his first prose fiction, *Kanthapura,* There is no village in India, however mean, that has not a rich *sthala-purana*, or legendary history, of its own.... One such story from the contemporary annals of a village I have tried to tell. Published in 1938, *Kanthapura* narrates, from the point of view of a spirited and garrulous South Indian grandmother, the effects of Mahatma Gandhi's ideas on the varied inhabitants of a small village in India. The voice of a narrator allows Rao to link traditional oral narrative, myths and legends, and social structures to create an impression of rural Indian which is also a microcosm of the nation as a whole, and the ways in which the Gandhi movement brings change. It is, as Robert Fraser remarks, "an early attempt, in Homi Bhabha's words, to "write the nation": to depict in vivid outlines, the writings, the jostlings and the uneasy birth pangs of the Indian collective consciousness". (38)

Raja Rao uses traditional stories, myths and beliefs of Indian people to write novels in English. Elleke Boehmer has a word of praise for Rao when she says, "Rao has composed a narrative in which story — line, generic structure, and nationalist resistance politics mutually reflect upon one another," (137). Mulk Raj Anand and R.K. Narayan too use Indian social conscious and popular beliefs to write fiction in English. All three of them tried to create a living myth of Gandhi in their fiction. We can now sit back and reflect upon the contribution of Anand, Narayan and Rao to Indian English fiction with satisfaction that they have laid the foundation of it and paved the way for other Indian English fiction writers to extend its horizon beyond the frontiers of the country.

It is true that recent Indian English novel has gained acceptance both at home and abroad. The migratory movement by writers all over the world has widened the horizon of fiction. If we look back, we also find that the 'great trio' has lived both at home and abroad and had exposure to English as a spoken language in the west. Their fiction can stand comparison with fiction in English written elsewhere in the world in the twentieth century. To conclude, I should say that as far as Indian English fiction is concerned, Anand, Narayan and Rao are the canon worthy of our emulation.

WORKS CITED

Anand, Mulk Raj. "Looking Back". *Journal of Literature and Aesthetics:* 4 : 1-2 (Jan.-Dec. 2004).

Appiah, Kwame Anthony. (cited) *In My Father's House.* New York: OUP, 1992.

Elleke, Boehmer. *Colonial and Postcolonial Literature.* Oxford: OUP, 1995.

Innes, C.L. *The Cambridge Introduction to Postcolonial Literatures in English.* New Delhi: Cambridge University Press India Pvt. Ltd., 2007.

Fisher, MarLene. *The Wisdom of the Heart: A Study of the Works of Mulk Raj Anand.* New Delhi: Sterling Publishers Private Limited, 1980.

Loomba, Ania. *Colonialism/Postcolonialism.* New York: Routledge, 1988.

Kohli, Surest. *Journal of Literature and Aesthetics.* 4 : 1-2 (Jan.-Dec. 2004).

Narasimhaiah, C.D. *The Swan and the Eagle: Essays on Indian English Literature.* New Delhi: Vision Books, 1999.

Rao, Raja. "Foreword". *Kanthapura.* Delhi: OUP, 1989.

Walsh, William. *Indian Literature in English.* London: Longman, 1990.

R.K. Narayan: A Critical Appreciation. New Delhi: Allied Publishers Pvt. Ltd., 1983.

Williams, H.M. *Indo-Anglian Literature: 1800-1970: A Survey.* Delhi: Orient Longman, 1976.

This paper is the revised version of the author's keynote address at U.G.C. Seminar organised by the Department of English, Khaira College, Khaira, Orissa, on October 07-08-2009.

23

Interrogating Sexuality and Reading Shiv K. Kumar's *Two Mirrors at the Ashram**

As I have observed in my book, *Postmodern Indian English Literature,*

> Kumar's art of writing fiction is influenced by Joseph Conrad. He chooses his characters from among the people whom he knows and only changes the proper names to avoid controversy. An element of autobiography is clearly discernible, and he makes a confession of it in course of an interview given to Saraswati Sabu. "I must confess that often I have written my stories with the names of original characters". (JASL 237) (74)

Shiv K. Kumar, creative writer, translator and literary critic of repute, is a Sahitya Akademi Award Winner for his book of verse, *Trapfalls in the Sky* for the year 1987. A playwright, short-story Writer, a Cambridge University Ph.D., on *Bergson and Stream of Consciousness Novel,* a distinguished Professor of English and Padma Bhushan, Kumar has four novels to his credit.

Two Mirrors at the Ashram depicts the life of Rajesh Sahni, a novelist and a pleasure seeker who finally becomes a seeker of truth after coming in contact with the Swamiji in the Ashram. A novelist is also true to his characters and honest to his feelings. Rajesh moves from place to place in search of characters and makes love to several women without marrying any one of them. Neera, Kulvinder, Sekeena, Susan — these are the women in Rajesh's life at different point of time. He made love to them and ran away.

---

* This chapter is the revised version of my lecture delivered at the national seminar on "Twenty-First Century Indian English Fiction" organized by the Department of English, Mahatma Gandhi Kashi Vidyapith, Varanasi on 5 February 2011.

Rajesh says, "Immediately after I've had a woman, I return to my writing — my real mistress, jealous and possessive" (37).

Both Rajesh and the Swamiji whose real name was Abhay Khanna became each other's confessor. The Swamiji confesses that he was in love with a Muslim girl, Nasreen, who denounced his love. And again he saw his mother in bed with his uncle. So he renounced the world and came to Vellore, where a South Indian Philanthropist gave him land to build his Ashram. Rajesh confesses that his first love was also a Muslim girl, Sakeena who studied medicine. She too refused to marry Rajesh on the plea that, "Won't our children to torn between Id and Diwali, She'd say — between her denial of idol-worship and my gods and goddesses" (81).

The violence caused in the body because of youth, finds a parallel in the physical violence caused by the assassination in Indira Gandhi. Chapter XVII begins with the graphic description of that violence.

> All hell broke loose in Delhi on the morning of 4 November, a little after nine I began to hear slogans just outside my window — 'Death to the killers of Indira Gandhi.... Har Har Mahadev!' It seemed as if every Sikh was an accomplice in the assassination, and the Hindu pantheon had given its blessings for the fanatic desire to wipe out the entire Sikh community. As I looked out, I saw hordes of men, armed with crowbars, hatchets, lathis, knives and daggers. On the curb were some cycle-rickshaws loaded with petrol cane. (*Two Mirrors at the Ashram* 114)

No doubt, Kumar is handling two difficult characters, Swami and Rajesh Sahni in the novel, in an interview with Mukund Padmanabhan, he says:

> You would have noticed that my protagonist is a pretty unusual man. A boozer, a womaniser, an agnostic. So is my Swami, an unusual character. My protagonist enjoys debunking the Swami and there is a transformation, which I feel is very critical and natural...Rajesh Sahani doesn't lend himself to any woman. I think I have tried to handle his character in a very restrained manner. He is a detached character from the very beginning. Women pursue him, but here is a man who is loyal to only one woman — his mother. When he seduces Susan, it is just to score over the Swami. It is a thing in his psyche. The only truth that he perceives and realizes is creative writing. (*The Hindu*, Monday 26 Feb. 2007)

No doubt, Kumar is giving a free play to sexuality in this novel. In course of an interview to me, when I suggested that, "a hint of love and sex could have been better than the explicit description of the physical union", he said:

> I agree with your observation that I have often "lapsed" into an explicit description of love and sex. As you have rightly observed that Arundhati Roy also lets herself go in the last scene (in *The God of Small Things*) may be, because sex is such an over-whelming thing that it tempts even such saints as Vishwamitra. Physical aspect of experience is also fundamental to all human beings. No wonder, we have raised such temples as Konark and Khajuraho as our tribute to Kamadeva. (*Studies in Postcolonial Literature* 244)

Kumar handles erotic images in poetic language, which is the saving grace of the novel. Here are a few examples:

> Fingers are indeed one of the most sensitive parts of the human body. They are like the keyboard of a piano, the brass-stops of a sitar. Like a blind man reading his Braille, I was now lost in my realm of imagination, mapping out the landscape of her legs and thighs, the contours of her breasts and the white spaces around her pink nipples. I imagined my fingers groping their way down to her waistline, and lower still to the point where all journeys end, where man descends into those dark caverns of peace, silence — and ecstasy. (*Two Mirrors at the Ashram* 61)
>
> Oh God, I said to myself, she's really stirred up. I responded by unbuttoning her blouse, her skirt. As our bodies touched, they almost burnt into flame. Deeper and deeper, we plunged into each other till I felt myself on the edge of eternity. I imagined the gods in Indraloka being consumed with jealousy. In the silence of the dawn, I fancied myself touching the epicenter of the universe. Not a word spoken, only fitful breathing, mute sounds, and our hands and lips communing. (*Two Mirrors at the Ashram* 67)

Kumar knows, as he tells in the novel that, "the truth reveals itself in the first cry of a new-born babe and in the last words of a dying man, that it is love experienced only at the moment of orgasm" (172) and therefore, he tries to reach divinity through body. He is like W.B. Yeats, who tries to transcend the body through sex and achieve the ultimate reality. Mythological references to Maneka and Viswamitra, are efforts in his direction.

Attitude to love (human love) brings a dichotomy between men and women. In patriarchal society certain norms were prescribed for women such as 'chastity' and 'constancy', without which love becomes lust for women and hence, they were looked down upon by men. Women have reacted against this patriarchal attitude by asserting that men don't know women. The bodies being different, men and women experience love and sex differently. One is not a Tiresias to say who among the two — man or woman — enjoys sex more. The emphasis on body brought out psychological difference between men and women in their attitude to love and life.

Previously class, gender and race were considered the norm to measure literature. Now a fourth category is added to it, namely sexuality Michel Foucault's multi-volume *History of Sexuality* (1976-84) became the master text for the study of sexuality. American Queer theorist, Judith Butler highlighted sexuality in literature in the book titled, *Bodies that Matter: On the Discursive Limits of Sex* (1993). Our fate lies not in our stars but in our body. This is the new mantra with which the novelists in 1990s and after have portrayed their characters. According to Alan Sinfield, "Sexuality is an unstable construct in our societies and hence produces endless textual work, such as awkward issue has continually to be revisited, disavowed, rediscovered, affirmed, closure, by definition, is always potentially unsatisfactory" (qtd. in *Bertens* 225). Shiv K. Kumar's *Two Mirrors at the Ashram* is a bright example.

Like Donne and Yeats, Kumar accepts body and wants us to transcend the body at some point of time to realise spirituality. Here are a few illustrations from the text:

> Swamiji, is it a sin to feel conscious of one's body?; She (Susan) asked.... No, my dear, the body is not sinful, nor is it evil to think of one's physical being. A beautiful human body is God's supreme creation, for isn't He an artist too? (p. 40)

Kumar wonders which is real India: Sexuality or spirituality? And Susan writes to Rajesh:

> Hi! I hate India! It's both a muddle and mystery. Your Janus — faced Country baffles me. Which of its two faces is real — spiritual or sexuality? Tirupati or Khajuraho? (p. 147)

The echo of E.M. Forster rings in our ears. Kumar being a poet at heart and critic in the head there are many lines of poetry (in fact, from his own poetry) in the text. Moreover, references to Eliot and Shakespeare are frequent.

One finds many a Freudian slip in the novel. Rajesh's background, love for the mother and his father's association with Arya Samaj, migration from Pakistan to India are cases in point. In this connection, I am reminded of Kenneth Patchen's words, "I think you will agree that I am alive in every part of this book; turn back twenty, thirty, one hundred pages — I am back here...there can only be one action: What a man is, when you have understood this, you will be through with novels". This is true of Kumar, the man behind fiction. Like E.M. Forster's *A Passage to India,* here Kumar reviews Christianity and Hinduism and makes apt observations Here are two examples.

> Let me (Swamiji tells Rajesh) tell you that I also know that just one confession does not absolve one of one's sins — unlike the Catholics who believe that you can get away with even single admission of guilt.... Hinduism in this respect, is must more demanding. We believe that we must atone for our sins with constant penance. Even then our sins will follow us into the next life, in the form of Karma. There is always rigorous punishment for our sins. (75-76)

...We Hindus have convenient explanation for everything — What you've done in our previous life conditions your present (*Two Mirrors at the Ashram*, 91).

The poet in Kumar takes the better of the novelist in him in describing the beauty of woman Kumar writes:

> She (Susan) was like a Greek vase in cut glass, a statute in marble. She looked like one of the apsaras from the Indraloka, a reincarnation of Maneka. (*Two Mirrors at the Ashram*, 55)

The significance of the title is symbolic, One mirror is the 'Self' though which we see ourselves, the other mirror is that of the 'spirit' which we can realise through renunciation. Thus we move between two mirrors in trying to see our image — it is a journey from body to spirit, from self to soul, a journey which we all have to undertake in order to understand the Truth, which alone triumphs. The ending is significant:

> *Let there be peace on earth, ...*
>
> *Om Shanti, Shanti this Shanti*! (223).

The echo of Eliot is unmistakable.

As we go through the novel, we experience a kind of transformation in our heart, if we are honest to our feelings and emotions.

Sex is not presented in the novel as a thing in itself but as a means to transcend reality and attain spirituality. Western Critics, Queer theorists like Judith Butler, Eve Kosofsky Sedgwick, Jonathan Dollimore, Alan Sinfield and others stop at the body as if it is the ultimate thing. Kumar goes beyond it by invoking, 'Shanti' through the realization of the body. There is lies the trimph of the novel and the novelist.

In *Politics, Philosophy, Culture,* Michel Foucault asks important questions about sex:

> How is it in a society like ours, sexuality is not simply a means of reproducing the species, the family and the individual? Not simply a means to obtain pleasure and enjoyment? How has sexuality come to be considered the privileged place where our deepest 'truth' is read and expressed? (qtd. in Brown 81)

Speaking about how the Greeks dealt with sexual ethics, Foucault argues:

> The great difference in sexual ethics for the Greeks was not between people who prefer women or boys or have sex in this way or another, but was a question of quantity and of activity and passivity. Are you a slave of your desires or their master? (Rabinow 349)

Kumar has aptly depicted how sex leads to our deepest truth and how mastering it a person attains spirituality.

The novel is foregrounded in Indian Culture. Hindu Philosophy of life is incorporated into the texture of the novel to explain the Karma (the action) of the principal characters, intertextual references to English poets, Shakespeare, Donne, Yeats and Eliot are discernable throughout the novel. There is an assimilation of the East and the West in terms of references to history and myth that transcends the space of the novel. The novelist, as it were, enters the text through a character to justify his position and establish his point of view Helen, Cleopatra, Venus, Menaka — they were all his miracles. His artefacts, says the novelist and then philosophizes that, "it's just that humans should also have the spiritual strength to transcend their physical being, to rise higher to Brahman. The body can be both our salvation as well as our damnation" (40). The ending of the novel fulfills the authorial intention by bringing peace (however contrived it may be) to the human heart and mind, Swamiji tells Rajesh: "You seem to understand me.... But then aren't we now two mirrors reflecting each other" (205). The novel has come 'full circle', it's better as it is.

WORKS CITED

Bertens, Hans. *Literary Theory: The Basics.* London: Routledge, 2001.

Brown, Alison Leigh. *On Foucault: A Critical Introduction.* Singapore: Thomson Asia Pvt. Ltd., 2004.

Das, Bijay Kumar. *Postmodern Indian English Literature.* New Delhi: Atlantic Publishers, 2006, Print.

Khan, M.Q. and Bijay Kumar Das, eds. *Studies in Postcolonial Literature.* New Delhi: Atlantic Publishers, 2007, Print.

Kumar, Shiv K. *Two Mirrors at the Ashram.* New Delhi: Penguin, 2006, Print.

——, Interview. *The Hindu.* Monday 26 Feb. 2007.

Rabinow, Paul. *The Foucault Reader.* New York: Pantheon Books, 1984.

Sabu, Saraswati. "Shiv K. Kumar: An Interview". *Journal of South Asia Literature.* 25 : 2 Summer, Fall, 1990 : 227-38.

24

Moving Frontiers of Postcolonial Studies

Post-colonialism is a protean term which defies exact definition. It is linked with several other questions. One, when does post-colonialism begin? Two, who are the critics or theoreticians behind this growth of this term and area of studies? Three, does it lead to neo-colonialism? Post colonialism owes its origin to the gaining of independence by former European and British colonies. The Commonwealth (i.e., the British Commonwealth) was established in 1948. Historically the 1948 marks the beginning of post-colonial studies and post-colonial literature. That is why Ireland and United States are excluded from the British Commonwealth and are not part of postcolonial studies.

The prefix 'post' in the word post-colonial is problematic. In one sense it means 'after' the end of colonialism. Ella Shohat explains the terms clearly in the following words:

> Echoing 'post-modernity,' 'post-coloniality' marks a contemporary, situation, condition or epoch. The prefix 'post,' then, aligns 'post-colonialism' with a series of other 'posts' — 'post-structuralism,' 'post-modernism,' 'post-marxism,' 'post-feminism,' 'post-deconstructionism' — all sharing the notion of a movement beyond. Yet while these 'posts' refer largely to the supersession of outmoded philosophical, aesthetic and political theories, the 'post-colonial' implies both going beyond anti-colonial nationalist theory as well as a movement beyond a specific point in history, that, of colonialism and Third World nationalist struggles. In that sense the prefix 'post' aligns the 'post-colonial' with another genre of 'posts' — 'postwar,' 'post-cold war,' 'post-independence,' 'post-revolution' — all of which underline a passage into a new period and a closure of a certain historical event or age, officially stamped with dates. (*Mongia* 323)

The term post-colonial historically means the end of colonialism in whatever form (i.e., by conquest or settlement) and critically means post-structuralist in approach, while post-colonial literature is a new nomenclature for Commonwealth literature. Elleke Boehmer makes a valid observation in the following words:

> the term post-colonial still draws support for its usefulness as an umbrella term, a way of bracketing together the literatures written in those countries which were once colonies of Britain. The United States is excluded because it won independence long before other colonial places, and its literature has therefore followed a very different trajectory. Ireland too is believed to represent a different case because its history has been so closely and so long linked to that of Britain. (4)

As stated above, different critics have different notions of post colonialism as an interdisciplinary study involving ideology, society, economics, literature and so on. If Russell Jacoby opines that post-colonial is the "the latest catchall term to dazzle the academic mind" (30), Ania Loomba defines it differently:

> It is true that the term 'postcolonialism' has become so heterogeneous and diffuse that it is impossible to satisfactorily describe what its study might entail. This difficulty is partly due to the interdisciplinary nature of post-colonial studies which may range from literary analysis to research in the archives of colonial government, from the critique of medical texts to economic theory, and usually combine these and other areas. (XII)

For Homi K. Bhabha "the term postcolonial is increasingly, used to describe that form of social criticism that bears witness to those unequal and uneven process of representation by which the historical experience of the once colonized Third World comes to be framed in the West" (qtd. in Mongia 1).

Postcolonial study is a multi-disciplinary activity. It is an international movement cutting across countries, races and continents. In the words of C.L. Innes, "it is the amalgamation of Commonwealth literary studies, Black Studies, and Third World Studies that has produced contemporary postcolonial literary studies..." (5). Postcolonial literary study is concerned with self-representation by the former colonized writers.

The question that baffles our minds is, who are the critics that shaped postcolonial theory? Four names' occur in this context: they are Frantz Fanon, Edward Said, Gayatri Spivak Chakravorty and Homi K. Bhabha. We may also recall the names of two well-known novelists, Raja Rao and Chinua Achebe in this context. Postcolonial critics like Edward Said, Gayatri Spivak (nee Chakravorty) and Homi K. Bhabha were influenced by European intellectuals like Helene Cixous, Jacques Derrida, Jacques Lacan, Jean-Paul Sarte, and Michel Foucault. Frantz Fanon whose origin lies in Africa was born in Martinique, a former colony of France in 1925 and was taught by Jacques Lacan. His book, *Black Skin, White Masks* (1952) is a psychological analysis of racism in colonial period. C.L. Innes makes an interesting observation on this book:

> This is a remarkable personal account and analysis of the effect of the 'colonial gaze' — of being seen, defined and stereotyped by the Europeans whose culture is deemed to be superior and to have greater authority than the cultures of Africa and the Caribbean. European appearance and culture is assumed to be the norm by which others are judged, making all others 'abnormal' and either exotic or inferior or both. (6)

Let us examine Fanon's statement:

> There is a fact: White men consider themselves superior to black men. There is another fact: Black men want to prove to white men at all costs,... the richness of their thought, the equal value of their intellect. How do we extricate ourselves? (10)

Fanon believes that African writing is governed by magnitude, and therefore, African writers write back to the centre by asserting their identity. The terms 'magnitude' is an ideology based on 'colonialist and racialist thinking' (Innes 7). Sartre's 'Preface' titled 'Black Orpheus' to an anthology of African poetry edited by Leopold Senghor influences Fanon's idea of negritude. Sartre writes:

> In fact, Negritude appears to be the weak stage of a dialectical progression: the theoretical and practical application of white supremacy is the thesis: the position of Negritude as antithetical value is the moment of negativity. But this negative moment is not sufficient in itself and the blacks who employ it well know it; they know that it serves to pave the way for the synthesis or the realization of a race less society. Thus, Negritude is dedicated to its own destruction, it is passage and not objective, means and not the ultimate goal. At the moment the black Orpheus most directly embraces this Eurydice, he feels her slip away from between his arms (Allen 50-51).

If *Black Skin, White Mask* (1952) centres around African identity *The Wretched of the Earth* (1961 French and 1965 English) concentrates on Algerians' struggle to liberate their country from French colonialism. Here Fanon makes a psychological study of both the colonized and the colonizers. In the words of Leela Gandhi:

> Fanon's *Black Skin, White Masks* invokes both Hegel and Sartre to diagnose the condition of the colonised slave as a symptom of 'imitativeness'. In Hegel's paradigm, the slave must ultimately turn away from the master to forge the meaning of his existence in labour. He can only regain his integrity by working over the density of matter to which he is henceforth confined. However, as Fanon argues, the racialisation of the master-slave relationship breeds a new and disabling discontent. For whenever the black slave faces the White master, she now experiences the disruptive charge of envy and desire (20).

In *The Wretched of the Earth,* Fanon argues:

> No, we do not want to catch up with anyone. What we want to do is to go forward all the time, night and day, in the company of Man, in the company of all men ... It is a question of the Third World starting a new history of Man, a history which will have regard to the sometimes prodigious theses which Europe has put forward, but which will also not forget Europe's crimes (Fanon 1968: 314-15).

Frantz Fanon's book, *The Wretched of the Earth* influenced African and Caribbean Writers to assert their identity and nationality with vehemence. C.L. Innes makes a pertinent observation in the following lines:

> While Bhabha, Said and Spivak, and more recently Kwame Anthony Appiah, Paul Gilroy, Édouard Glissant and Stuart Hall, have most strongly influenced the critics of postcolonial literatures, it is Fanon who has perhaps most influenced writers — particularly in Africa and the Caribbean, and particularly in the earlier phases of resistance to colonization and the creation of a national consciousness. (And for this reason this study places particular emphasis on Fanon's analysis of colonialism and its effects.) *Ngugi* has written about Fanon, and his later fiction and drama follows many of Fanon's precepts regarding the role of a revolutionary writer. Walcott's *Dream on Monkey Mountain* can be read

> as a dramatization of Fanon's analysis of black subjectivity in Black Skin, White Masks. Lamming's novel *In the Castle of My Skin* (1953), published one year after Fanon's first book, shows its influence in the title as well as the portrayal of the internalization of racism by Barbadians. (12-13)

Anthony Kwame corroborates this in the book, *In my Father's House: Africa in the Philosophy of Culture:*

> All aspects of contemporary African cultural life including music and some sculpture and painting, even some writings with which the west is largely not familiar — have been influenced — often powerfully — by the transaction of African societies through colonialism, but they are not all in the relevant sense postcolonial. For the post in post-colonialism like the post in postmodernism is the post of the space — clearing gesture. (240-41)

I have referred to the observations made by different critics and quoted a few of them to show what they mean by post-colonialism, particularly with reference to Africa. Post-colonialism is a broad term and postcolonial study is an all-inclusive discipline that defies exact location, and time. That is the reasons why Australian Critics like Ashcroft, Griffiths and Tiffin in their book, *The Empire Writes Back* use the term 'post-colonial' with a hyphen "to cover all the cultures affected by the imperial process from the moment of colonialization to the present day" (2). They further stated their point of view in the following words:

> *The Empire Writes Back* argued that the term post-colonial might provide a different way of understanding colonial relations: no longer a simple binary opposition, black colonized vs. white colonizers; Third World vs. the West, but an engagement with all the varied manifestations of colonial power, including those in settler colonies. The attempt to define the post-colonial by putting barriers between those who may be called 'post-colonial' and the rest, contradicts the capacity of post-colonial theories to demonstrate the complexity of the operation of imperial discourse. We have suggested above that we need to ground the post-colonial in the 'fact' of colonial experience. But it is probably impossible to say absolutely where that experience and its effects begin or end. If we take the example of slavery, we can see that it was clearly a major incentive for imperial expansion, but it

> was also in existence before and after that period. Can we really say that slavery and its effects (e.g. the black diaspora) are not a legitimate element of the colonial and should not be part of what we study to try and understand how colonialism worked? (200)

Post-colonialism, being an off-shoot of colonialism varies from country to country. That is because colonies were set up both by conquest and settlement. If Australia, Canada were colonies by settlement, India was a British colony by conquest. In Australia, the British established a penal colony in 1788 and took possession of the entire continent in 1829. These white people who came to Australia deprived the Aborigines of their own rights. After the World War II, a large number of immigrants from Europe and particularly from the United Kingdom came to Australia. It was only in 1967 that the Aborigines got citizenship in their own country. In India the foundation of the British Empire was laid in 1757 after Robert Clive defeated the Nawab of Bengal in the Battle of Plassey. But India came under the direct rule of the British crown and became a colony in 1858 after the First War of Independence in 1857. The whole of India was a British Colony only for 90 years, after which it got freedom in 1947. The two cases cited here, Australia and India represent two dimensions of colonialization. Unlike the Australian Aborigines, Indians were never deprived of their citizenship in their own country. No doubt that India imbibed British laws, literature and to some extent British Culture during the colonial period, but it retained its native literatures and culture in spite of the onslaught of the British.

Moving from post colonialism to postcolonial studies, one is reminded of the vastness of the subject which is interdisciplinary in nature. Before I turn to evaluate postcolonial literature let us examine two important statements. One, to a question, "When is postcoloniality supposed to have begun"? Arif Dirlik replied, "When Third World intellectuals have arrived in First world academe?" (qtd. in Mongia 2). Two, the term postcolonial, "is simply a polite way of saying not-write, not-Europe, or perhaps not-Europe-but-inside-Europe" (Ahmad 8). The first statement of Dirlik means that postcoloniality is a migratory movement from the former colonies to the west (particularly to UK and USA). The second statement means that postcolonial is an off-shoot of colonial and also neo-colonial. In other words, postcolonialism refers to migrants, immigrants, expatriates and diasporans. For example, during the colonial era, the people of lower strata of society were sent to other parts of the world as indentured labourers. V.S. Naipaul's grandfather went to Trinidad from Mumabi during that period. In the postcolonial era, our intellectuals, writers, scientists, engineers, doctors and intellectuals go to UK, USA and the west for improving their prospects and gaining international visibility. Thus, they became neo-colonials in the west.

Neil Lazarus explains the growth of Postcolonial Studies in a lucid language in the following passage:

> Before the late 1970s, there was no field of academic specialization that went by the name of "postcolonial studies". Today, by contrast, postcolonial studies occupy a position of legitimacy and even relative prestige, not only within the Euro-American academy but also in universities in many countries of the formerly colonized world. Postcolonial studies centers have been set up in many institutions — mostly linked to departments of literature but inviting significant input also from scholars based in cultural studies, history, anthropology, art, and other disciplines — and innumerable conferences and colloquia have been — convened. Advertisements for academic positions in postcolonial studies have become fairly routine. Several dedicated academic journals have begun publication, and any number of other journals have devoted special issues to "postcolonial literature," "postcolonial theory," or "the postcolonial condition." Literary anthologies and critical readers, as well as compilations of essays in the field, have been published, and many of these have sold very well,' And in addition to the hundred; of scholarly books and thousands of critical articles that might be Said to be in the field or indeed to make it up from the works of Edward W. Said, Homi K. Bhabha, Benedict Anderson, V.Y. Mudimbe, Peter Hulme, and Gayatri Chakravorty Spivak to the mass of less influential work on particular authors, periods, situations, events, and concepts — there has recently emerged a burgeoning production of scholarly texts that take the *critical field itself* as their object (1).

Bruce King explains the importance of the age of postcolonialism and its impact on both the former colonies as well as the colonizers leading to the growth of new literatures in English in the following lines:

> Age of Postcolonialism was brought about by the new political and economic importance of former colonies after the Second

> World War and the rapid spread of communications and international business during the last third of the twentieth century. Local cultures in the process of modernization and under-going the crisis of identity that accompanies hasty transformation were increasingly, if uneasily, in direct contact with an expanding Western culture and economy themselves undergoing mercuric changes including their relationships to former colonies and their own crisis of identity. The results were liberating, energizing, at times contradictory, as traditions crumbled and were constructed. During the first phase national political and cultural liberation was the goal. In the second phase cultural and economic liberation became the ideal for groups and movements within and across national boundaries, including black nationalism, feminism, and recent immigrants, each of which claimed its own literature. Although a similar process could be seen in the cultures of other former imperial languages, it was in English-speaking nations that this development most rapidly and visibly took place. 'English literature' now meant such writers as Wole Soyinka, Chinua Achebe, Nadine Gordimer, I.M. Coetzee, Derek Walcott, V.S. Naipaul, Margaret Atwood, Michael Ondaatje, Les Murray, Salman Rushdie, Vikram Seth, Anita Desai and Janet Frame, none of whom was British, American, or even Irish. As English was the main international language of business, science, politics, travel, education and social change, even nations that were not former English colonies produced English-language writers. The new national literature, national multicultural literatures and International English literature were parts of a developing urban global culture, produced by international politics, communications and a world-wide economy, which in clouded a heightened awareness of difference partly to assert identity. (1)

Having defined what constitutes postcolonialism and the area of postcolonial studies by taking into consideration, the views expressed by critics, let me explore the frontiers of postcolonial literature and criticism. What is postcolonial literature? Literature presupposes a language and the nationality of the writer. In India if English becomes the medium of postcolonial literature, then it excluded indigenous literatures written in Hindi, Oriya, Bengali, Telugu, Tamil etc. This is also the case with some other former British colonies. Secondly, each literature presupposes a nation to which its writer belongs. W.B. Yeats makes it clear in his poem "Under Ben Bulben":

Many times man lives and dies
Between his two eternities,
That of race and of soul
And ancient Ireland knew it all.

We can define postcolonial literature as an international literature written in English by the people whose country was once upon a time a colony of a European country. That means to describe someone a postcolonial writer, is to mention a period, a historical background that reveals the change from colonial to postcolonial era. Period wise, Post World War II may be taken as a dividing period between colonial and postcolonial literature. Let us take the case of Indian English writers in the postcolonial era. They belong to three groups: One group of writers write in English and live in India (Jayanta Mahapatra, Kamala Das, Shashi Deshpande, Arundhati Roy, Mahesh Dattani and a host of others), the second group of writers are expatriate, immigrant and diasporic writers of Indian origin (Bharathi Mukherjee, R. Parthasarathy, Kiran Desai, Salman Rushdie and so on) and the third group of writers such as Amitav Ghosh, Vikram Seth, Anita Desai and so on, who divide their time between India and the west. What's common among them? English language and homeland (now or before). Thus, we can say that postcolonial literature is a transnational literature written in English language.

Coming to the treatment of themes of postcolonial literature written in different countries and continents such as India, Africa, Australia, Canada, West Indies and in UK and USA by the writers of former colonies, we can say that search for identity — personal as well as national — feminist assertion of rights personal as well as political and the interplay of local and global issues are some of the key themes that occur in prose, poetry and fiction. If Raja Rao and Chinua Achebe have asserted their rights to use English language in their own way to bring their native tradition and socio-political situation alive in the modern period, the postcolonial writers in 1980s and beyond being conscious of double audience — one at home, their own people and second, the international readers, abroad have chosen transnational themes. Writers like Margaret Atwood, Anita Desai, Vikram Seth, Kiran Desai, V.S. Naipaul, Derek Walcott, Michael Ondaatje, Salman Rushdie, and a host of others have written keeping in mind the double audience and became successful. It is here that postcolonial literature differs from Anglo-American literature. Feminism and multiculturalism became an integral part of postcolonial literature. Anita Desai, Margaret

Atwood, Arundhati Roy and a host of others have tried to make an assertion of feminine the Patriarchal world. Atwoods's *Surfacing* and Roy's *The God of Small Things* can be cited as examples.

Postcolonialism and Feminism have something in common. That is both postcolonial writers and feminist writers are pre-occupied with thought of making their voice heard by those who once dominated them and subjected them to harsh treatment. Deepika Bahri makes a pertinent observation on the closeness between postcolonial and feminist studies:

> Feminist studies and postcolonial studies sometimes find themselves in a mutually investigative and interactive relation with each other, especially when either becomes too narrowly focused, i.e., when feminist perspectives are blind to issues pertaining to colonialism and the international division of labor and when postcolonial studies fails to include gender in its analysis. On the one hand, thus, feminists sometimes complain that analyses of colonial or postcolonial exits fail to consider gender issues adequately, bracketing them in favor of attention to supposedly more significant issues, such as empire building, decolonization, and liberation struggle (in the colonial context), and nation-building (in the postcolonial context) (Lazaras 201).

It may be mentioned here that both postcolonial theory and feminist theory seek to give voice to the marginalized people. The question of representation, voice and resistance to colonialists are major concerns of postcolonial theory and feminist theory.

Postcolonial theory (say, criticism) has an impact on postcolonial writers in different parts of the world. African and Caribbean writers are much influenced by Frantz Fanon's theory, while Indian English Writers are drawn towards the writings of Said, Spivak and Bhabha. Australian and Canadian writers have different priorities in their writings. Moreover, writers of Postcolonial diaspora who live in UK and mostly in USA are more influenced by neo-colonialism and the writings of Said, Spivak and Bhabha. *The Routledge Dictionary of Literary Terms* has stated that "Postcolonialism is the 'Cultural logic' of neo-colonialism Writ small in the language of metropolitan academy. Certainly, the theoretical sophistication of post-colonial theory, and its sometimes difficult and opaque language, extends itself to criticism that postcolonialism is an overelaborate, abstracted and self-indulgent form of cultural analysis that does little to address the politically urgent problems of formerly colonized world" (184-85).

In the concluding part of the paper I would like to reflect on postcolonial theory and criticism. It has two dimensions: Postcolonial literary history and postcolonial criticism. Literary histories such as *Indian Writing in English* (1962) (which had gone into several editions) by K.R.S. Iyengar, *A History of Indian English Literature* (1982) by M.K. Naik, *Indian English Literature 1980-2000* (2001) by M.K. Naik and Shyamala A. Narayan, *Post-Modern Indian English Literature* (1999, Second Edition 2007) by Bijay Kumar Das, *A History of Australian Literature* by H.M. Green, *The Oxford History of Australian Literature* (1981) by Leonie Kramer and *The Oxford History of New Zealand Literature in English* (1991) by Terry Strum are meant for interpreting postcolonial literature in India, Australia and New Zealand. Similar literary histories are available on Canadian and Caribbean postcolonial literature. When it comes to the postcolonial theory proper, we turn to the works of Edward Said, Gayatri Spivak Chakravorty, and Homi K. Bhabha. Here, the 'holy trinity' (as they are called) of postcolonial theory turn from literary criticism proper to culture and imperialism to explicate postcolonial literature. Postcolonialism criticism is a social criticism which lays emphasis more on culture than on literature. It is interdisciplinary in nature.

Colonial history, politics, ideology, feminism, neo-colonialism are some of the important traits of postcolonial criticism. Books on postcolonial studies written and edited by critics such as *The Empire Writes Back* by Bill Ashcroft, Gareth Griffiths and Helen Tiffin, *Colonial and Postcolonial Literature* by Elleke Boehmer, *Colonialism/ Postcolonialism* by Ania Loomba, *Post-colonial Literatures in English* by Dennis Walder, *The Cambridge Introduction to Postcolonial Literatures in English* by C.L. Innes, *Postcolonial Literary* Studies edited by Neil Lazarus, *New National and Postcolonial Literatures: An Introduction* edited by Bruce King, *Contemporary Postcolonial Theory* edited by Padmini Mongia, *Postcolonial Theory* edited by Leela Gandhi and *Post-colonial Studies: The Essential Glossary* by John Theme interpret postcolonial literature terms of colonialism, postcolonialism, and neo-colonialism — i.e., history, and ideology.

To conclude, I would like to make a few observations. One, Postcolonial literature is not merely a re-naming of Commonwealth literature. Two, Postcolonial literature means postcolonial literature in English, which excludes literatures written in other languages in former colonies, such as Bhasha Literatures in India. Three, postcolonial literature is not a single identity and therefore, we have to state postcolonial literatures in English in former colonies which gained independence after the World War II. Imperialism, Culture, socio-political conditions, economics and above all, feminism are important clues to postcolonial studies. Postcolonial studies encompass Human Sciences of which literature is only a part. Therefore, the Frontiers of postcolonial Studies are ever widening making us conscious of the factors that went into the making of literary texts in the post-World War II era.

WORKS CITED

Ahmad, Aijaz. "The Politics of Literary Postcoloniality". *Contemporary Postcolonial Theory*. Ed. Padmini Mongia. Delhi: OUP, 1997.

Appiah, Kwame Anthony. "Is the Post in Postmodernism the Post in Postcolonial?" *Contemporary Postcolonial Theory*. Ed. Padmini Mongia. Delhi: OUP, 1997.

Ashcroft, Bill Gareth Griffiths & Helen Tiffin. *The Empire Writes Back*. London: Routledge, 1989 rpt. Chennai: Chennai Micro Print Pvt. Ltd., 2003.

Bahri, Deepika. "Feminism in and Postcolonialism". *Postcolonial Literary Studies*. Ed. Neil Lazarus. Cambridge: Cambridge University Press, 2004.

Boehmer, Elleke. *Colonial and Postcolonial Literature*. Oxford: OUP, 1995.

Childs Peter and Roger Fowler, ed. *The Routledge Dictionary of Literary Terms*. New York: Routledge 2006 (Indian rpt. 2008).

Fanon, Frantz. *Black Skin, White Masks*. Trans. Charles Lam Markmann. New York: Grove Press, 1967.

Fanon, Frantz. *The Wretched of the Earth*. Trans. Constance Farrington. New York: Grove Press, 1968.

Gandhi, Leela. *Postcolonial Theory: A Critical Introduction*. Delhi: OUP 1999.

Innes, C.L. *The Cambridge Introduction to Postcolonial Literatures in English*. New Delhi: Cambridge University Press, 2007.

Jacoby, Russell. "Marginal Returns: The Trouble with Postcolonial Theory". *Lingua Franca*. Sept./Oct. 1995.

King, Bruce. "New Centres of Consciousness: New Post-colonial International English Literature". *New National and Post-Colonial Literatures: An Introduction*. Ed. Brace King, Oxford: Clarendon Press, 1996.

Lazarus, Neil. "Introducing Postcolonial Studies". *Postcolonial Literary Studies*. Ed. Neil Lazarus. Cambridge: Cambridge University Press, 2004.

Loomba, Ania. *Colonialism/Post-colonialism*. London: Routledge, 1998.

Mongia, Padmini, ed. *Contemporary Postcolonial Theory*. Delhi: OUP 1997.

Sarte, Jean-Paul. *Black Orpheus*. Trans. Samuel Allen. Paris: Présence Africaine, 1956.

Shohat, Ella. "Notes on the 'Post-colonial'". *Contemporary Postcolonial Theory*. Ed. Padmini Mongia. Delhi: OUP, 1997.

25

Keki N. Daruwalla in Conversation with Bijay Kumar Das

Keki N. Daruwalla (b. 1937-) is a major Indian English poet with ten volumes of poems to his credit. He won Sahitya Akademi Award for his book of verse, *The Keeper of the Dead* for the year 1984. Poet, anthologist and fiction writer, he has made immense contribution to Indian English Literature.

BKD. In your poem "The Hebrew Professor" you have stated: "In 48 my teacher said to me,/if you don't belong to a city,/a country, an age, you must surely belong to a language!".

I would like to begin with the statement that underlines the question of identity.

What gives an identity to a poet? Is it the country or the language he writes in?

KND. I think both. Identities are individual and personal. These days we are very concerned about identities. The Pakistanis can never get over their wretched identity problems. They have no idea what to do with Taxila. They want to access the heritage of the Moguls blah blah. Did Kabir ever think of identity? Or Tuka? Or Villon? Why are we modems so obsessed with identity?

In the final analysis I think it is the personal consciousness of the poet, his interior self that gives him an identity. But the markers are the country, language and religion. I hope the poetry of a writer also gets him his identity!

BKD. In the introduction to *Two Decades of Indian Poetry 1960-80* you have mentioned:

"My poems are rooted in landscape which anchors the poem. The landscape is not merely there to set the scene but to lead to an illumination. It should be the eye of the spiral. I try that poetry, relate to the landscape both on the physical and on the plane of the spirit. For me riot stricken town is landscape."

How do you relate landscape to the making of a poem?

KND. I think it is unfair to trot out what a writer says 30 years ago and ask him about it. In my early days landscape was very important to my writing — both fiction and poetry. I imbibed the landscape as it were. I was seeing the land as if for the first time. But after all one is not painting a sugar cane field. If landscape enters a poem or a story, there has to be a purpose behind it.

In fiction I like to cite a story. And the place will modulate what you are writing about. The timbre and texture of the piece would be affected by the place — the Terai, or Rohilkhand or the Himalayas will exercise their influence on what you are writing about. So will Tibet.

BKD. You began publishing books of poems in 1970s. So far you have published 10 collections of poems including *Collected Poems 1970-2005* (2006). Do you recognize any influence on your poetry?

KND. Please don't forget that till 1974 I was living in small towns where there was no one to interact with. Yes I spent 3 years in Lucknow (1971-74) but never interacted with any writer.

As for reading one had to keep away from the 19th century poets. I kept T.S. Eliot also at a distance. Indians, especially writing in our languages, have tried to follow him far too much. I kept to myself. The reader has to find if I have been influenced. Its not for me to say. On the other hand what is tradition if not 'influence' in some manner or the other?

BKD. Were you conscious of any kind of Indian English poetic tradition when you started writing poetry?

KND. None. There was no poetry tradition here.

BKD. You have written on a number of themes — Love, Death and contemporary reality. Why is it that most of the poems are written in the ironic mode?

KND. Not most. Some. Irony is a good antidote to sentimentalism. And a lot of our Indian language poetry drips with sentiment. And irony comes naturally to me. If you are rational in this mad world you've got to be ironic, Pal.

BKD. You once said, "Writing a poem is like a clot going out of the blood". Do you mean to say that a poem is an integral part of the poet's life which moves from filiations to affiliation (Vico's term popularized by Edward Said) when it is published?

KND. This is a bit too much for me. Forget what I said forty years ago. Yes, but there is quite a cathartic feeling once you get the poem out after it has churned within you.

BKD. What contributes more to the making of a poem — language or culture?

KND. Both again. Languages also have their culture. For instance, English is known for its understatement, and also irony.

BKD. Your poem "The Ghaghra in-Spate" reminds us of A.K. Ramanujan's poem "River" in its depiction of the reality that stares us in our face. Should you take it as a topical poem?

KND. I don't know what you mean. Have forgotten Ramanujan's poem.

BKD. You are the third Indian English poet (after Jayanta Mahapatra and Nissim Ezekiel) to win the Sahitya Akademi award for your book of verse, *The Keeper of the Dead* for the year 1984. In a poem called the "The Parsi Hell" you have said:

"Through out life a man carried his death even as a woman carries her child".

Is it correct to say that death is the central metaphor that underlines this volume?

KND. The last line should have been mentioned. "A Parsi carries his hell." The earlier two lines are there where they are because the last line had to come.

No I may be bleak, and death appears in quite a few poems. If you write about life, death too comes in.

BKD. In recent years you have written some memorable poems on contemporary reality for instance you have written on the theme of migration in two poems. In a poem called "Migration" you have said:

Migrations are always difficult
Ask any drought
Any plague
Ask the year 1947

Ask the chronicles themselves
If there had been no migration
Would there have been enough
History to munch on?

Do you think that immigrant and expatriate poets face a kind of identity crisis? Do you think poets like A.K. Ramanujan and R. Parthasarathy feel an anxiety of Indianness?

KND. Ramanujan didn't. I have a whole essay on him which makes that point. I haven't read Paratha's second volume so can't comment. But most diaspora writers have this anxiety of Indianness, as you phrase it.

BKD. In "A millennium Poem" you have said that "What have we to do with the spool of time/which like Draupadi's Sari unwinds, unwinds and unwinds"?

KND. Yes, I said that.

BKD. Coming to the art of writing poetry would you please tell me whether you revise your poems as a rule or you stick to the first draft?

KND. With the coming of the PC, one keeps looking at what one wrote and rectifications, changes become the norm. I tend to cut out a few words, sometimes a line. The effort is to make the poem terse. Can it do without this word or line? If it can, cut the wretched thing out. But there are no major changes — the alterations are miniscule.

BKD. Do you agree with Paul Valéry when he says that, "A poem is not complete, it is abandoned"?

KND. Wish I could write such poems. Mine are too definitive. Formerly I planned my last lines. That is a handicap, for the poem has to willy-nilly move towards the last lines I penned, like a man to his grave. Now I have shed this habit. The ending comes of itself.

BKD. In "Prologue 1" "Island poems" you have stated that "A poem is an Island itself". Do you think that a poem is an autonomous entity?

KND. Never thought of it that way. But why not, you can argue both ways. But it is an entity, you can't deny that.

BKD. Is your poem "Draupadi" a criticism of feminism and feminists?

KND. It's a light poem and should be taken as such. Makes people laugh. Though the way we (Political leaders and Indian language writers mostly) go on and on about Eklavya and Draupadi does embarrass me.

BKD. Who among your contemporaries — Ezekiel, Ramanujan, R. Parthasarathy, Jayanta Mahapatra, Shiv K. Kumar — according to you has contributed most to Indian English poetry?

KND. Ezekiel and Ramanujan.

BKD. Do you think that Indian English Poetry has declined after 1980s?

KND. It would be very presumptuous of me to agree to that. There are very fine poets today — the women lead — Imtiaz Dharker, Arundhathi Subramaniam, Rukmini Bhaya Nair, Meena Alexander, Sujatha Bhatt. Jeet Thayeel and Ranjit Hoskote are exceptional — Jeet's anthology is a proof of the kind of writing that's available. And he and Ranjit are excellent poets. Jeet's anthology is a defining volume. There's a lot of good diaspora writing. Among the less known ones I have considerable regard for Anand Thakore, Sridala Swami.

BKD. What are the real challenges before Indian English poetry? Is it Postcolonial poetry, Third World poetry or Bhasha Poetry in India?

KND. Have no worthwhile comments to make.

BKD. What do you think about the reception and reviewing of Indian English Poetry in our country?

KND. Not good enough. And the reviewing is so parochial — Bengali reviewers for the Bongos, Malayali for the Malayalis and so on and so forth. Second rate poets are extolled by third rate reviewers — as long as poet and critic are of the same clan, or are cronies — or sharers of the bottle, rum mostly, (*hum-pyala, hum-Divala*).

BKD. My last question is: What you are involved in writing now?

KND. Another novel.

26

Multi-theoretical Approaches to Five Seminal Twentieth Century Novels Across the World

Let me begin with Michael Ondaatje's statement that "Fiction is always the unofficial story" to show how multi-theoretical approaches to twentieth century fiction facilitate the study of it in the twenty-first century. Reading convention varies from age to age. We have come a long way from reading fiction from the standpoint of story, plot, character and E.M. Forster's *Aspects of the Novel* is no longer the arbitrator of reading fiction.

Readers of fiction could be broadly divided into three types: common reader, academic reader and fictionist as reader. Common readers read for stories and characters in fiction. For them, fiction (i.e., novel) could be summarized and characters could be imitated. First language readers excel in this kind of reading and memorise the story. Academic readers do not read fiction for the story element in it but they take the opinion of the critics to analyse the work of fiction theoretically from one angle to another emphasizing the idea that no reading of fiction could be conclusive. Traditionally, novels were read on the basis of plot, character, theme, language and setting. Now in the late twentieth century and early twenty-first century novels are read on the basis of theoretical frame work such as formalistic criticism, structuralist criticism, deconstructive criticism, reader-response criticism, gender theory, feminist criticism, new historicism, dialogic criticism, postcolonial theory, modernism, post-modernism, ecocriticism and above all, humanistic criticism.

Novelists do not follow a particular theory to write novels. They tend to assimilate the story, the plot and characters of other novelists creatively in order to write their novels in their own way. What Robert Liddell says in his well-known book, *A Treatise on the Novel*, "A writer may gather experience in the world, but it is in the 'ivory tower' that he learns what part of his experience falls within his range" (49), is true of every great fiction writer. That means, a fiction writer combines his own experience with his reading of others' fiction and in the process creates his own fiction. Keeping this in view let us analyse the five seminal novels, *Things Fall Apart* (Chinua Achebe), *Kanthapura* (Raja Rao), *The English Patient* (Michael Ondaatje), *A House for Mr Biswas* (V.S. Naipaul) and *Surfacing* (Margaret Atwood), in the light of various critical theories such as postcolonialism, feminism, gender studies, ecocriticism, and above all, anti-colonial nationalism.

I

Let us begin with *Things Fall Apart* (1958), the title of which has been borrowed from W.B. Yeats's "The Second Coming". It is the meeting point of indigenous history, Ibo Culture with Colonizer's (British) Culture. The story of the novel is the story of Okonkwo who rises to a high position in his village called Umuofia until a disaster forces him into a seven-year exile during which White missionaries, followed by White colonial administrators move in and seize the village. That leaves him with no other alternative than to resist the White minority invasion which ultimately drives him to commit suicide. The novel begins with the description of the protagonist's achievement and fame in the following words:

> Okonkwo was well known throughout the nine villages and even beyond. His fame rested on solid personal achievements. As a young man of eighteen he had brought honour to his village by throwing Amalinze the Cat. Amalinze was the great wrestler who for seven years was unbeaten, from Umuofia to Mbaino. He was called the Cat because his back would never touch the earth. It was this man that Okonkwo threw in a fight which the old man agreed was one of the fiercest since the founder of their town engaged a spirit of the wild for seven days and seven nights (*TFA* 3).

The three-part novel deals with, 'ceremony of innocence' depicting Okonkwo as a hero, a criminal and finally, a rebel against colonial rule respectively. V.A. Shahane makes an apt analysis of the novel in the following words:

> The division of the novel, *Things Fall Apart* in three parts is itself a movement of clock-time, a linear development of the history of Iboland. It opens when Okonkwo is at the height of his fame, position and power. As a result of his accidental killing of a boy, Okonkwo is banished from his village for

> a period of seven years. He leaves before dawn and goes to his mother's village for a stay of seven years. The second part finds Okonkwo in exile, involved in his efforts towards resettlement at Mbanta. On his return to Umuofia he finds that the new religion, Christianity, has made many inroads into the traditional strongholds of Ibo society. The arrival of the white man, the missionaries and the Commissioner, the religious and the secular arms of the western civilization's domination over Africa, dismayed him. In fact, it created a major crisis of Okonkwo's life (34).

In course of an interview to Kwame Anthony Appiah in 1982, Chinua Achebe says,

> I'm an Ibo writer because this is my basic culture; Nigerian, African and a writer...no, black first, then a writer. Each of these identities does call for a certain kind of commitment on my part. I must see what it is to be black — and this means being sufficiently intelligent to know how the world is moving and how the black people fare in this world. This is what it means to be black. Or an African — what docs Africa mean to the world? When you see an African, what does it mean to a white man? (qtd. in Innes 208).

Achebe turns to indigenous history and culture to counter the onslaught of British Colonialism. It is in this sense *Things Fall Apart* stands out as an exemplary text of anti-colonial nationalism. This novel can also be read on the basis of gendered violence as Okonkwo beats his wife, in spite of the protests of his other two wives. As Richard J. Lane has rightly observed:

> Achebe's *Things Fall Apart* has also triggered important feminist research. In other words, the colonial encounter is not perceived as something that happened in a 'gender-neutral' domain; instead, gender roles constitutive of indigenous and invader societies come into contact and conflict. While early feminist accounts of *Things Fall Apart* argued that the novel was inherently sexist, more recent feminists have turned to a closer reading of Achebe's texts to recover 'inscriptions of women's oppositional narratives of resistance to both the Igbo masculine tradition and its patriarchal discourses' (45-46).

Things Fall Apart reinforces the trajectory of the protagonist, Okonkwo's fall from an adored hero to a victim of a condemned colonized who was driven to desperation to end his own life. He has a Satanic fall for his evil action of onslaught on a woman (his wife) and human killings from time to time. C.D. Narasimhaiah amply sums up the fall of Okonkwo in the following passage:

> The most terrific sight of all is that they cannot touch the dangling body of Okonkwo. Obierika, one of the elders and a good friend of Okonkwo, bursts out ferociously at the District Commissioner:
>
>> That man was one of the greatest men in Umuofia. You drove him to kill himself. And now he will be buried like a dog.
>
> They cannot bury him. Only strangers can, because it is a sin against the Earth, his body is evil. Such is the ignoble end of Okonkwo. Things *have fallen* 'apart'. But we have witnessed things falling apart almost from the beginning of the novel — Okonkwo has committed a series of offences against his father, son, and wife. He killed his neighbour's son, though inadvertently and suffered exile. He killed a refugee who looked up to him as 'Father'. He killed the white man's messenger. And to top it all, accepted ignominious treatment from the white man, paid the fine and let the whole clan pay a fine too. Unbecoming of one whose fame had spread like bush-fire (163).

Things Fall Apart is a Colonial African novel which influenced other colonial writers to write on the theme of anti-colonial nationalism. In a sense, it is both an archetypal and canonical novel of the twentieth century.

II

Raja Rao's *Kanthapura* (1938) precedes Chinua Achebe's *Things Fall Apart* (1958) by two decades but its influence is limited to India only. The anti-colonial nationalism is manifest in both the novels. Both the novelists have traveled in Europe and settled for long in USA. But Achebe is more widely known than Raja Rao in the English-speaking world. "Introduction" to *Kanthapura* is an anti-colonial manifesto. Both Achebe and Rao insisted on writing in English in their own way. In other words, they insisted on creating an African English idiom and Indian English idiom respectively and hoped that, "time alone with justify it". In fact, time has justified it.

Kanthapura can be better understood, if read in the light of humanistic criticism. If K.R.S. Iyengar, a humanistic critic calls it a Gandhian novel, the theme of which could be summed up as "Gandhi and our Village" (391), C.D. Narasimhaiah opines that no

Indian English novel of the scope and size of *Kanthapura* pictures "so vividly, truthfully and touchingly the story of the resurgence of India under Gandhi's leadership" (Naik et al. 236). William Walsh and H.M. Williams link *Kanthapura* with the Indian puranic tradition.

Raja Rao adopted the narrative method in which the old woman tells the story, to depict the impact of Gandhian moral values of non-violent struggle for freedom on the people of a small village, Kanthapura, through his hero, Murti. The bardic narrative in the novel is fused with the speaking-acting-dramatic flow of speech recorded the crisis of change in every character through the impact of Gandhi. The novelist is talking in the person of the old woman so that through her vibrant words, he is able to merge his flow into the village woman's speech quite successfully with ease to carry the narrative.

The grandmother describes goddess Kenchamma with devotion and adoration:

> 'Kenchamma' is our goddess. Great and bounteous is she. She killed a demon ages, ages ago, a demon that had come to ask our young sons as food and our young women as wives...she has never failed us, I assure you, our Kenchamma (*Kanthapura* 1:2).

Raja Rao makes an attempt to create national myth around Gandhi to suit the fictional mode. Gandhi has been deified by being likened to Lord Krishna, who killed the serpent Kali. Gandhi's fight against the British symbolizes the fight between good and evil. The novel begins with creating a myth around Gandhi and ends with the merging of this modern myth with that of the national myth in the persons of Rama and Sita who have passed into Hindu consciousness as God and Goddess. The novel comes a full circle when the old woman affirms her unfailing faith in the leadership of Gandhi who is hailed as the saviour of India.

> We are all for the Mahatma. Pariah Rachanna's wife, Rachi and Seethamma and Timmamma are all for the Mahatma. They say there are men in Bombay and men in Punjab and men and women in Bombay and Bengal and Punjab, who are all for the Mahatma. They say the Mahatma will go to the Redman's country and he will get us the Swaraj.... And Rama will come back from exile and Sita will be with him for Ravana will be slain...brother Bharatha will go to meet them with the worshipped sandal of the Master on his head.

> And as they enter Ayodhya there will be rain of flowers (*Kanthapura* 189).

Kanthapura almost becomes an epic in prose when characters are described in terms of gods and demons representing good and evil, virtue and vice respectively. *Kanthapura* has been variously described as 'Sthala Purana' (legendary history of the village called Kanthapura) and a politico-religious novel but it is all these and perhaps much more. Raja Rao succeeds in transcending the limitations of time and place in *Kanthapura* by transforming a small village, Kanthapura into a mini India, and deifying Gandhi, turning him into a demi-god. Gandhi becomes a saviour like Rama and Krishna and Kanthapura becomes the microcosm of India.

III

The English Patient (1992) Michael Ondaatje's Booker Prize Award Winning novel is foregrounded in the World War II. Ondaatje's idea of creating fictional characters not handcuffed to history makes this novel significant. In course of an interview with Maya Jaggi, he makes his preference clear as a postcolonial novelist:

> Our newspapers are full of official stories, and what the novelist is responsible for is something unhistorical, unofficial — what goes on in private. That's what interests me (Nasta 254)...
>
> I'm sure I wouldn't have become a writer if I'd stayed in Sri Lanka, or in England. When I came to Canada I met young writers who worked on little magazines and worked at small presses, so I thought I could try this (Nasta 259).

The English Patient begins with Hana (aged 20), a nurse of Canadian origin taking care of the English patient with severe burns because of plane crash in an Italian Vila, San Girolamo and ends with Kip (Kripal) an Indian (a bomb defuser) brooding over his love relationship with Hana (aged 34) and the time span of the novel is fourteen years. The narrative is interspersed with present and past with all the important characters taking recourse to flashbacks. The novel is about the devastation of war and the intrigue of love relationship between people of different nations. Failure in love and extramarital love affair spoil personal lives of individuals resulting in death.

In *The English Patient*, Almasy is in love with Katharine, the wife of Geoffrey Clifton which enrages the latter leading to a plot to kill all three of them, by crashing a plane on the English patient.

His plan failed and he died in action. His wife Katharine could not be saved in spite of the English patient's attempt to keep her alive.

Almasy-Katharine love affair reveals how love (i.e., extramarital love) and war are intertwined in the novel. Continual flashbacks of important characters reinforce this point. The opening sentence of Chapter IX ("The Cave of Swimmers"), "I promised to tell you how one falls in love" opens the door of Almasy's heart and nostalgically he harks back to the past. The following two extracts show how love and war are embedded into the texture of the novel:

> I sank to my knees in the mosaic-tiled hall, my face in the curtain of her gown, the salt taste of these fingers in her mouth. We were a strange statue, the two of us, before we began to unlock our hunger. Her fingers scratching against the sand in my thinning hair. Cairo and all her deserts around us (251).
>
> Women want everything of a lover. And too often I would sink below the surface. So armies disappear under sand. And there was her (Katharine's) fear of her husband, her belief in her honour, my old desire for self-sufficiency, my disappearances, her suspicions of me, my disbelief that she loved me. The Paranoia and Claustrophobia of hidden love (252).

Hana-Kip love relationship runs parallel to Almasy-Katharine affair, reinforcing the idea of how love and war can co-exist. Here are two extracts from the novel:

> Wherever Hana is now, in the future, she is aware of the line of movement Kip's body followed out of her life. Her mind repeats it. The path he slammed through among them. When he turned into a stone of silence in their midst. She recalls everything of the August day — What the sky was like, the objects on the table in front of her going dark under the thunder (300)...
>
> When Hana comes into the roofless chapel he is sitting there leaning his back and head against the wheel.
> Kip.
> He says nothing, looking through her
> Kip, it's me. What did we have to do with it? He is stone in front of her.
> She kneels down to his level and leans forward
> into him, the side of her head against his chest, holding herself like that.
> A beating heart.
> When his stillness does not alter she rolls back onto her knees.

> ...
> He leans to his side away from her, his face stopping a few inches from a rain puddle.
> A boy and a girl (307).

In *The English Patient,* the characters are drawn from different countries such as India, Canada, America, England, German and Hungary, who are involved in World War II. The novel deals with war and the devastation of war, the action shifting from desert to Italian Villa. Between nurse and patient, spy and bomb defuser, individual and country, cruelty and compassion, violence and love, the novel is exquisitely balanced.

IV

A House for Mr Biswas (1961) is a postcolonial novel. It is foregrounded in Naipaul's father's story, "They Named him Mohun". Naipaul acknowledges his literary indebtedness to his father in course of an interview:

> The writing that has mattered most to me is that of my father, which has been published. It taught me to look at things which had never been written about before, and seemed dull in life, yet when transferred to paper became very surprising. A great deal of my vision of Trinidad has come straight from my father (qtd. in Salgado 317).

The novel (*A House for Mr Biswas*) begins (as stated in The Prologue) with the Protagonist Mohun Biswas, a sacked journalist dying at the age of 46 in his irretrievable mortgaged house in Sikkim Street, St. James Port of Spain, Naipaul writes:

> Mr. Biswas was forty-six and had four children. He had no money. His wife Shama had no money. On the house in Sikkim Street Mr. Biswas owed, and had been owing for four years, three thousand dollars. The interest on this, at eight per cent, came to twenty dollars a month; the ground rent was ten dollars. Two children were at school. The two older children, on whom Mr. Biswas might have depended, were both abroad on scholarships (Naipaul 7).

> Mr. Biswas's stories, with their recurrent fantasies of escape from the marriage trap, bear an obvious relevance to the novel's wider theme and link up interestingly with its major structural metaphor, the building of a house. For the house represents not only a recognizable location and identity for the displaced second-generation colonial out of sympathy

> with his Indian roots and unable to identify with his new surroundings. It also stands for the acceptance of the roles of husband, father and breadwinner which both circumstance and temperament invite Mr. Biswas to resist for so long. It is only when that resistance is abandoned that Mr, Biswas succeeds in attaining a home which survives him and can become a point of growth for the new generation of Savi and Anand (Salgado 318).

Mr. Biswas began his career as a signboard painter. It is as a signboard painter he went to Mrs. Tulsi's house. And it is in this house he met a sixteen-year-old shop-assistant Ms Shama, who instantly fell in love with him. They got married in no time.

> Mr. Biswas finds himself a complete misfit in Mrs. Tulsi's household. His marriage proved to be unsuccessful. Shama, his wife never understood him till he purchased a house of his own. Mr. Biswas tried to negotiate with a newspaper, *Trinidad Sentinel* through Misir. He initially refused to work for the Tulsis who were blood suckers. He would rather catch crabs or sell coconuts than work under any of the Tulsi's. He abused his in-laws. He referred to his two brothers-in-law as 'the little gods', to Seth as 'the big boss', and to Mrs. Tulsi as 'the old queen' then as 'the old hen' and next as 'the old cow' and more insultingly a 'she-fox' (This kind of behaviour and attitude brought discord among the Biswas couple). He further told Shama that her two brothers looked like monkeys and that Hanuman house was a real zoo where all kinds of animals dwelt. He referred to Hari, one of Tulsi's sons-in-law, as "the constipated holyman". In retaliation Shama told him that he was a "barking Puppy dog" (98-99).

Mr. Biswas after being shunted out of the Hanuman house began to realize the hierarchy of the Tulsi family. Then only he understood the importance of owning a house. Moreover, he made amends by coming closer to Shama. Naipaul emphasizes this in his "preface" to the novel:

> He didn't now care to do anything against his wife's wishes. He had grown to accept, her judgement and to respect her optimism. He trusted her. Since they had moved to the house. Shama had learned a new loyalty, to him and to their children; away from her mother and sisters, she was able to express this without shame, and to Mr. Biswas this was triumph almost as big as the acquiring of his own house (8).

After he bought a house by borrowing from Ajodha he realised that his dream had come true. He planted a laburnum free in the extra space. There is something romantic about it. As Naipaul puts it:

> It grew rapidly. It gave the house a romantic aspect, softened the tall graceless lines and provided some shelter from the afternoon sun. Its flowers were sweet, and in the still hot evenings their smell filled the house (584).

The death of Mohun in his house in the end marks victory for him. In the postcolonial era, the colonized sought to establish their identity both politically and economically. Naipaul visualized the situation:

> How terrible it would have been, at this time, to be without it, to have died among the Tulsis, amid the squalor of that large, disintegrating and indifferent family; to have left Shama and the children among them, in one room; worse, to have lived without even attempting to lay claim to one's portion of the earth; to have lived and died as one had been born, unnecessary and unaccommodated (13-14).

In course of a chapter in my book, *Aspects of Commonwealth Literature*, what I said about the novel, remains valid for me even today.

> This is written within the great tradition of humanist novel in the post-colonial era. While writing the novel the empirical self (i.e., biographical 'self') goes extinct and the 'implied self' (i.e. the point of view embodied in the work) emerges. Naipaul's father's story becomes the story of any post-colonial man displaced from his origin by chance or choice. The 'unhoused' condition creates a kind of uncertainty among the people of contemporary diaspora and hence there is a need for overcoming this uncertainty by owning 'a house'. In spite of the autobiographical design of the novel, it succeeds in transcending that individual 'self' by universalizing the issue of 'alienation' and 'rootlessness' in the Post-Colonial World (103).

V

Margaret Atwood's *Surfacing* (1972) has been variously interpreted as a feminist, eco-feminist, post-colonial and above all, manifest novel. Writing for Atwood is a matter of faith and hope. In *Second Words: Selected Critical Prose,* Atwood states:

> Writing, no matter what its subject, is an act of faith, the primary faith being that someone out there will read the results. I believe it's also an act of hope, the hope that things can be better than they are (*Second Words* 349).

Let me cite a few academics for their insight into the novel. M. Prabhakar calls *Surfacing* a 'distinct feminist voice'. Richard J. Lane goes a step ahead to say that, "it is a voice which articulates issues of gender, subjectivity, madness, nationality, ecology and narrative power. Often read in conjunction with Atwood's work of literary theory, *Survival* which was published in the same year, it is possible in retrospect to see how *Surfacing* created a schema through which key feminist and other critical debates in Canada could take place" (71). M. Prabhakar regards this schema as a 'blue print of revolt' (*LHY* 71). Erinc Ozdemir opines that, "the novel valorizes feminity against masculinity, while at the same time it paradoxically dramatizes a desire to destroy all dichotomies and dualistic thinking" (*English Studies* 58).

Surfacing is also read in the light of environmentalism. In the words of Shannon Hengen, "Environmentalism in the works of Atwood becomes a concern with the urgent preservation of human place in a natural world in which the term 'human' does not imply 'superior' or 'alone' and in which what is fabricated or artificial is less satisfying than what has originally occurred" (Howells 74). The landscape of South-Western Quebec, where the novel, *Surfacing* is set in is near the border Ontario. The setting of the novel is in the forest land. In my book Chapter VI, "Margaret Atwood's *Surfacing* as an Eco-Feminist Novel" (*Critical Essays on Post-Colonial Literature* 64-71). I have tried to bring feminism and ecology together in interpreting *Surfacing* as an eco-feminist novel. Colonialism and Patriarchy are seen as power structures that exploit and therefore, the former is seen as a paradigm of the latter in feminist literary criticism.

In Canada colonial exploitation is seen as a kind of exploitation of both nature and women. To Northrop Frye, Canada is "the only country left in the world which is a pure colony, colonial in psychology, as well as mercantile economics" (1971: III). Margaret Atwood goes a step ahead when she says that, "Canada as a whole is a victim, or an 'oppressed minority' or 'exploited', a colony for someone else's profit" (1972: 35). Colonial power-structures have gone deep into the collective unconsciousness of Canada and have become a metaphor for feminine and nature exploitation for women writers in that country. The kind of attitude that links colonial exploitation of female and nature together gives rise to Eco-feminism.

Surfacing is divided into three parts and this division corresponds to shift in tense from present (Part-I) to past (Part-II) and again to present (Part-III). The unnamed female protagonist describes the trip made by her along with her boyfriend Joe, and two other friends, Anna and David to North Quebec to find out what happened to her father after the death of her mother. During the journey she recalls her past how her art teacher concealing his marital status proposed to her and made her pregnant. Then she was forced to undergo an abortion. She became bitter about it and took it as an assault by patriarchy, which denies her to grow independently as an artist and have a claim over the child. It seemed to her that woman is a toy in the hands of men to be used, abused and abandoned. That is why she decided to get pregnant by Joe, her boyfriend. Now she has acquired a mind of her own and refused to be a victim. She has decided to give birth this baby. "I cannot know yet; it is too early. But I assure it: if I die it dies, if I starve it starves with me. It might be the first one, the first true human, it must be born, allowed" (*Surfacing* 206).

Surfacing can be taken as a novel of protest against patriarchy's violence against women and nature and a triumph of feminine assertion of independent identity and dignity in the twentieth century. The novel is not written according to feminist theory. On the contrary the feminist theory issues out of it. Such a novel could be written by a woman who is both a creative writer and a critic. Atwood is a novelist-critic like Eliot as a poet-critic. *Surfacing* is a seminal novel which influenced generation of novelists and paved the way for new novels across the English speaking world in the last forty-five years.

VI

In the last section of my paper, an attempt has been made to connect the above five texts, *Things Fall Apart*, *Kanthapura*, *The English Patient*, *A House for Mr Biswas* and *Surfacing* on the basis of the creative use of English language in an indigenous way, which leads to the creation of distinct idioms not in British English but in other English(es). Raja Rao's clarion call in his introduction to *Kanthapura* to 'write in English in our own way' has its unconscious echoes in Achebe, Atwood, Ondaatje and V.S. Naipaul. The result is that postcolonial fiction has come of age in no time. It stands on par with British fiction, a fact well acknowledged and authenticated by the conferment of Booker Prize (now renamed as Man Booker Prize) on postcolonial writers. It may be noted that three of the above five canonical novelists (Naipaul, Atwood, and Ondaatje) are Booker Laureates. It is a pity that Achebe and Rao were overlooked by the Booker Jury.

Achebe's use of African English, metaphor and proverbs are, to say the least, is superb. Here are a few examples from *Things Fall Apart*:

> Let us take a few sayings and proverbs used in the novel: "our elders say that the sun will shine on those who kneel under him" (7). "As the elders said, if a child washed his hands he could eat with kings" (8). This proverb makes us aware of the fact that Okonkwo was a self-made man who "had won fame as the greatest wrestler in the nine villages" and whose "achievement was reversed". "As our people say, a man who pays respect to the great paves the way for his own greatness" (18). Ogbuefi Idigo referring to the palm-wine tapper, Obiako who gave up his trade said, "There must be a reason for it. A toad does not run in the day time for nothing" (19). Okonkwo justifies his self-praise while asking for a loan. "I know what it is to ask a man to trust another with his yams, especially these days when youngmen are afraid of hard work. I am not afraid of work. The lizard that jumped from the high iroko tree to the ground said he would praise himself if not one else did" (20). Nwakibie uses another proverb to answer Okonkwo: "Eneke the bird says that since men have learnt to shoot without missing, he has learnt to fly without perching. I have learnt to be stingy with my yams"... (20). "When the moon is shining the cripple becomes hungry for a walk" (10). "Never make an early appointment with a man who has just married a new wife" (128). "A child cannot pay for its mother's milk" (151).

Achebe has insight into life of things that happen around us. He writes: 'whenever you see a toad jumping in broad day light then know that something is after its life'. "The clan was like a lizard, if it lost its tail it soon grew another" (*TFA* 155).

Raja Rao precedes Achebe to create an Indian English idiom in *Kanthapura*. Expressions like "as honest as an elephant", "the pumpkin moon", "so you are a traitor to your salt givers", "your humble servant", "I lick your feet", "son of a concubine", "son of a widow", "you donkey's husband", "you son of my woman", "sour-milk", "dung-eating curs", "a crow and sparrow story", "to stich up one's mouth", "to eat mud", "every squirrel has his day", "not a mosquito moved", "my right eyewinks", "heart — it beat like a drum", "heats squeezed like a wet cloth" the affectionate tag "brothers" is atypical Indian address to fellow citizens in public meetings, etc. gives evidence to the fact that Raja Rao is deliberately making an effort to create an Indian English idiom which will be acceptable to Indians for it acclimatizes an indigenous tradition to English language.

The free flowing language in *The English Patient* adds to the charm of the novel. The English patient, the protagonist of the novel, who "fell burning into the desert" says,

> I have spent weeks in the desert forgetting to look at the moon...as a married man may spend days never looking into the face of his wife. These are not sins of omission but signs of preoccupation (4).
>
> This is a story of how I fell in love with a woman, who read a specific story from Herodotus. I heard the words she spoke across the fire, never looking up, even when she teased her husband (247).

If Almasy is in love with Katharine, Kip broods over his love for Hana:

> She is a woman of honour and smartness whose wild love leaves out luck, always taking risks, and there is something in her brow now that only she can recognize in a mirror. Ideal and idealistic in that shiny dark hair! People fall in love with her (320).

In "Characters in Fiction", Mary McCarthy stated that "the fictional experiments of the twentieth century went in two directions: sensibility and sensation.... The novel of sensibility was feminine and the novel of sensation was masculine". McCarthy believes that British fiction of the twentieth century is feminine but American fiction is masculine (Kumar and McKean 64). The five novels analysed above are a combination of both feminine and masculine fiction. They are the fiction of sensibility as well as sensation.

To conclude, I should say that the five novels analysed above clearly show the impact they have on the minds of fiction writers and readers across the English-speaking world. No wonder Achebe, Raja Rao, Naipaul, Ondaatje and Atwood found their way to the syllabuses of colleges and universities all over the English world, where the above-mentioned novels are prescribed texts in the curriculum.

WORKS CITED

Achebe, Chinua. *Things Fall Apart*. New Delhi: Allied Publishers, 1993. Print.

Atwood, Margaret. *Surfacing*. Ontario: Paperbacks Ltd., 1980. Print.

——. *Second Words: Selected Critical Prose*. Toronto: House of Anansi Press, 1982. Print.

Das, Bijay Kumar. *Aspects of Commonwealth Literature*. New Delhi: Creative Books, 1995. Print.

——. *Critical Essays on Post-Colonial Literature*. New Delhi: Atlantic Publishers, 2007 rpt. 2012. Print.

Hengen, Shannon. "Margaret Atwood and Environmentalism". *The Cambridge Companion to Margaret Atwood*. Ed. Coral Ann Howells. Cambridge: Cambridge University Press, 2006: 72-85. Print.

Innes, C.L. *The Cambridge Introduction to Postcolonial Literatures in English*. New Delhi: Cambridge University Press India Pvt. Ltd., 2007. Print.

Iyengar, K.R.S. *Indian Writing in English*. New Delhi: Sterling Publishers Pvt. Ltd., 1984. Print.

Kumar, Shiv K. and Keith, McKean, ed. *Critical Approaches to Fiction*. New Delhi: Atlantic Publishers, 2004. Print.

Lane, Richard J. *The Postcolonial Novel*. Cambridge: Polity Press, 2006. Print.

Liddell, Robert. *A Treatise on the Novel*. London: Jonathan Cape, 1947. Print.

Narasimhaiah, C.D. *Essays in Commonwealth Literature: Heirloom of Multiple Heritage*. Delhi: Pencraft International, 1995. Print.

——. "Raja Rao's *Kanthapura*: An Analysis", *Critical Essays on Indian Writing in English*. Ed. M.K. Naik et al. Dharwad: Karnatak University, 1972. Print.

Ondaatje, Michael. *The English Patient*. London: Blooms Bury Publishing, 1992. Print.

——. (Interview) "Michael Ondaatje with Maya Jaggi". *Writing Across Worlds: Contemporary Writers Talk*. Ed. Susheila Nasta. New York: Routledge, 2004.

Ozdemir, Erinc. "Power, Madness and Gender Identity in Margaret Atwood's *Surfacing*". *English Studies* 84:1 (2003): 57-79. Print.

Prabhakar, M. "Margaret Atwood's *Surfacing*: Blue Print for Revolt", *The Literacy Half-Yearly* 36:1 (January 1995): 70-79. Print.

Rao, Raja. *Kanthapura*. Delhi: Oxford University Press, 1989, Print.

Salgado, Gamini. "V.S. Naipaul and the Politics of Fiction." *The New Pelican Guide to English Literature 8. The Present*. Ed. Boris Ford. London: Penguin Books, 1987. Print.

Shahine, V.A. "*Things Fall Apart*: Chinua Achebe's Art of Fiction". *Scholar Critic* 1:1 (January 1981): 32-39. Print.

27

Reconfiguring Partition Narratives in Three Select Indian English Novels

The partition of Indian subcontinent in August 1947 gave rise to two independent sovereign countries — India and Pakistan. Independence was achieved not without bloodshed and violence. The partition was thrust upon the people by a handful of power-hungry leaders in connivance with the colonizer. Partition affected the geography of the country and distorted its history. The result was bloody communal violence and onslaught on innocent people boiling down to wholesale killing of men, women, children and rape of women. At the political level new governments were formed, evacuees and refugees on both sides accelerated migration, perhaps the largest one in human history and at social level families were broken, houses were deserted and captured simultaneously. Religious bigotry made people blind to reason resulting in infinite sufferings of humanity on both sides of the border and their cries went unheeded. The repercussion of partition was terrible, reminding us of Eliot's warning, "human kind cannot bear very much reality" ("Burnt Norton"). Creative writers responded to the holocaust of partition and its aftermath in portraying the human sufferings in their works. New kind of literature was born which is called Partition Literature all over the Indian subcontinent.

Partition writings include canonical Indian English novels like Khushwant Singh's *Train to Pakistan*, Attia Hosain's *Sunlight on a Broken Column*, B. Rajan's *The Dark Dancer*, Manohar Malgonkar's *A Bend in the Ganges*, Raj Gill's *Rape*, Amitav Ghosh's *The Shadow Lines*, Chaman Nahal's *Azadi* and host of others in Indian Bhasa Literature and in Pakistani writings such as Bapsi Sidhwa's *Ice-Candy Man*.

The title of Attia Hosain's magnum opus, *Sunlight on a Broken Column* (1961) is taken from T.S. Eliot's *The Hollow Men*. It is fore-grounded in her family and in the family of her father-in-law, against the backdrop of inevitable partition in 1947. It is not quite autobiographical but unmistakably an admixture of personal and the impersonal in which the tradition shapes the individual talent. Hosain's Cambridge-educated father, a friend of Motilal Nehru, the well-known freedom fighter and Jawaharlal Nehru's father, was a taluqdar of 'Oudh', while her mother came from an intellectual family grounded in Persian and Urdu tradition. Thus, her parents juxtaposed in themselves English education and Urdu culture, a confluence of tradition and modernity. Her cousin turned husband was Cambridge educated, while her father-in-law was also a 'taluqdar' like her father, who played a prominent role in the political, civil and social life of UP. What is of utmost importance was that he was also a Vice Chancellor of Lucknow University. Her family witnessed the course of freedom movement and the inevitable partition of the country. She being a nationalist decided to stay back in India and when her husband was posted to the Indian High Commission in London, she went there and joined the Eastern Service of BBC.

In *Sunlight on a Broken Column*, Baba Jan's family reminds us of Attia Hosain's own family. It is a multi-dimensional novel with a variety of themes: generation gap leading to credibility deficit, communal divide, gender discrimination and above all, the fall out of partition. All these themes are woven around Baba Jan's family. Laila, the narrator of the novel, is its central character. Everything is seen through her eyes and from her point of view. The novel is in four parts with linear progression. A fifteen year old girl, Laila views things from her angle. Growing up in a joint family with uncles, aunts, cousins, *ayas*, servants and patriarchal head of the family, she begins to understand life slowly but steadily and sees it whole.

An orphan who lost her parents quite early in life, Laila was raised by her aunt (Piusi) Abida. But her 'agony abides'. She says,

> It was my fifteenth birthday. Not that it mattered to anyone else. My birthday was remembered only by me, and while at school, by the teachers when forms had to be filled up (*Sunlight on a Broken Column* 16).

Aunt Abida's admonition to Laila shows how the elders want the younger generation to obey the traditional norms of family without questioning them. She says,

> My child, there are certain rules of conduct that must be observed in this world without question...you must never forget the traditions of your family no matter to what outside influences you may be exposed. I have been responsible for you since the day God willed you to be without a father and

> mother.... Never forget the family into which you were born (*SBC* 38).

Laila like her creator revolted against the society which never allowed Muslim girls to come out of home and to choose their mate. Laila refused to abide by that rule and had her education at Aligarh Muslim University. Regarding her marriage she told politely but firmly, "I won't be paired off like an animal" (*SBC* 29). She further stated that, "I joined the University for post-graduate studies with my uncle's indifferent consent and my aunt's passive disapproval" (*SBC* 225). Her education had given her courage to choose Ameer for her husband, disregarding his family condition. Laila-Ameer love description is high water mark in the novel. The free flowing poetic language heightens the intensity of love, which justifies K.R.S. Iyengar's apt observation that, "Attia Hosain writes with a feeling for places, events and words" (464). Laila says,

> The moment when Ameer kissed me had no beginning; it was as pure and eternal as the snows we had been watching in deep communicative silence. It was a part of every moment before it, the moment for which I had been born to become a part of existence before and after it, to know its meaning and fulfil its purpose. I knew a sense of such completeness and harmony that it seemed I was the earth, the sky, the light and the snow (*SBC* 222).

Here, one is reminded of John Keats's love description in "The Eve of St. Agnes" absolutely calm, poise, beautiful and romantic. Being conscious of his lower social status and family background, when Ameer said, "Laila, I have nothing to offer you, nothing but my love", Pat came Laila's reply, "What more do I want?" (*SBC* 223). True to her words she remained true to her love both in his life and also in his death.

Then comes the most important theme of the novel — preparation for partition, communal divide, breaking up families and finally the partition and its aftermath. The assertion of religion as a weapon of communities, the rise of political parties like Congress and newly formed Muslim League opened debates not only at political level but also at the social level bringing discord in families as well. Hamid and his sons Kemal and Saleem, Baba Jan's (Syed Mohammed Hasan) son and grandsons respectively argued violently among themselves over the partition of the country and the creation of Pakistan. Hamid's house became the mini India where the pulse of the people of the country was felt through them. Part III Chapter XII is the most crucial chapter of the novel in which different viewpoints were discussed violently — not without rancor.

Laila, the protagonist and narrator of the novel puts things in their perspectives:

> A new type of person now frequented the house. Fanatic, bearded men and young zealous would come to see Saleem, rough country-dwelling landlords and their 'courtiers' would visit my uncle. Saleem had, metaphorically, discarded his old school tie and my uncle his spats and gloves.... Had both father and son not been so strong-willed, their conflicting ideas would not have led to so many wordy quarrels (*SBC* 230).

Saleem joined the Muslim League as a reaction to what he called the Congress's anti-Muslim sentiment. But Hamid, his father said sarcastically "This Muslim League in which you are so interested, I have heard it called communal and reactionary by nationalist Muslims" (*SBC* 233). In an argument with Kemal, Saleem went on to say, "Muslims who are in the Congress are being used as dupes to give it a secular appearance" (*SBC* 255).

Liberal nationalist muslims like Baba Jan and Hamid are progressive, while communal muslims like Saleem are regressive. As Laila puts it:

> At the end of the last century Baba Jan had been influenced by ideas of reform among Muslims and had sent his sons to English Universities. He had thought the weapons of the foreigners should be used against them to preserve inherited values and culture. To copy their alien ways was abhorrent to him (*SBC* 86).

Hamid was westernized, so was wife Saira. They sent their two sons Kemal and Saleem to England. In course of their quarrel, Hamid told Saleem "I always found it was possible for Hindus and Muslims to work together on a political level and live together in friendship" (*SBC* 234).

Saleem subscribed to the other viewpoint put forward by the people who form the Muslim League, which states,

> The majority of Hindus have not forgotten or forgiven the Muslims for having ruled over them for hundreds of years. Now they can democratically take revenge. The British have ruled about two hundred years, and see how much they are hated (*SBC* 234).

Saira, Saleem's mother subscribes to this view when she says, "Oh dear, there is no question, it would be better to have the British stay on than the Hindus ruling" (*SBC* 234).

The division in Hamid's family on the question of partition of the country is an index of the mind of the people who are torn apart in the country between, “to be or not to be” while deciding to stay back or leave the country. Saleem and Kemal represent two diverse opinions in the country at the time of partition. Kemal hit the nail when he said, “there will still be millions of Muslims here”. The argument went on as follows:

> Saleem tried to calm him. “Kemal, let’s not become emotional about this, You wanted us to speak frankly. I admit Nadira has gone off rather at a tangent, but I am facing this quite objectively. I think we have no future here, and our children have even less.”
>
> Kemal’s voice quivered with suppressed emotion. “I see my future in the past. I was born here, and generations of my ancestors before me. I am content to die here and be buried with them” (*SBC* 288).

Nadira, Saleem’s wife was in favour of migrating to Pakistan, which according to her for most of the muslims of Indian subcontinent, “something different from other countries of the world.” She further argues that their “ancestors left their homes when they first came here”. Migration, for her is a simple thing for ‘people do migrate from one country to another’. Laila retorted he “then let us return to our ancestors’ homeland. Let us return to Arabia, Turkestan, Persia” (*SBC* 289).

Laila, who clearly is the authorial voice makes a very significant statement in the following words:

> How can we live together as a nation if all the time only the differences between the different communities are being preached? (*SBC* 245).

Partition took place. People like Saleem and Nadia left for Pakistan, while nationalists like Kemal and Laila stayed back. The aftermath of partition was terrible. Victimized by communal violence, people suffered endlessly and their sufferings would melt stones, if stones could be melted. Beneath this human agony, there was a saving grace of humanity when Hindus rescued the Muslims who have stayed back in India, their homeland. Laila shouted at her cousin, Zahira:

> Do you know who saved me and my child? Sita, who took us to her house, in spite of putting her own life in danger with ours. And Ranjit, who came from his village, because he had heard of what was happening in the foothills and was afraid for us. He drove us back, pretending we were his family, risking discovery and death. What were you doing then? ...Do you know who saved all the others who had no

> Sitas and Ranjits? Where were all their leaders? Safely across the border. The only people left to save them were those very Hindus against whom they had ranted. Do you know what 'responsibility' and 'duty' meant? To stop the murderous mob at any cost, even if it meant shooting people of their own religion (*SBC* 304).

Zahira pointed out that the same thing happened on the other side also. "Do you think we did not have the same sense of duty on our side? Do you think the same things did not happen there?" (*SBC* 304-05).

The partition and the traumatic violence had left a scar in the body and mind of the people — particularly nationalist people like Laila who, 'bought hideous saris with the national flag printed around the borders', during freedom struggle. Coupled with the national suffering was the personal tragedy of Laila who lost her husband, Ameer, who was killed while trying to escape from the Army captivity. No wonder, Laila said, "I lived and moved through an endless tunnel with no exist" (*SBC* 317). As William Walsh has rightly observed that, "Laila evokes in her character and suffering the experience and the pain of so many in the subcontinent, the subjected women, just as she makes us understand the astonishing toughness their life can breed in women" (103).

What is the significance of this novel and its relevance to the twenty-first century? It reminds us of sufferings of people who had become victims to fanatics' fury and violence. The novel dovetails the past into the present, and reminds us of the importance of independence. It is a warning to all Indians not to fall a prey to communal politics. Religion, one should do well to remember is personal not above nationalism. This inward looking novel enlightens the Indians about the consequences of partition and reminds the British, our colonizers, of terrible loss of life and property in the wake of creation of another country carved out of India with their connivance. The communal feelings which led to partition of India is now back with terrorists attacking the country in the name of religion. The debate of nationalism is back in the country, when National Flag and song are not given the due honour even on some University Campuses. The wheel has come full circle. The relevance of *Sunlight on a Broken Column* is now more than ever before.

Amitav Ghosh's *The Shadow Lines* reminds us of partition in all its horrors evoking, "a fear that comes of the knowledge that normalcy is utterly contingent, that the spaces that surround one, the street one inhabits, can become, suddenly and without warning, as hostile as a desert in a flash flood" (204). Like Attia Hosain's *Sunlight on a Broken Column* this novel tells us of a family story which is the microcosm of the stories of partition at the national level.

The novel begins with the recollection of the unnamed narrator of his father's aunt, Mayadebi, who 'went to England with her husband and son, Tridib' (3) in 1939, the year in which the World War II broke out that was thirteen years before the narrator was born. The novel revolves around the narrator's early admiration of his uncle Tridib, who died in a communal riot. In his book, *Amitav Ghosh*, Anshuman A. Mondal writes candidly about Tridib's death and the narrator's haunting memory in the following words:

> The narrator himself, however, was not present at Tridib's death so his attempt to make sense of it is haunted by this absence. Around this absent centre, the narrator's swirl of memories is constructed through the assimilation of other people's recollections of the event: Tridib's younger brother, Robi, and May Price, an Englishwoman with whom Tridib was becoming romantically involved. It is through their narratives that his own is assembled and the novel discloses how an identity is patched up — or woven, to use Ghosh's favourite metaphor — through interconnecting narratives which may or may not add up to something: at the end of the novel, the narrator is still, to all intents and purposes, at a loss to explain what happened to Tridib (10).

Border for Amitav Ghosh is an imaginary one with many implications. It could be geographical, cultural, linguistic and similarly boundaries could be national and communal when the narrator's grandmother enquired, whether she would be able to "see the border between India and East Pakistan from the plane" while flying to Dhaka, his father laughed and said, why, did she really think the border was a long black line "with green on one side and scarlet on the other, like it was in a school atlas", she was "puzzled". She further went on to say, "But there's something — trenches perhaps, or soldiers or guns pointing at each other, or even just barren strips of land. Don't they call it no — man's land?" (151).

In a perceptive article, "Who is Afraid of Shadow Lines?" A.N. Kaul observes:

> Its (*The Shadow Lines's*) story-line is woven around two families, the Datta-Chowdharys of Bengal and the Princes of London, the relationship between whom spans three generations and involves several passages to and from India on both sides. The story towards the end also negotiates the

> newly sprung up frontier between India and Bangladesh, engaging or acknowledging along the way the presence of other foreign countries and continents via the diplomatic or U.N. postings of two of the Datta-Chowdharys. But to Ghosh all national and communal demarcations are shadow lines, arbitrary and unreal divisions which can lead to terrible consequences (as in Dacca or Calcutta) or, more pervasively, to those many Indian-English, East-West dilemmas which bedevil interpersonal relations in earlier novels but which simply do not exist in *The Shadow Lines* (*IL* 89).

The burden of the novel is to show how people suffered, separated from relatives and uprooted from their native place because of lack of trust among two dominant communities — Hindus and Muslims — giving rise to violence. Partition is no solution to human hatred and distrust. It can lead to further partition creating another border line. This was anticipated by the grand oldman, Jethamoshai of the narrator's grandmother, who came to Dhaka to take him to Calcutta (Kolkata):

> Once you start moving you never stop. That's what I told my sons when they took the trains. I said: I don't believe in this India-Shindia. It's all very well, you are going away now, but suppose you get there they decide to draw another line somewhere? What will you do then? Where will you move to? No one will have you anywhere. As for me, I was born here and I'll die here (215).

As Priyamvada Gopal has pointed out:

> This is, of course, precisely what happens to Pakistan a few years later when it undergoes yet another division into two nations, generating Bengali Bangladesh. Partitions happen over and over again: once the difference is privileged as the basis for nationhood, there open up endless possibilities for fissure (81).

A novel has two sections: "Going Away" and "Home". In Section-I when Mayadebi and Tridib left she was twenty-nine and Tridib was eight. The narrator tried to connect his past and the present through his imagination. In the end the truth was revealed to him, when May told him that Tridib was killed by the mob, while trying to save his grand uncle (Mayadebi's uncle) who was attacked by the mob while driving the rickshaw. They had, "Cut Tridib's throat from ear to ear" (251). This is the outcome to partition, when cruelty run supreme.

Partition has become an inseparable part of living memory affecting not the people of one generation but the generation that has followed. As A.N. Kaul rightly says:

> And yet the hero's growing boy's experience in this novel is not after all his experience, and the same is true of his imagination and perception. It has all been foretold, forelived. Tridib being, so to speak, the novel's ur-imagination, ur-hero, ur-narrator (*IL* 91).

The much talked about and discussed novel in Indian English Literature is Khushwant Singh's *Train to Pakistan* (1956). This novel describes in realistic terms the horrors of partition involving people of three religions — Hinduism, Islam and Sikhism and two countries — India and Pakistan. It depicts the actual transfer of about ten million people as a consequence of communal divide in the wake of partition in 1947. The result is that one million people were killed in the process. The locale of the novel is Mano Majra, a tiny village in the undivided Punjab. This village housed majority of Sikhs, and a number of Muslim families and only one Hindu family of Ram Lal, the moneylender. According to V.A. Shahane, "this realistic masterpiece (*Train to Pakistan*) contains, among other things, a well thought out structure, an artistically conceived plot, an absorbing narrative and imaginatively realized characters" (68).

The novel begins with an ominous note: "The Summer of 1947 was not like other Indian Summers". The novelist takes a detached stand and describes how partition has affected the people in clear and unmistakable words:

> The summer before, communal riots, precipitated by reports of the proposed division of the country into a Hindu India and a Muslim Pakistan, had broken out in Calcutta, and within a few months the death toll had mounted to several thousand. Muslims said the Hindus had planned and started the killing. According to the Hindus, the Muslims were to blame. The fact is, both sides killed. Both shot and stabbed and speared and clubbed. Both tortured. Both raped. From Calcutta, the riots spread north and east and west: to Noakhali in East Bengal, where Muslims massacred Hindus; to Bihar, where Hindus massacred Muslims. Mullahs roamed the Punjab and the Frontier Province with boxes of human skulls said to be those of Muslims killed in Bihar. Hundreds of thousands of Hindus and Sikhs who had lived for centuries on the Northwest Frontier abandoned their homes and fled

> toward the protection of the predominantly Sikh and Hindu communities in the east (*Train to Pakistan* 1).

The novel is divided into four parts: (i) "Dacoity", (ii) "Kalyug", (iii) "Mano Majra" and (iv) "Karma". Mano Majra, 'a tiny place', has only 'three brick buildings'. They are the moneylender Lala Ram Lal's house, the Sikh temple and the mosque. Dacoity in Ram Lal's house and two love scenes occur simultaneously. As V.A. Shahane puts it:

> The shunting of the goods train was in progress when Malli and his gang were involved in house breaking and murder, when Jugga and Nooran were locked in each other's arms and when Hukum Chand and Haseena were engaged in an attempt at physical contact.... The train thus constitutes the principal rhythm in the novel.... The repetitive movements, whistles, and sounds of the train act as a refrain to the progression in stages of action and character in the novel (81).

There are two prominent views on partition:

Sikh Inspector's view and Hukum Chand's counseling.

> Sometimes, sir, one cannot restrain oneself. What do the Gandhi-caps in Delhi know about the Punjab? What is happening on the other side in Pakistan does not matter to them. They have not lost their homes and belongings; they haven't had their mothers, wives, sisters and daughters raped and murdered in the streets (*TP* 21).
>
> "We must maintain law and order," he answered after a pause. "If possible, get the Muslim to go out peacefully. Nobody really benefits by bloodshed. Bad characters will get all the loot and the government will blame us for the killing. No, Inspector Sahib, whatever our views and God alone knows what I would have done to these Pakistanis if I were not a government servant — we must not let there be any killing or destruction of property (*TP* 21).

Events move swiftly and the catastrophic events of partition affect the fate of individual men in Mano Majra. The arrival of ghost train filled with corpses from Pakistan at Mano Majra unnerved both Sikhs and Muslims. Their age-old belief in each other gave rise to suspicion. Notwithstanding Sikh-Muslim age-old friendship and love, Muslims were evacuated to Chandanpur refugee camp to be transported to Pakistan later on. Hindu fanatics got an opportunity to take revenge upon Muslims and what Pakistani Muslims did to Hindu there. Hukum Chand came to know that Haseena would be on that train. He set Jugga free and violently reacted:

> What were the people in Delhi doing? Making fine speeches in the assembly! Loud-speakers magnifying their egos; lovely-looking foreign women in the visitors' galleries in breathless admiration. "He is a great man, this Mr. Nehru of yours. I do think he is the greatest man in the world today. And how handsome! Wasn't that a wonderful thing to say? 'Long ago we made a tryst with destiny and now the time comes when we shall redeem our pledge, not wholly or in full measure but very substantially.'" Yes, Mr. Prime Minister, you made your tryst. So did many others (*TP* 176).

When Jugga learnt that Nooran would be on that train to Pakistan, he decided to let it pass braving the fanatics. As K.R.S. Iyengar has rightly observed that, "we begin with Jugga and Hukum, a budmash and a rake, and it is thanks to them — for Hukum sets Jugga free and Jugga snaps the rope — that the refugee train crosses over safely to Pakistan" (520).

The act of Jugga's sacrifice of his life, 'the train went over him and went on to Pakistan', justifies the title of the novel, *Train to Pakistan.* It is not an easy novel to write because the facts stated come within the purview of journalism. Khushwant Singh an acclaimed journalist turned writer knows how to turn journalistic writing into creative art. The two love episodes — Jugga and Nooran, the Hukum and Haseena redeem the stark realism into an art of fiction. Jugga would not have sacrificed his life and saved the lives of host of Muslims on the train but for Nooran and Hukum would not free Jugga but for Haseena. Love is positive — it connects when religion, particularly organized religion divides. That is the implicit message of the novel.

WORKS CITED

Ghosh, Amitav. *The Shadow Lines*. Delhi: Ravi Dayal Publisher, 1988. Print.

Gopal, Priyamvada. *The Indian English Novel: Nation, History and Narration*. Oxford: Oxford University Press, 2009. Print.

Hosain, Attia. *Sunlight on a Broken Column*. Gurgaon: Penguin Random House India Pvt. Ltd., 1961 rpt. 1988. Print.

Iyengar, K.R.S. *Indian Writing in English*. New Delhi: Sterling Publishers Pvt. Ltd., 1984. Print.

Kaul, A.N. "Who is Afraid of Shadow Lines?" *Indian Literature* 33:4 (July-Aug. 1990). Print.

Mondal, A. Anshuman. *Amitav Ghosh*. New Delhi: Viva Books, 2010 rpt. 2011. Print.

Shahane, V.A. *Khushwant Singh*. New York: Twayne Publishers Inc, 1972. Print.

Singh, Khushwant. *Train to Pakistan*. New Delhi: Time Books International, 1956 rpt. 1989. Print.

Walsh, William. *Indian Literature in English*. London: Longman, 1990. Print.

28

Two Centuries of Indian English Poetry: The Making of a Canon

The subject of this paper is vast in scope encompassing three periods in history: colonial, postcolonial and neocolonial. The origin of Indian English poetry dates back to 1827 when the first Indian English poet, Henry Derozio published his book of verse, *Poems* in 1827. I have excluded E.V. Rieu's anthology, *India in Song: Eastern Themes in English Verse by British and Indian Poets* (1920) because it includes British poets. Since then, Indian English poetry spans over a period of one hundred and twenty years (i.e., from 1827-1947), which may legitimately be called the colonial era. Apart from Henry Derozio, the other poets who belong to colonial period are Kasiprasad Ghose, Michael Madhusudan Dutt, Toru Dutt, Aru Dutt, Harindranath Chattopadhyaya, Joseph Furtado, Sarojini Naidu, Manmohan Ghose and Sri Aurobindo. Of these only three stand out as poets of consequence. They are Toru Dutt (1856-77), who, "has an undisputed claim to be regarded as the first Indian poet in English" (Parthasarathy 1), Sarojini Naidu (1879-1949) and Sri Aurobindo (1872-1950).

Poet-anthologists like R. Parthasarathy, P. Lal, Adil Jussawalla, Keki N. Daruwalla, and a few others denounce the colonial Indian English poetry of Toru Dutt, Sarojini Naidu and Sri Aurobindo, lock, stock and barrel for following the British Romantic and Victorian poets. Dom Moraes too joined them in questioning the competence of these poets to write verse in English. On the other hand, C.D. Narasimhaiah in his well-known book, *The Swan and the Eagle* speaks in admiration of the above three poets. He lauded both Toru Dutt and Sarojini Naidu as pioneers in the field of Indian English poetry. C.D. Narasimhaiah is more eloquent in his praise of Sri Aurobindo who he considers not only as a distinguished poet but critic too. He goes a step forward to tell that English language has gained from Sri

Aurobindo and compares him with Joseph Conrad who broadened the descriptive range of the English language. He says, "it may be said of Sri Aurobindo that he made the English language accommodate certain hitherto unknown (inconscient) areas of experience both through his prose work, *Life Divine* and through his epic *Savitri*, not to speak of the numerous translations from Sanskrit poetry and drama as well as his other less known but important works" (47). It is interesting and important to remember that Sri Aurobindo nearly succeeded in creating an idiom in English which is peculiar and unique to the genius of Indian people. Well known scholars and critics like K.R.S. Iyengar, Sisirkumar Ghose and M.K. Naik too praise Sri Aurobindo and Sarojini Naidu as poets of importance. In the course of an article entitled "Indian Poetry in English, Yesterday — Today — Tomorrow" (*The Literary Criterion*, Vol. XVIII, No. 3. 1983: 9-18), Professor K.R.S. Iyengar takes R. Parthasarathy, Keki N. Daruwalla and Adil Jussawalla to task for criticizing Sri Aurobindo and earlier poets in English for wrong reasons. In his article, "Indian Writing in English: A Reply to Dom Moraes" (*The Literary Criterion*, Vol. 12, Nos. 2-3, 1976: 6-15), Narasimhaiah takes Moraes to task for the latter's arrogance to run down Indian writing in English in general and poetry in particular in the following words:

> Toru Dutt, whom he (Moraes) breezily dismisses as of no consequence and argues what Toru did many school girls can do better and remain unknown. School girls apart, had Keats died before he was 21 by which time Toru had given unmistakable promise of her genius (the Keastian ring of her letters collected by Harihar Das can hardly be missed) what would the world have had of the poet who is now "with Shakespeare"? (8).

What Narasimhaiah says about Moraes, "one thing clearly emerges from this criticism, it is that Mr Moraes who criticizes the critics has proved himself inept for the critical function" (9), could be applied equally to the other poet-anthologists as well.

If the spiritual mode of Sri Aurobindo's *Savitri* or Sarojini Naidu's romantic mode in *The Temple: A Pilgrimage of Love* or mythical writings of Toru Dutt are unacceptable to the post-Independence poet-anthologists of our country, they need to make an introspective study of themselves how much they have followed (should we say imitated?) Eliot, Pound, Auden and other Anglo-American poets. R.W. Desai in course of an article "Contemporary

Indian English Poetry: A Critique" (*The Critical Endeavour*, Vol. 17, Jan. 2011) too questions the post-independence Indian English poets for the lack of form and rhyme in their poetry. Let us be objective in our assessment of colonial Indian English poets. It is not true to say that they are all bad and imitative. Likewise it is not that all postcolonial (Post-Independence) poets are all good. The earlier was not leaden and the latter is not golden. A good deal of good and bad poetry was written in both the periods.

FIRST GENERATION POST COLONIAL INDIAN ENGLISH POETS

Nissim Ezekiel's *A Time to Change* (1952) (published by Fortune Press, London) heralded a new dawn for post-colonial (post-independence Indian English poetry. In 1960s Ezekiel's two significant books of verse, *The Unfinished Man* (1960), and *The Exact Name* (1965), were closely followed by Kamala Das's *Summer in Calcutta* (1965) and A.K. Ramanujan's *The Striders* (1966). The trio laid the foundation of modern Indian English poetry. We may say now that Nissim Ezekiel, A.K. Ramanujan, Kamala Das, R. Parthasarathy, Jayanta Mahapatra, Adil Jussawalla, Shiv K. Kumar, Keki N. Daruwalla, Dom Moraes, Arun Kolatkar, A.K. Mehrotra, P. Lal and Pritish Nandy who wrote between 1950s and 1990s produced quite a few remarkable poems. Most of these well-known poets have won Sahitya Akademi Awards and brought out collections of their poems under the title, *Collected Poems*. These include Nissim Ezekiel's *Collected Poems 1952-1988* (OUP, 1989), A.K. Ramanujan's *The Collected Poems of A.K. Ramanujan* (OUP, 1999), Keki N. Daruwalla's *Collected Poems 1970-2005* (Penguin Books, 2006), Dom Moraes's *Collected Poems 1954-2004* (Penguin Books, 2004), Kamala Das's *Collected Poems*, Vol. 1 (1984) and *Only the Soul Knows How to Sing* (DC Books, 1996), Jayanta Mahapatra's *Selected Poems* (OUP, 1982) and *The Life of Dawns, 1974-2008* (Authors Press, 2009). The nine poets who won the Sahitya Akademi Award are Jayanta Mahapatra for *Relationship* (1981), Nissim Ezekiel for *Latter — Day Psalms* (1983), Keki N. Daruwalla for *The Keeper of the Dead* (1984), Kamala Das for *Collected Poems*, Vol. 1 (1985), Shiv K. Kumar for *Trapfalls in the Sky* (1987), Dom Moraes for *Serendip* (1994), A.K. Ramanujan for *The Collected Poems of A.K. Ramanujan* (1999), Jeet Thayil for *These Errors are Correct* (2012) and Adil Jussawalla for *Trying to Say Goodbye* (2014).

First generation of Postcolonial Indian English poets can be broadly divided into two groups. One, those who dive deep into Indian culture, tradition, history and time, and two, those who lay emphasis on Indian geography, people, places and contemporary reality. Poets who belong to the first group include Kamala Das, Jayanta Mahapatra, A.K. Ramanujan, R. Parthasarathy and a few others. They, as it were, make a voyage within. Jayanta Mahapatra's *Relationship*, Arun Kolatkar's *Jejuri* and R. Parthasarathy's *Rough Passage* are bright examples of this kind of poetry. Poets who belong to the second group include Nissim Ezekiel, Keki N. Daruwalla, Adil Jussawalla, Shiv K. Kumar, O.P. Bhatnagar and a few others. They lay emphasis on contemporary India of their time highlighting geography, people, places and above all, the reality that engulfs them. Most of them excel in ironic mode.

Poems that have appealed to the readers and gained their appreciation belong to poets of both the above-mentioned groups. They are Jayanta Mahapatra's *Relationship*, "A Country", "The Lost Children of America", "A Pastoral Perhaps", "The Abandoned British Cemetery at Balasore", and "Hunger", Nissim Ezekiel's "Night of the Scorpion", "Jewish Wedding in Bombay", "Nudes 1978", "Hymns in Darkness", "Poet Lover, Birdwatcher", "Background, Casually," "The Visitor" and "In India", A.K. Ramanujan's "A River", "Small Scale Reflections on a Great House", "Second Sight", "Love Poem for a Wife, 1", "Some Indian Uses of History on a Rainy Day", Keki N. Daruwalla's "The Ghaghra in Spate", "Crossing of Rivers", "Death of a Bird", "Migrations", "The Parsi Hell", "The Hebrew Professor", Dom Moraes's "Landscape", "Painter", "Homo Sapiens", "Myth", Kamala Das's "An Introduction", "The Looking Glass", "Home is a Concept", "Blood", "Substitute", Shiv K. Kumar's "Lord Krishna to Arjuna", "Twenty-fifth Wedding Anniversary", "I say it on Oath, your Lordship", "R. Parthasarathy", "Exile" and "Home Coming".

Theory of Diaspora and Postcolonialism can be applied to Kamala Das's "Home is a Concept", O.P. Bhatnagar's "Look Homeward Angel", Keki N. Daruwalla's "Migrations". In "Home is a Concept", "Kamala Das describes the plight of expatriate, immigrant and diasporic writers for whom the concept of home has become burdensome. An immigrant or diasporic writer may accept another country as his home but does that country accept him as its' own on par with the natives?" Some are torn between the country they left behind and the country they adopt as their own. Hence, they are suspended between two words — neither at home, here or there.

> The unwanted wait here, and there for aeroplanes
> clutching at heavy briefcase that hold
> the papers to be read at seminars,
> passports, visas and photographs of laughing
> children. The unwanted carry heavy bags
> and overcoats but the heaviest language
> they tote is pain. If home is a concept
> they shall not know it... (*Only the Soul Knows How to Sing* 105).

If Kamala Das's "Home is a Concept" explains diasporic situation, O.P. Bhatnagar's "Look Homeward Angel" exposes the intention behind migration and disastrous consequences of migratory movements. The poem opens with a clear statement:

> I don't blame my friends settled abroad
> Far off in England and Mozambique,
> America, Australia or Madrid,

Bhatnagar compares the migrant Indians to the migratory birds and regrets that unlike the birds, these people never return home. They forget the "country that once brought them up/ splitting water with sun rays" and build 'homes away from home'. The poet thinks that one of the reasons behind migration is to earn more. So these people fail to 'look beyond glamour and gold'. Making a reference to history and myth, Bhatnagar says,

> Even Greece had its Ulysses
> Who brought his ships back home
> but our Heroes make no myths
> And our imagination no Homer
> (*An Anthology of Indian English Poetry*,
> Ed. M.Q. Khan and B.K. Das, OUP, 1992: 37-38).

SECOND GENERATION OF INDIAN ENGLISH POETS

Now let me turn to the second generation of postcolonial Indian English poets who appeared on the Indian literary scene in nineteen eighties. They are Bibhu Padhi, C.P. Surendran, Ranjit Hoskote, Robin S. Ngangom, Niranjan Mohanty, Makarand Paranjapee, Gopi Kishan Kottoor, and a few others, who live in the country and write poetry in English. Of these Bibhu Padhi stands out with eight collection of poems to his credit. He has come a long way from his first book of verse, *Going to the Temple* (1989) to *Midnight Diary*

(2015). His poetry has variety of themes starting from family poems to landscape of the place, to mythology, to art, and between history and geography it is exquisitely balanced. Pain is a recurring theme in his poetry. Pain keeps us awake. It revives our memory of people and places dear to us. Pain comes from the migraine that occurs 'every third day', from the early death of his father, the nervous breakdown of the mother and the moving away of brothers from the parental house, and not receiving letters from friends living in 'Calcutta or Bhopal' but not from anything in particular. Pain comes from everywhere like the 'wife's neuralgia returning every winter' but nothing in particular, 'Not these, not here'.

Bibhu Padhi's poetry has variety ranging from love poetry to contemporary reality, landscape of places and the changing nature of people from tradition to modernity. He is firmly rooted in the soil of Odisha — Cuttack is the nerve centre of his poetry. All kinds of theories ranging from New Criticism, Structuralism and Post-Structuralism to Eco-Criticism can be applied to his poetry. Apart from the themes, the techniques of employing imagery and symbols in his poetry have an appeal to the readers. Like Nissim Ezekiel's scorpion, an ordinary creature like house lizard is well portrayed in Padhi's poetry, bringing the traditional beliefs into its modern connotations. House Lizard saying 'true, true, true' in course of talks or conversations between two individuals often comes true. What is striking in Padhi's poetry is the choice of words and the evocation of images in their contexts, which endear him to the readers. The readers respond to his poetry, the way they do to Ezekiel's poetry or Ramanujan's poetry. He successfully recreates the Odisha scene in his "Home" and "House" poems.

Ranjit Hoskote (1969-) is in the line of first group of postcolonial poets such as Jayanta Mahapatra, Kamala Das, R. Parthasarathy and others, who speak of history, tradition and culture of the country. He is also an elegiac poet who laments the death of pioneering poets such as Nissim Ezekiel and Ghalib. He has also a sense of history and dives deep into the pages of it, to recreate the past in the present. The last life of Ezekiel was very painful, when he suffered from Alzheimer which ultimately claimed him. Hoskote's poem, "Passing a Ruined Mill" brings out the agony of suffering to the surface. The poem begins:

> His mind's gone black as a fax
> left untouched for months in a drawer,
> his faded words a defeat

of grammar and the continuities we prize.
(Thayil 298)

History and memory are happily blended in another poem, "Ghalib in the Winter of the Great Revolt" (Delhi 1957). This war reminds us of Timur who had 'broken Delhi walls', 'the profits of betrayal' and 'penalties of defeat'. This poem is linked with the other Agha Shahid Ali Memorial Poem, "Colours for a Landscape Held Captive" evoking the old days of captivity. Thus, he writes:

They never knew you, who only recall...
you never meant to trap us in that country
without a post office, where boatmen and saints
trade stories to while away the days
of khaki captivity (Thayil 306)

C.P. Surendran (1959-) has a number of books of verse to his credit which include *Gemini II*, *Posthumous Poems*, *Canaries on the Moon*, and *Portraits of the Space We Occupy*. He sees life steadily and sees it whole. He takes his poems as 'a way of belief'. A sense of sadness overwhelms his poems. He is not a pessimist but a realist who understands life as it unfolds before him. He says, "In time, our goodness may/ Reconcile us to our failure" ("Departure"). He realizes that all our grief end in death. Thus, he writes:

There is no grief
Death cannot redress.
("Solution", *Posthumous Poems* 92)

He wants to live in his work. No wonder, he says in his "Introduction" to *Posthumous Poems*, "Talk true. In our speech we rise again".

Robin S. Ngangom (1959-) has three collections poetry, *Words and the Silence*, *Time's Crossroads* and *The Desire of Roots* to his credit. He is a very promising Indian English poet from North-East. In a poem called, "House", Ngangom states how he is rooted in the soil. He writes:

Relentlessly a dream has hemmed me in these hills.
While the future has cast me as a bleak interpreter of signs.
("House", Sen 373)

The second generation of Indian English poetry are in the direct line of the first generation of poets beginning with Nissim Ezekiel, Kamala Das, A.K. Ramanujan, Jayanta Mahapatra and the host of other eminent Indian English poets. Jeet Thayil's (*60 Indian Poets*) and Sudeep Sen's (*The HarperCollins Book of English Poetry*), recent anthologies of poetry highlight the second generation of poets in the same way the anthologies of R. Parthasarathy (*Ten Twentieth Century Indian Poets*), Keki N. Daruwalla (*Two Decades of Indian English Poetry, 1960-1980*) and Arvind Krishna Mehrotra's (*Twenty Indian Poems* and *The Oxford India Anthology of Twelve Modern Indian Poets*) have highlighted the first generation of poets. The second generation of poets are "full of promise and potentiality" but limited in achievement.

NON-RESIDENT / DIASPORIC INDIAN ENGLISH POETS

Significant Indian poets who live abroad in the US, UK, Germany, Australia and some other countries could be divided into two groups. Non-Resident Indian English poets and poets of Indian origin (Diasporic poets). They are Meena Alexander, Shanta Acharya, Sujata Bhatt, Tabish Khair, Sudesh Mishra, Leela Gandhi and Imtiaz Dharker. Not only these poets are of Indian origin but they are deeply connected with the land of their birth or the birth of their ancestors.

Meena Alexander's collections of poems include *Stone Roots* (1980), *House of a Thousand Doors* (1985), *River and Bridge* (1995), *The Shock of Arrival* (1996) and her latest collection of poems is titled, *Atmospheric Embroidery* (2015). A strong political awareness is another striking feature of Alexander's poetry, and this is a trait which few of the contemporary women poets share. In "News of the World," a woman from Cambodia remembers how during the political trouble there, "I/ my mother's head in a sack/ ran three days and nights/ through a rice-field." "The Young of Tiananmen" is a moving tribute to martyrs of the notorious Tiananmen Square massacre, "as blood swallowed them whole." "Prison Cell" is an imaginative reconstruction of Nelson Mandela's experience in prison, whether "even an ant, a fly/ would be company". There are quite a few good poems in *Atmospheric Embroidery*. Alexander's title poem takes the world as a work of embroidery linking the rivers of the world and the trees to evoke the landscape of the world in our mind. Thus, she says

> In The Thousand Longest Rivers
> The Nile is the hardest water
> Then comes the Mississippi — Missouri
> Once we lived by brilliant waters
>
> (*Atmospheric Embroidery* 5)

In "Aesthetic Knowledge" she says, 'the landscape becomes us' and states man's position in the universe.

> We are creatures of this world
> An invisible grammar holds us in place
> When God shows his face
> Even mountains start to blaze
>
> (*Atmospheric Embroidery* 6)

Sujata Bhatt (1956-), who now lives in Germany found a place in *The Harvill Book of Twentieth-Century Poetry in English* (2000) edited by Michael Schmidt. Bhatt, a promising poet has a number of collections of poems to her credit such as *Brunizem* (1988), *Monkey Shadows* (1991), *The Striking Rose* (1995), *Point No Point: Selected Poems* (1997) and *My Mother's Way of Wearing a Sari* (2000). A widely travelled poet, she reflects on her experiences both inside the country and abroad in her poetry.

All the five poems included in the above-mentioned anthology are good poems by any standard. They are, "Muliebrity", "A Different History", "Understanding the Ramayana", "White Asparagus" and "The Stinking Rose". Let me, analyse one of them, "A Different History" which is written in the ironic mode. The superstition prevalent in India is reflected in the following lines:

> Here, the gods roam freely
> disguised as snakes or monkeys
> every tree is sacred
> and it is a sin
> to be rude to a book.
>
> ("A Different History")

Shanta Acharya (1952-) has a number of collections of poems which bear testimony to her potentiality to be called a good poet of Indian diaspora. In *Not this, Not that* (1994) and *Numbering our Day's Illusions* (1995), there is a longing for serenity, and calm of mind. She tries to come to terms with herself. Eliot once said, 'People may change and smile but the agony abides.' This seems to be true in case of Shanta Acharya. Memory is a burden that needs to be overcome. Poem after poem she tries to redeem her past and come to terms with reality that baffles her. In "Highgate Cemetery" she says,

> In the unmapped terrain within us we bury
> in terraced catacombs painful memories.
> If only we could let them grow out of us like trees.

She harks on the same theme in another poem called "Sleep".

It is terrible to live with memory
the beginning of all our suffering.

With the advancing years comes the regret for the past and uncertainty of the future. Thus, she writes:

I travel towards what end I cannot say—
along the way, those I meet and those I don't,
all that happens and all that I wait for to happen
keep defining me in some inexplicable way
Daily mirror mocks my wrinkles and streaks of grey.
("Shringara", *Journal of Literature and Aesthetics*, Jan-June 1998: 63)

The voice in her poetry is controlled and submerged, looking before and after. Hence, the prayer to understand the meaning of life and bear sufferings with courage and determination.

... I have to pray and wait
for life's meaning to unfold itself to me
("The Poet's RSVP")
Teach me how to find myself in these palaces of
art, that I may learn to love and suffer with my heart
("An Italian Prayer")

Apart from the thematic contents, the language is highly evocative of the scenes depicted in her poetry. The form in her poetry is controlled, and the choice of words and images is appropriate. Acharya has contributed to the creation of an Indian English idiom by using innovative language in her poetry and that is not a mean achievement.

Imtiaz Dharker's well-known books of poems are *Purdah* (1989), *Postcards from God* (1994), *The Terrorist at my Table* and *Over the Moon* (2014). She is conscious of the political atmosphere around her. To Adil Jussawalla's observation, "Imtiaz, you have talked about women's issues in your work", she says,

> I have talked about issues like *Purdah* etc. but in a wider political context, no just gender politics. I think every act is political. The act of writing poetry is political, even lack of action is political. Where we take the poem is finally what its about. Even when I was writing *Purdah*, and especially in my later work, I have moved into a wider arena. It's finally about not belonging to any group, not needing to identify with any group, religion or country. It's about being an outsider,

> writing and working from the position of an outsider, in the most positive sense (*Gentleman*, Jan. 2001: 61)

We live in the age of global terror with some countries aiding and abetting the terrorists. Dharker in her poem, "The Terrorist at my Table" tells as much like a detached observer of horror and violence.

> At my back, the news is the same
> as usual. A train
> blown up, hostages taken.

Leela Gandhi's *Measure of Home* (2001) contains forty poems on a number of themes. It makes an interesting story. The book begins with "Invocation", "Let my vowels resonate/ my verbs resound/ until the singing is done,/ my song sung" (1). She seeks to speak of the 'fractured past'. Unlike Kamala Das's "Looking Glass", which urges women to gift their all to men, Leela Gandhi's "The Looking Glass" asserts, "there's more my story to being loved than loving", and concludes, "In love, the looking glass is our nemesis". Leela Gandhi takes the feminist view of life, and says, "Daughters are verbs and sons ciphers". In her poem, "Katha" she says:

> Poems and poets both, practice promiscuity,
> There is no fidelity in either man or words.
> (*Measures of Home* 37)

CONCLUSION

Coming to the question of canon formation in Indian English poetry, I am reminded of Harold Bloom's well known book, *The Western Canon*. Here, he ponders over the question, 'What makes the author and the works canonical' and says, "the answer more often than not, has turned out to be strangeness, a mode of originality that either cannot be assimilated or that so assimilates us that we cease to see it as strange" (Bloom, 3). He further states that, "One mark of an originality that can win canonical status for a literary work is a strangeness that we either never altogether assimilate, or that becomes such a given that we are blinded to its idiosyncrasies. Dante is the largest instance of the first possibility, and Shakespeare, the overwhelming example of the second" (4).

The question is wherein does the greatness of a poet lie? It lies in his appeal to the readers beyond his life time and involves the question of influence over succeeding generation of poets. As far as the two centuries of Indian English poetry is concerned, Nissim

Ezekiel and A.K. Ramanujan can be said to achieve the canonical status. They are the canon to whom both contemporaries and succeeding generations of poets have looked up for inspiration. In course of my article, "T.S. Eliot and Nissim Ezekiel: The Making of the Poetic Canon" (*The Critical Endeavour*, Vol. XVIII, 2012), I have stated the importance of Ezekiel as a canonical poet by putting him by the side of T.S. Eliot.

> Eliot and Ezekiel have something in common — that is, both of them brought everyday conversational language into the realms of poetry. If for Eliot, the poet is involved 'with the intolerable wrestle/with words and meanings', for Ezekiel, 'the best poets wait for words'. Poems like "Night of the Scorpion", "Enterprise", "Poet, Lover, Birdwatcher". "The Professor" and "Very 'Indian' Poems in Indian English" bring conversational language into the realms of poetry. Irony and parody became favourite mode in Ezekiel's poetry (Das 28).
>
> Eliot and Ezekiel have influenced poets who succeeded them. Eliot's influence is international but Ezekiel's is national. Jayanta Mahapatra, Keki N. Daruwalla, Dom Moraes, Shiv K. Kumar — all acknowledge their indebtedness to Ezekiel. In course of an interview given to me (*The Critical Endeavour*, Vol. XVII, Jan. 2011), Keki N. Daruwalla acknowledges Nissim Ezekiel's greatness as a poet and humanist. Both Eliot and Ezekiel began as poets who looked life from negative point of view, finally ended as great humanistic poets. They fashioned a new vocabulary for poetry and set the taste for the age. Eliot and Ezekiel brought the readers of their own countries close to poetry. This is a significant achievement by any standard, anywhere in the world (Das 30).

Similarly, I have emphasized the greatness of Ramanujan by putting him by the side of Eliot in course of my article, "Intersecting Tradition with the Individual Talent: Reading the poetry of T.S. Eliot and A.K. Ramanujan" (*The Critical Endeavour*, Vol. XVI, 2011). Both Eliot and Ramanujan were polyglots, who knew a number of languages. I have stated that

> If Eliot laid emphasis on history and time, Ramanujan spoke about Indian myths, folklore and history, which gave a shape to his poetry. Both the poets spoke about tradition but broke it when the need arose. Both of them toyed with the idea of becoming Buddhists, but resisted later on.... If Eliot's art is

> 'the way up' through detachment from the self, things and persons, Ramanujan's is the 'way down' to family bond, relations and body. The attachment with the body makes him cry, dear body, you brought me/ curled in womb and memory, 'do not leave me/ behind'. Primary opposites like body and mind, history and contemporaneity, nature and culture are juxtaposed in Ramanujan's poetry.... Both Eliot and Ramanujan spoke about tradition but broke traditional form of poetry by deviating from the rigorous metrical verse. The greatest contribution of both Eliot and Ramanujan is that they brought everyday conversational language into realms of poetry (Das 106, 111-12).

Ramanujan would continue to inspire the poets in the twenty-first century for showing the way how national myths and folklore can be used in making poems in English. In "Mythologies I", and "Mythologies II", Ramanujan has demonstrated clearly how Puttana and Hiranya Kasyap could be effectively used as myths in poetry. Ramanujan interprets myth in terms of life in death — not death in life as Eliot does in *The Waste Land*.

> The breast she offered was full
> of poison and milk...
> She changed, undone by grace
> from deadly mother to happy demon
> found life in death
>
> ("Mythologies I")

To conclude, I should say, that for thematic variation, felicity of expression, inwardness with language and technical virtuosity Nissim Ezekiel and A.K. Ramanujan are the canon of Indian English Poetry.

WORKS CITED

Bloom, Harold. *The Western Canon*. London: McMillan, 1995. Print.

Das, Bijay Kumar. *Interpreting Poetry and Evaluating Criticism*. New Delhi: Atlantic Publishers, 2015. Print.

——. *Perspectives on the Poetry of A.K. Ramanujan*. New Delhi: Doaba House, 2013. Print.

——. "T.S. Eliot and Nissim Ezekiel: The Making of the Poetic Canon". *The Critical Endeavour* 18 (2012): 286-96. Print.

——. "Intersecting Tradition with the Individual Talent: Reading the Poetry of T.S. Eliot and A.K. Ramanujan". *The Critical Endeavour* 17 (2011): 256-66. Print.

Das, Kamala. *Only the Soul Knows How to Sing*. Kottayam: DC Books, 1996. Print.

Gandhi, Leela. *Measures of Home*. Delhi: Ravi Dayal Publisher, 2000. Print.

Jussawalla, Adil. "Memos and Reminders". Panel Discussion. *The Gentleman* 21:1 (Jan. 2001). Print.

Khan, M.Q. and B.K. Das. *An Anthology of Indian English Poetry*. Calcutta: Oxford University Press, 1992. Print.

Narasimhaiah, C.D. *The Swan and the Eagle*. 3rd Ed. New Delhi: Vision Books Pvt. Ltd., 1999. Print.

——. "Indian Writing in English: A Reply to Dom Moraes". *The Literary Criterion*. 12: 2-3 (1976): 6-15. Print.

Parthasarathy, R. ed. *Ten Twentieth Century Indian Poets*. New Delhi: Oxford University Press, 1976. Print.

Sen, Sudeep, ed. *The Harper Collins Book of English Poetry*. Noida: Harper Collins Publishers, 2012, Print.

Surendran, C.P. *Posthumous Poems*. New Delhi: Penguin Books India (P) Ltd., 1999. Print.

Thayil, Jeet, ed. *60 Indian Poets*. Gurgaon: Penguin Books, 2008. Print.

This paper is the revised version of the Plenary Lecture delivered at the UGC sponsored National Seminar on Contemporary Indian English Poetry: Culture and Identity organised by the University Department of English, T.M. Bhagalpur University, Bhagalpur on 7-8 July 2017.

29

An Era of Darkness: A Journey from Colonialism to Postcolonialism

Shashi Tharoor's book, *An Era of Darkness: The British Empire in India* (2017) grew out of his participation in a debate on, "Britain Owes Reparations to Her Former Colonies" on 28 May 2015 organised by the Oxford Union at Oxford. The title of the book is foregrounded in V.S. Naipaul's *An Area of Darkness* (1964). The Chapter 6 of the book, "The Remaining Case for Empire" is relevant to trace the path from the beginning of Colonialism to Postcolonialism in India. Here one is reminded of Elleke Boehmer's *Colonial and Postcolonial Literature* (1995) and Ania Loomba's *Colonialism and Postcolonialism* (2009). How English language and literature influenced Indians to learn English and write literature in English called Indian English Literature is the focus of this chapter. Let us, first take the following statement of the author:

> I had my English schooling in India and I learned it without the shadow of the Englishman judging my prose. I delighted in the language on its own terms, as a pan-Indian language today, and not as a symbol of colonial oppression. In any case, most English-educated Indians, including myself, will not repudiate Shakespeare and P.G. Wodehouse: we must concede we couldn't have enjoyed their master works without the English language (235).

This is a valid statement in the Indian context. Let us take the case of Raja Rammohan Roy. After being grounded in Bengali (his mother tongue) Sanskrit, Persian and Arabic, Roy learnt English and adapted "to the British system of education in India at which he excelled" (217) observes Tharoor. Macaulay's famous (should we say infamous?) "Minute on Education" (1835) legitimized the teaching of English "to a small minority of Indians" (218).

Macaulay has clearly stated his objectives in the following words:

> We must do our best to form a class who may be interpreters between us and the millions whom we govern, a class of persons, Indians in blood and colour but in English in taste, in opinions, in morals and intellect (218-19).

When we look back into the past, Macaulay's "Minute on Education" boomeranged on the British when Indian leaders who learnt English used it as a vehicle to fight against the British to make India free from the colonial rule. All our freedom fighters of the highest order R.C. Dutta and Dadabhai Naoroji in the last part of the nineteenth century and Mahatma Gandhi, Jawaharlal Nehru, C. Rajagopalachari and a host of other leaders used to write and protest against the British in the English language. Rajaji is reported to have said, "the English language is Goddess Saraswati's gift to us". Mahatma Gandhi was of the view that, "say your say in any language you like".

British colonialism has brought two things simultaneously. One, British imperialism, economic exploitation and subjugation of Indian people and two, English language and rich English literature and above all, Bard of Avon (William Shakespeare). Orientalists looked down upon Indians, while Anglicists appropriated British values, culture and lauded English literature. Anti-colonial nationalism united Indians and finally, brought independence, though a truncated one (Pakistan broke away from India due to the evil design of the British). Britishers left the country — not their language and literature. English has become our acquired language (second language) through which we received our education at the school, more so at college and university level — to be precise, the language of our mind if not our heart. We will do well to remember that it is not the British alone but the Americans who are responsible for the globalization of the English language. As Shashi Tharoor has rightly observed:

> By virtue not so much of British colonization, as of American twentieth-century dominance, English has become the language of globalization, the benefits of which are also accruing to India. But though the world wide adaptation of English has 'certainly facilitated more global exchanges and business transactions among English speakers everywhere' including India... (234).

Tharoor thinks that non-English speaking subjects were discriminated against.

English is no less ours' for primarily it being an Englishman's or an American's. If 'language speaks the man' (Heidegger) language becomes the man. In choosing the language, the language becomes the man. Here, I am reminded of A.K. Ramanujan who said:

> English has distorted our traditions, but it has also made us look at our traditions. It's not enough to say that it is all colonialism and has done nothing but distort. This whole question of colonial distortion has been formulated in English. It requires a dialogue with English. English has been the 'other' through which we have returned to ourselves. English has become a part of us. To say we want to return to a pre-English state is chimerical. The anti-colonial discourse is all done in English. Nobody's writing this in Kannada. In India, there is a wonderful group of new historians called the Subalterns who are looking at all the distortion of the colonial intellectual practices. But all their work is done in English. Isn't the English in which they are writing distorting what they are writing about? English has made us self-critical and made us critical of English itself (*Uncollected Poems and Prose* 79).

Since in this chapter of the book, I am concerned with post-colonial literature, I will concentrate on finding out how English writers have influenced Indian writers in the colonial and post-colonial period, and American writers have influenced Indian writers in the neo-colonial era (i.e., from the second part of the twentieth century to the present time).

Indian English writers of colonial period, Mulk Raj Anand, R.K. Narayan, Raja Rao, B. Rajan, Manohar Malgonkar, Attia Hosain, and a host of others have come under the influence of British writers. It is E.M. Forster who helped Anand and in a way showed the way by asking the latter to visit Gandhi's Ashram at Sabarmati, Gujarat before finalizing the manuscript of *Untouchable* and later helped him to publish the book in London. R.K. Narayan owes a lot to Graham Greene to publish his novels — *Swamy and Friends, The Bachelor of Arts* and *Guide*. The Indian English writers have learnt from the British writers how to use English as a medium of creative expression. Raja Rao took a stand to write fiction in English in our own way which stated clearly in his *Preface to Kanthapura* (1938).

Indian English poets in the colonial period such as Michael Madhusudan Dutt, Toru Dutt, Sarojini Naidu and Sri Aurobindo have learnt a lot from British poets. British Romantic and Victorian poets cast their spell on them. Sri Aurobindo went in Miltonic way to write his immortal epic, *Savitri.* Modern Indian English poets — particularly the leader of the Indian English poetic movement of 1950s and 1960s, Nissim Ezekiel began writing poetry under the shadows of T.S. Eliot and W.H. Auden. The 'city' as in Eliot and Auden became the nerve centre of Ezekiel's poetry. Eliot's spell was also unmistakable on the poets of Indian Bhasha literatures as well. This is the gain of colonialism — plain and simple.

In the realms of Indian English prose writers — Jawaharlal Nehru, Nirad C. Chaudhuri, S. Radhakrishnan and the host of their contemporaries and succeeding generation of prose writers the influence of English writers is discernable. To my mind, Nehru, the greatest Indian English prose writer could not have written his all time classics like *The Discovery of India* (1946), *An Autobiography* (1936) and *Glimpses of World History* (1934) without English influence. British critics and public figures are full of praise for Nehru's use of idiom, prose-style. Nehru's *An Autobiography* is a masterpiece, unparalleled in English language and literature. In the words of K.R.S. Iyengar, "Personal history was fused with national history and we were privileged to watch the evolution of Nehru's personality" (303).

Tharoor says, "One cannot denounce British colonialism and celebrate the doyen of English humourist at the sametime" (236). But this is possible because material and imperialistic colonialism which sprang from Orientalism was denounced by anti-colonial nationalism. The English of Queen Victoria had to go back from the Indian soil and it went back. But the England of Shakespeare, Donne, Wordsworth, Keats, Tennyson, Dickensian, Hardy, Eliot, Lawrence, Forster, Orwell, Ted Hughes, Larkin, William Golding, Beckett and host of other writers was bound to stay back and it stayed back.

Postcolonialism issues out of colonialism and looks forward to neo-colonialism. In the concluding chapter of the book, Tharoor asks a rhetorical question: "What do we do about colonialism, other than understand it?" (279). As I have pointed out in this chapter there are two kinds of colonialism — materialistic and intellectual (including our thought and literature). Tharoor refers to two important books — one, Pankaj Mishra's, *From the Ruins of Empire: The Revolt against the West and the Remaking of Asia* (2012) and two, Niall Ferguson's, *Empire: The Rise and Demise of the British World Order and the Lessons for Global Power* (2003) to justify how much Britain owes Reparations to India. He cites the case of the Kohinoor, 'the world's largest diamond' (280), which should be returned to India.

As I have stated that this chapter is not concerned with materialistic colonialism, but postcolonial literature(s) in India — Indian English literature and Bhasha literatures. A large number of writers from India have voluntarily left the country, as expatriates, emigrants and diasporas to settle in the US and also in the UK and Canada. The names of writers like Attia Hosain, Kamala Markandaya, Nirad C. Chaudhuri, Salman Rushdie, A.K. Ramanujan, R. Parthasarathy, Bharati Mukherjee, Jhumpa Lahiri, Rohinton Mistry, Kiran Desai, Meena Alexander, and also a number of writers who divide their time between the west and India contribute immensely to the making of postcolonial Indian English literature. These writers are internationally known and recognized and some of them have won awards like Booker Prize and Pulitzer Prize.

The question which haunts us after the World War II is that what are the subjects of postcolonial literature which emerged after the withdrawal of the British empire from the former colonies including India. Elleke Boehmer makes an apt observation in the following passage:

> Rather than simply being the writing which 'came after' empire, *postcolonial* literature is that which critically scrutinizes the colonial relationship. It is writing that sets out in one way or another to resist colonialist perspectives. As well as a change in power, decolonization demanded symbolic overhaul, a reshaping of dominant meanings. Postcolonial literature formed part of that process of overhaul. To give expression to colonized experience, Postcolonial writers sought to undercut thematically and formally the discourses which supported colonization — the myths of power, the race classifications, the imagery of sub-ordination, Postcolonial literature, therefore, is deeply marked by experiences of cultural exclusion and division under empire. Especially in its early stages it can also be a nationalist writing. Building on this, *postcoloniality* is defined as that condition in which colonized peoples seek to take their place, forcibly or otherwise, as historical subjects (3).

Postcolonial literature seeks to explore indigenous history, culture and tradition as opposed to the colonizer's history, culture and tradition. It is based on anti-colonial culture and tradition. It emphasizes alternative history and culture. Moreover, postcolonial writers write in their own way taking liberty with British English. The creation of Indian English idiom has widened the range and scope of English language and literature. Indian English literature has helped to widen the scope of the new literatures in English.

In the concluding paragraph of this chapter let me say that Tharoor's book which is foregrounded in the Oxford debate on, "Britain Owes Reparations to Her Former Colonies", for "Centuries of rapacity in their lands" (Tharoor's words 282), demands not financial compensation in terms of economic aid but atonement of the sins committed in the past like Jallianwala Bagh Killings in 1919. Thus writes Tharoor:

> It is getting late for atonement, but not too late: I, for one dearly hope that a British Prime Minister will find the heart, and the spirit, to get on his or her knees at Jallianwala Bagh in 2019 and beg forgiveness from Indians in the name of his or her people for the unforgivable massacre that was perpetuated at that site a century earlier (XXIII).

Tharoor speaks in terms of economic exploitation and political subjugation of our people at the hands of the British for nearly 200 years and appropriately concludes the *Preface* "...as an Indian I find it far easier to forgive than to forget" (XXVI).

But the question is, how our own Indigenous literatures were suppressed by the imposition of English language and literature on us. Now that Indian Bhasha literatures are getting translated into English for the benefit of Indians at home and also for the benefit of bringing it to the notice of the English speaking people abroad including the former colonizer's progeny, is the right kind of atonement that English language has made for suppressing them during the colonial period. Postcolonial Indian English literature and regional literatures in English translation go hand in hand fulfilling the journey from colonialism to postcolonialism, and again to neo-colonialism.

WORKS CITED

Boehmer, Elleke. *Colonial and Postcolonial Literature*. Great Clarendon Street: Oxford, 1995. Print.

Iyengar, K.R.S. *Indian Writing in English*. New Delhi: Sterling Publishers Pvt. Ltd., 1984. Print.

Nehru, Jawaharlal. *An Autobiography*. New Delhi: Jawaharlal Nehru Memorial Fund, Oxford University Press, 1982. Print.

Ramanujan, A.K. *Uncollected Poems and Prose*. Eds. Molly Daniels-Ramanujan and Keith Harrison. New Delhi: Oxford University Press, 2000. Print.

Tharoor, Shashi. *An Era of Darkness: The British Empire in India*, New Delhi: Aleph Book Company, 2016. Print.

Select Bibliography

Ashcroft, Bill, Gareth Griffiths and Helen Tiffin. *The Empire Writes Back*. London: Methuen, 1987. Print.

Atwood, Margaret. *Survival: A Thematic Guide to Canadian Literature*. Toronto: Anansi, 1972. Print.

——, ed. *The Oxford Book of Canadian Verse*. Toronto: Oxford University Press, 1982. Print.

Beier, Ulli, ed. *Introduction to African Literature*. London: Longman, 1967. Print.

Benson, Eugene and L.W. Conolly, eds. *The Encyclopedia of Post-Colonial Literatures in English*. London: Routledge, 1994. Print.

Bharucha, Nilufer E. and Vrinda Nabar. *Mapping Cultural Spaces: Post-Colonial Indian Literature in English*. New Delhi: Vision Books, 1998. Print.

Boehmer, Elleke. *Colonial and Post-Colonial Literature*. New Delhi: Oxford University Press, 1995. Print.

Cook, David. *African Literature: A Critical View*. London: Longman, 1977. Print.

Cox, H.M.L., ed. *Ten Modern New Zealand Poets*. Auckland: Longman Paul, 1982. Print.

Curnow, System, ed. *Essay on New Zealand Literature*. Auckland: Heinemann, Educational Book, 1973. Print.

Darby, Phillip. *The Fiction of Imperialism: Reading Between International Relations and Postcolonialism*. London and Washington: Cassell, 1998. Print.

Das, Bijay Kumar. *Critical Essays on Research Methodology, Interdisciplinarity and Indian Literature*. New Delhi: Atlantic Publishers, 2017. Print.

——. *Interpreting Poetry and Evaluating Criticism*. New Delhi: Atlantic Publishers, 2015. Print.

Das, Bijay Kumar. *Perspectives on the Poetry of A.K. Ramanujan*. New Delhi: Doaba Publishers, 2013. Print.

——. *Post-modern Indian English Literature*. New Delhi: Atlantic Publishers and Distributors, 2006, 3rd Edn. 2013. Print.

——. *Form and Meaning in Mahesh Dattani's Plays*. New Delhi: Atlantic Publishers and Distributors Pvt. Ltd., 2008. 2nd Edn. 2012. Print.

——. *The Poetry of Jayanta Mahapatra*, Calcutta: Writer's Workshop, 1992. (Revised and Enlarged Edition. New Delhi: Atlantic Publishers, 2009).

——. *Critical Essays on Poetry*. New Delhi: Kalyani Publishers, 1993, 2003. Print.

——. *Shiv K. Kumar as a Post-Colonial Poet*. New Delhi: Atlantic Publishers and Distributors, 2001. Print.

——. *The Horizon of Nissim Ezekiel's Poetry*. New Delhi: B.R. Publishing Corporation, 1995. Print.

——. *Aspects of Commonwealth Literature*. New Delhi: Creative Books, 1995. Print.

——. *Perspectives on Indian English Poetry Criticism*. Bareilly: Prakash Book Depot, 1993. Print.

——. *Modern Indian English Poetry*. Bareilly: Prakash Book Depot, 1992. Print.

——, ed. *Perspectives on the Poetry of R. Parthasarathy*. Bareilly: Prakash Book Depot, 1983, 1997. Print.

——, ed. *New Readings in Indian English Literature*. Bareilly: Prakash Book Depot, 2011. Print.

Davin, D.M., ed. *New Zealand Short Stories*. New Zealand: Oxford University Press, 1976. Print.

Dhawan, R.K., ed. *Commonwealth Fiction*. New Delhi: Classical, 1988. Print.

Elliott, Brian. *The Landscape of Australian Poetry*. Melbourne: Cheshire, 1967. Print.

Ford, Boris, ed. *The New Pelican Guide to English Literature: Present*. England: Penguin Books, 1983. Print.

Frye, Northrop. *The Bush Garden: Essay on the Canadian Imagination*. Toronto: Anansi, 1971. Print.

Gopal, Priyamvada. *The Indian English Novel: Nation, History and Narration*. New York: Oxford University Press, 2009. Print.

Grace, Sherrill. *Violent Duality: A Study of Margaret Atwood.* Montreal: Vehicle Press, 1980. Print.

Hammer, Robert D. *V.S. Naipaul.* New York: Twayne Publishers Inc., 1973. Print.

Hankin, Cherry, ed. *Critical Essay on the New Zealand Short Stories.* Auckland: Heinemann, 1982. Print.

Heywood, Christopher, ed. *Perspectives on African Literature.* London: Heinemann Educational Books, 1971. Print.

Hope, A.D. *The Cave and the Spring: Essay on Poetry.* Sydney: University Press, 1965. Print.

Hughes, Peter. *V.S. Naipaul.* New York: Routledge, 1988. Print.

Innes, C.L. *Chinua Achebe.* Cambridge: Cambridge University Press, 1990. Print.

——. *The Cambridge Introduction to Postcolonial Literatures in English.* New Delhi: Cambridge University Press, 2008. Print.

Iyengar, K.R.S. *Indian Writing in English.* Bombay: Asia Publishing House, 1962. Print.

Jain, Jasbir. *The Diaspora Writes Home: Subcontinental Narratives.* Jaipur: Rawat Publications, 2015. Print.

Jain, Jasbir and Veena Singh, ed. *Contesting Postcolonialisms.* Jaipur: Rawat Publications, 2000. Print.

Jones, Elders. *The Writing of Wole Soyinka.* London: Heinemann, 1973. Print.

Khan, M.Q. and Bijay Kumar Das, ed. *Studies in Post-Colonial Literature.* New Delhi: Atlantic Publishers, 2007. Print.

Killam, G.D. *An Introduction to the Writing of Nuggi.* London: Heinemann, 1980. Print.

King, Bruce, ed. *Introduction to Nigerian Literature.* London: Evans, 1972. Print.

——, ed. *Literature of the World in English.* London: Routledge and Kegan Paul, 1974. Print.

——, ed. *New National and Post-Colonial Literatures.* New York: OUP, 1996 rpt. 2002. Print.

——. *The New English Literatures — Cultural Nationalism in a Changing World.* New York: St. Martin's Press, 1980. Print.

——. *Modern Indian Poetry in English.* Delhi: Oxford University Press, 1987. Print.

King, Bruce. *Three Indian Poets*. Madras: Oxford University Press, 1991. Print.

Kumar, Shiv K. *Contemporary Indian Literature in English*. Shimla: Indian Institute of Advanced Study, 1992. Print.

Kumar, Shiv K. and Keith McKean, ed. *Critical Approaches to Fiction*, New Delhi: Atlantic Publishers, 2003 rpt. 2014. Print.

Lane, Richard J. *The Postcolonial Novel*. Cambridge: Polity Press, 2006. Print.

Lazarus, Neil, ed. *The Cambridge Companion to Postcolonial Literature Studies*. New York: CUP, 2004. Print.

Lindfors, Bernth and Bala Kothandaraman, eds. *South Asian Responses to Chinua Achebe*. New Delhi: Prestige Books, 1993. Print.

Loomba, Ania. *Colonialism/Postcolonialism*. New York: Routledge, 1999. Print.

Loomba, Ania, et al., ed. *Postcolonial Studies and Beyond*. Ranikher: Permanent Black, 2007. Print.

Madsen, Deborah, ed. *Post-colonial Literatures: Expanding the Canon*, London: Pluto, 1999. Print.

Mandel, Eli, ed. *Contexts of Canadian Criticism: A Collection of Critical Essays*. Toronto: University Press, 1971. Print.

McAuley, James. *A Map of Australian Verse*. Melbourne: Oxford University Press, 1975. Print.

McLeod, John. *Beginning Postcolonialism*. New Delhi: Viva Books Pvt. Ltd., 2011 rpt. 2013. Print.

Mongia, Padmini, ed. *Contemporary Post-Colonial Theory: A Reader*. New Delhi: Oxford University Press, 1999. Print.

Moore, Gerald. *Wole Soyinka*. New York: Africana Publishing Corporation, 1971. Print.

Moore-Gilbert, Bart. *Postcolonial Theory: Contexts, Practices, Politics*. London and New York: Verso, 1997. Print.

Mukherjee, Meenakshi, ed. *Considerations*. New Delhi: Allied Publishers, 1977. Print.

——. *The Twice-born Fiction: Themes and Techniques of the Indian Novel in English*. Ind. Ed. New Delhi: Arnold-Heinemann, 1971. Print.

——. *Perishable Empire*. New Delhi: OUP, 2000. Print.

Mukherjee, Meenakshi, ed. *Elusive Terrain: Culture and Literary Memory*, New Delhi: OUP, 2008. Print.

Naik, M.K., ed. *Aspects of Indian Writing in English*. New Delhi: Macmillan, 1979. Print.

——. *Perspectives on Indian Poetry in English*. New Delhi: Abhinav Publications, 1984. Print.

——. "Mulk Raj Anand," *Indian Writer Series*. New Delhi: Arnold Heinemann, 1973. Print.

Nandi, Ashis. *The Intimate Enemy*. New Delhi: Oxford University, 1983.

Narasimhaiah, C.D. *Commonwealth Literature: A Handbook of Select Reading List*. Delhi: Oxford University Press, 1976. Print.

——, ed. *The Awakened Conscience*. New Delhi: Sterling Publishers, 1978. Print.

——, ed. *An Anthology of Commonwealth Poetry*. Madras: Macmillan India Ltd., 1990. Print.

——. "Raj Rao", *Indian Writer Series*. New Delhi: Arnold Heinemann, 1973. Print.

——. *Essays in Commonwealth Literature*. Delhi: Pencraft International, 1995. Print.

O'Donell, Margaret J. *An Anthology of Commonwealth Verse*. Madras: Blackie and Sons Publishers Pvt. Ltd., 1984. Print.

Palmer, Eustace. *The Growth of the African Novel*. London: Heinemann, 1979. Print.

Panikar, Kenneth. *The South African Novel in English*. London: Macmillan, 1978. Print.

Parry, Benita. *Postcolonial Studies: A Materialist Critique*. London: Routledge, 2004. Print.

Parthasarathy, R., ed. *Ten Twentieth Century Indian Poets*. Delhi: Oxford University Press, 1977. Print.

Paterson, Alistair, ed. *Contemporary New Zealand Poets*. New Zealand: Pilgrims South Press, 1980. Print.

Pres, John, ed. *Commonwealth Literature*. London: Heinemann, 1965. Print.

Punter, David. *Postcolonial Imaginings: Fictions of a New World Order*. Edinburgh: Edinburgh University Press, 2000. Print.

Rai, Soudha. *V.S. Naipaul: A Study in Expatriate Sensibility*. Atlantic Highlands, NJ: Humanities Press, 1982. Print.

Rajeshwar, M. *The Novels of Wole Soyinka*. New Delhi: Prestige Books, 1992. Print.

Ramaswamy, S. *Exploration: Essay on Commonwealth Literature*. Bangalore: MCC Publications, 1988. Print.

Rao, A. Ramakrishna and C.R. Visweswara Rao. *Indian Response to African Writing*. New Delhi: Prestige Books, 1993. Print.

Rao, K. Damodar. *The Novels of Ayi Kwei Armah*. New Delhi: Prestige Books, 1993. Print.

Sertima, Ivan Van. *Caribbean Writers: Critical Essays*. London: New Beacon Books, 1968. Print.

Sethi, Rumina. *Myths of the Nation: National Identity and Literary Representation*. New Delhi: OUP, 1999. Print.

Shahane, V.A. *Khushwant Singh. Twayne's World Authors Series*. New York: Twayne, 1972. Print.

Shahane, V.A. and M. Sivaram Krishna, eds. *Indian Poetry in English: A Critical Assessment*. Madras: Macmillan, 1982. Print.

Smith, A.J.M., ed. *Masks of Poetry: Canadian Critics on Canadian Verse*. Toronto: McClelland and Steward, 1968. Print.

——, ed. *The Oxford Book of Canadian Verse*. Toronto: Oxford University Press, 1965. Print.

Stead, C.K. *In the Glass Case: Essays on New Zealand Literature*. Auckland: Auckland University Press, 1981. Print.

Sundaram, P.S. *R.K. Narayan. Indian Writers Series*. New Delhi: Arnold Heinemann, 1974. Print.

Thiong'o, Ngũgĩ wa. *Globalectics: Theory and the Politics of Knowing*. New York: Columbia University Press, 2014. Print.

Trivedi, Harish and Meenakshi Mukherjee, eds. *The National Across the World: Postcolonial Literary Representations*. New Delhi: OUP, 2007. Print.

Udoeyop, N.J. *Three Nigerian Poets*. Ibadan University Press, 1973. Print.

Walder, Dennis. *Post-Colonial Literatures in English: History, Language Theory*. New Delhi: Atlantic Publishers & Distributors Pvt. Ltd., 2005. Print.

Walsh, William. *A Manifold Voice: Studies in Commonwealth Literature*. London: Chatto and Windus, 1970. Print.

——. *Commonwealth Literature*. Oxford Paperback. University Series, London: Oxford University Press, 1973. Print.

——. *R.K. Narayan. Writers and their Work Series*. London: Longman, 1971. Print.

——. *V.S. Naipaul*. Edinburgh: Oliver and Boyd, 1973. Print.

——, ed. *Readings in Commonwealth Literature*. Oxford: Clarendon Press, 1973. Print.

——. *Indian Literature in English*. London: Longman, 1990. Print.

White, Landegg. *V.S. Naipaul: A Critical Introduction*. London: Macmillan Press, 1975. Print.

Williams, Patrick and Laura Chrisman, eds. *Colonial Discourse and Post-Colonial Theory: A Reader*. London: Harvester Wheatsheaf, 1993. Print.

Woodcock, George. *Odysseus Ever Returning: Essay on Canadian Writers and Writings*. Toronto: McClelland and Stewart, 1970. Print.

Wright, Judith. *Pre-occupations in Australian Poetry*. Melbourne: Oxford University Press, 1966. Print.

Young, Robert J.C. *Colonial Desire: Hybridity in Theory, Culture and Race*. London: Routledge, 1995. Print.

Index

L

M

N

O

P